First Edition 2005.

The Clay Sanskrit Library is co-published by
New York University Press
and the JJC Foundation.

Further information about this volume
and the rest of the Clay Sanskrit Library
is available on the following websites:
www.claysanskritlibrary.com
www.nyupress.org

ISBN 0-8147-8814-9

Artwork by Robert Beer.
ver design by Isabelle Onians.
typesettting by Somadeva Vasudeva.
at Britain by St Edmundsbury Press Ltd,
munds, Suffolk, on acid-free paper.
nter & Foulis, Edinburgh, Scotland.

THE CLAY SANSKRIT LIBRARY
FOUNDED BY JOHN & JENNIFER CLA

EDITED BY

RICHARD GOMBRIC

C
Layout &
Printed in Gre
Bury St Ed
Bound by Hu

WY

THREE SATIRES

NĪLAKAṆṬHA, KṢEMENDRA & BHALLAṬA

EDITED AND TRANSLATED BY
SOMADEVA VASUDEVA

NEW YORK UNIVERSITY PRESS
JJC FOUNDATION
2005

Library of Congress Cataloging-in-Publication Data
Nīlakaṇṭha Dīkṣita, 17th cent.
[Kalividambana. English & Sanskrit]
Three satires / Nilakantha, Ksemendra & Bhallata ;
edited and translated by Somadeva Vasudeva.
p. cm. – (The Clay Sanskrit library)
In English and Sanskrit; includes translations from Sanskrit.
Includes bibliographical references and index.
ISBN 0-8147-8814-9 (cloth : alk. paper)
I. Title: 3 satires. II. Vasudeva, Somadeva.
III. Kṣemendra, 11th cent. Kalāvilāsa. English & Sanskrit.
IV. Bhallaṭa, 9th cent. Bhallaṭaśataka. English & Sanskrit.
V. Title. VI. Series.
PK3798.N54K313 2005
891'.23–dc22 2004029512

CONTENTS

A *sandhi* grid is printed on the inside of the back cover

SANSKRIT ALPHABETICAL ORDER

Vowels:	*a ā i ī u ū ṛ ṝ ḷ ḹ e ai o au ṃ ḥ*
Gutturals:	*k kh g gh ṅ*
Palatals:	*c ch j jh ñ*
Retroflex:	*ṭ ṭh ḍ ḍh ṇ*
Labials:	*p ph b bh m*
Semivowels:	*y r l v*
Spirants:	*ś ṣ s h*

GUIDE TO SANSKRIT PRONUNCIATION

a	b*u*t
ā, â	r*a*ther
i	s*i*t
ī, î	f*ee*
u	p*u*t
ū, û	b*oo*
ṛ	vocalic *r*, American p*ur*dy or English p*re*tty
ṝ	lengthened *ṛ*
ḷ	vocalic *l*, ab*le*
e, ê, ē	m*a*de, esp. in Welsh pronunciation
ai	b*i*te
o, ô, ō	r*o*pe, esp. Welsh pronunciation; Italian s*o*lo
au	s*ou*nd
ṃ	*anusvāra* nasalizes the preceding vowel
ḥ	*visarga*, a voiceless aspiration (resembling English *h*), or like Scottish lo*ch*, or an aspiration with a faint echoing of the preceding vowel so that *taiḥ* is pronounced *taih*^{i}

k	lu*ck*
kh	blo*ckh*ead
g	*g*o
gh	bi*gh*ead
ṅ	a*n*ger
c	*ch*ill
ch	mat*chh*ead
j	*j*og
jh	aspirated *j*, he*dgeh*og
ñ	ca*ny*on
ṭ	retroflex *t*, *t*ry (with the tip of tongue turned up to touch the hard palate)
ṭh	same as the preceding but aspirated
ḍ	retroflex *d* (with the tip of tongue turned up to touch the hard palate)
ḍh	same as the preceding but aspirated
ṇ	retroflex *n* (with the tip of tongue turned up to touch the hard palate)
t	French *t*out
th	ten*t h*ook

d	*d*inner	*r*	trilled, resembling the Italian pronunciation of *r*
dh	guil*dh*all	*l*	*l*inger
n	*n*ow	*v*	*w*ord
p	*p*ill	*ś*	*sh*ore
ph	u*ph*eaval	*ṣ*	retroflex *sh* (with the tip of the tongue turned up to touch the hard palate)
b	*b*efore	*s*	hi*ss*
bh	a*bh*orrent	*h*	*h*ood
m	*m*ind		
y	*y*es		

CSL PUNCTUATION OF ENGLISH

The acute accent on Sanskrit words when they occur outside of the Sanskrit text itself, marks stress, e.g. Ramáyana. It is not part of traditional Sanskrit orthography, transliteration or transcription, but we supply it here to guide readers in the pronunciation of these unfamiliar words. Since no Sanskrit word is accented on the last syllable it is not necessary to accent disyllables, e.g. Rama.

The second CSL innovation designed to assist the reader in the pronunciation of lengthy unfamiliar words is to insert an unobtrusive middle dot between semantic word breaks in compound names (provided the word break does not fall on a vowel resulting from the fusion of two vowels), e.g. Maha·bhárata, but Ramáyana (not Rama·áyana). Our dot echoes the punctuating middle dot (·) found in the oldest surviving samples of written Sanskrit, the Ashokan inscriptions of the third century BCE.

The deep layering of Sanskrit narrative has also dictated that we use quotation marks only to announce the beginning and end of every direct speech, and not at the beginning of every paragraph.

CSL PUNCTUATION OF SANSKRIT

The Sanskrit text is also punctuated, in accordance with the punctuation of the English translation. In mid-verse, the punctuation will not alter the *sandhi* or the scansion. Proper names are capitalized, as are the initial words of verses (or paragraphs in prose texts). Most Sanskrit metres have four "feet" *(pāda):* where possible we print the common *śloka* metre on two lines. The capitalization of verse beginnings makes it easy for the reader to recognize longer metres where it is necessary to print the four metrical feet over four or eight lines. In the Sanskrit text, we use French *Guillemets* (e.g. *«kva saṃcicīrṣuḥ?»*) instead of English quotation marks (e.g. "Where are you off to?") to avoid confusion with the apostrophes used for vowel elision in *sandhi*.

Sanskrit presents the learner with a challenge: *sandhi* ("euphonic combination"). *Sandhi* means that when two words are joined in connected speech or writing (which in Sanskrit reflects speech), the last letter (or even letters) of the first word often changes; compare the way we pronounce "the" in "the beginning" and "the end."

In Sanskrit the first letter of the second word may also change; and if both the last letter of the first word and the first letter of the second are vowels, they may fuse. This has a parallel in English: a nasal consonant is inserted between two vowels that would otherwise coalesce: "a pear" and "an apple." Sanskrit vowel fusion may produce ambiguity. The chart at the back of each book gives the full *sandhi* system.

Fortunately it is not necessary to know these changes in order to start reading Sanskrit. For that, what is important is to know the form of the second word without *sandhi* (pre-*sandhi*), so that it can be recognized or looked up in a dictionary. Therefore we are printing Sanskrit with a system of punctuation that will indicate, unambiguously, the original form of the second word, i.e., the form without *sandhi*. Such *sandhi* mostly concerns the fusion of two vowels.

In Sanskrit, vowels may be short or long and are written differently accordingly. We follow the general convention that a vowel with no mark above it is short. Other books mark a long vowel either with a bar called a macron (*ā*) or with a circumflex (*â*). Our system uses the macron, except that for initial vowels in *sandhi* we use a circumflex to indicate that originally the vowel was short, or the shorter of two possibilities (*e* rather than *ai*, *o* rather than *au*).

When we print initial	*â*,	before *sandhi* that vowel was *a*
	î or *ê*,	*i*
	û or *ô*,	*u*
	âi,	*e*

âu,	*o*
ā,	*ā* (i.e., the same)
ī,	*ī* (i.e., the same)
ū,	*ū* (i.e., the same)
ē,	*ī*
ō,	*ū*
āi,	*ai*
āu,	*au*
’, before *sandhi* there was a vowel *a*	

FURTHER HELP WITH VOWEL SANDHI

When a final short vowel (*a*, *i* or *u*) has merged into a following vowel, we print ’ at the end of the word, and when a final long vowel (*ā*, *ī* or *ū*) has merged into a following vowel we print ” at the end of the word. The vast majority of these cases will concern a final *a* or *ā*.

Examples:

What before *sandhi* was *atra asti* is represented as *atr’ âsti*

atra āste	*atr’ āste*
kanyā asti	*kany” âsti*
kanyā āste	*kany” āste*
atra iti	*atr’ êti*
kanyā iti	*kany” êti*
kanyā īpsitā	*kany” ēpsitā*

Finally, three other points concerning the initial letter of the second word:

(1) A word that before *sandhi* begins with *ṛ* (vowel), after *sandhi* begins with *r* followed by a consonant: *yatha” rtu* represents pre-*sandhi* *yathā ṛtu*.

(2) When before *sandhi* the previous word ends in *t* and the following word begins with *ś*, after *sandhi* the last letter of the previous word is *c* and the following word begins with *ch*: *syāc chāstravit* represents pre-*sandhi* *syāt śāstravit*.

(3) Where a word begins with *h* and the previous word ends with a double consonant, this is our simplified spelling to show the pre-*sandhi*

form: *tad hasati* is commonly written as *tad dhasati*, but we write *tadd hasati* so that the original initial letter is obvious.

COMPOUNDS

We also punctuate the division of compounds (*samāsa*), simply by inserting a thin vertical line between words. There are words where the decision whether to regard them as compounds is arbitrary. Our principle has been to try to guide readers to the correct dictionary entries.

WORDPLAY

Classical Sanskrit literature can abound in puns *(śleṣa)*. Such paronomasia, or wordplay, is raised to a high art; rarely is it a *cliché*. Multiple meanings merge *(śliṣyanti)* into a single word or phrase. Most common are pairs of meanings, but as many as ten separate meanings are attested. To mark the parallel senses in the English, as well as the punning original in the Sanskrit, we use a *slanted* font (different from *italic*) and a triple colon *(⁝)* to separate the alternatives. E.g.

> Yuktaṃ Kādambarīṃ śrutvā kavayo maunam āśritāḥ
> *Bāṇa|dhvanāv* an|adhyāyo bhavat' îti smṛtir yataḥ.
>
> "It is right that poets should fall silent upon hearing the Kádambari, for the sacred law rules that recitation must be suspended when *the sound of an arrow ⁝ the poetry of Bana* is heard."
>
> Soméshvara·deva's "Moonlight of Glory" I.15

EXAMPLE

Where the Devanagari script reads:

कुम्भस्थली रक्षतु वो विकीर्णसिन्दूररेणुर्द्विरदाननस्य।
प्रशान्तये विघ्नतमश्छटानां निष्ठ्यूतबालातपपल्लवेव॥

Others would print:

kumbhasthalī rakṣatu vo vikīrṇasindūrareṇur dviradānanasya /
praśāntaye vighnatamaśchaṭānāṃ niṣṭhyūtabālātapapallaveva //

We print:

Kumbha|sthalī rakṣatu vo vikīrṇa|sindūra|reṇur dvirad'|ānanasya
praśāntaye vighna|tamaś|chaṭānāṃ niṣṭhyūta|bāl'|ātapa|pallav" êva.

And in English:

"May Ganésha's domed forehead protect you! Streaked with vermilion dust, it seems to be emitting the spreading rays of the rising sun to pacify the teeming darkness of obstructions."

Padma·gupta's "Nava·sáhasanka and the Serpent Princess" I.3

INTRODUCTION

THE THREE SATIRISTS translated in this volume chose to pursue three very different strategies in their compositions. We may surmise that they wrote to fulfil three equally different aims, but these are not as clear-cut as might have been expected.

All three were members of privileged and learned aristocracies linked to the royal court. While Bhállata suffered a humiliating fall from his high rank of court-poet, Ksheméndra was an independently wealthy man of leisure, and Nila·kantha endured a number of vicissitudes.

BHÁLLATA

Bhállata was a *protégé* of King Avánti·varman of Kashmir (*reg.* 855–883CE) a celebrated patron of eminent poets.[1] The chronicler Kálhana reports that his successor, King Shánkara·varman (*reg.* 883–902CE) discontinued this royal patronage and that Bhállata and his poet peers were henceforth forced to support themselves with lowly work.[2] While Kálhana portrays the new king Shánkara·varman as boorish (he preferred to speak vernacular dialects instead of cultivated Sanskrit), a quite different picture of him can be gleaned from the *Āgama/ḍambara*, an historico-philosophical drama written by the logician Bhatta Jayánta, a contemporary of Bhállata's. There it is rather the learned elites who are being ridiculed, and Shánkara·varman is portrayed as interested in statecraft rather than the fine arts.

"Bhállata's Hundred Allegories" is a collection of "detached poems" *(muktaka)*, each complete in itself, composed in sophisticated courtly Sanskrit in various metres. "Detached poems" are usually classified as being "free of context" *(a/nibaddha)*, so that there is no narrative linking them. It is a common practise, however, to group verses that are thematically related into units (sometimes called *paryā* or *vrajyā*).

"Bhállata's Hundred Allegories" is the earliest known collection of detached poems devoted entirely to allegorical satire *(anyāpadeśa)*. The poet Bhállata is heir to a sophisticated verbal art, and both he and his intended audience expect literature to be crafted with genius within the bounds of formal rules. These verses of his allegories depend primarily on a few figures of speech *(alaṅkāras*, as taught in Sanskrit rhetorics) that relate two separate senses. The relation of the two senses can be of various kinds: "fusion" *(śleṣa* = paronomasia); the "intended sense" and the "unintended sense" *(prakṛta-aprakṛta* in *aprastuta/praśaṃsā*, lit. "presentation of a topic not under discussion"); "compounding" (in *samās'/ôkti* lit. "compounded speech") etc.

This second sense, that serves as a pretext, is usually quite easy to interpret. Trees, which give shade and fruit to weary travellers, represent charitable donors; gleaming jewels are learned scholars ablaze with learning; hissing, venomous serpents are miscreants whispering falsehoods, etc.

The general tone of the collection is one of resigned criticism, Bhállata laughs not so much at the folly of his contemporaries as that he suffers from their mistakes. Bhállata emphasises this pain by occasionally using tortuous syntax for effect.

Bhállata's verses are difficult, and they need to be read slowly and carefully.

KSHEMÉNDRA

The Kashmirian poet Ksheméndra (*fl. ca.* 990/1010–1070 CE),[3] was a prolific writer[4] whom recent scholars have variously charged with vulgarity and bad taste.[5]

Many of Ksheméndra's compositions may offend modern tastes, but a consequent vilification of his works' literary merit may be premature (he fares better if his work is judged with the literary criteria prevalent in his time and milieu).

We need to take into account that no work of Kshéméndra's has ever been critically edited, that he had studied literary theory with Abhínava·gupta, one of the greatest Sanskrit rhetoricians,[6] and that his contemporaries credited his works with poetic merit. One sure measure of Kshéméndra's popularity among traditional Sanskrit aesthetes is the large number of his verses which are current in poetic anthologies.[7] Even when the chronicler Kálhana censures a lack of historical accuracy in Ksheméndra's now lost "List of Kings " he fairly acknowledges that it was "the work of a poet."[8] Kálhana has even flattered Kshemendra by reworking a number of his verses.

How, then are we to account for such discrepant receptions of his work?

Is it just the case that, as with so many other Sanskrit poems, recent literary evaluations of Ksheméndra's satires are based on current notions of what a literary work should be? The short reply to such a reception, namely, that the work was not written for the modern reader, will avail little, for it is here presented to the modern reader. Nor would it be fair to exhort readers to immerse themselves into the world of the work, to understand the premises and prejudices of the author and his millieu. That, of course, is the job of the editor and translator.

The reader must, however, be warned that one may not blithely approach the works produced by one ancient classical civilisation with readily preconceived norms derived from another.[9] When LAPANICH[10] laments that the so-called "didactic" verses in the "Grace of Guile" interrupt the flow of the narrative, this tells us merely something about what she believed poetic satire ought to be. To the trained Sanskrit ear that Kshemėndra was addressing, smoothly flowing stories would have seemed fine in epic or Puranic narrative, or as refreshing interludes. But Kshemėndra was no mere story-teller in the market-place. Like Bhállata, he was a learned, aristocratic wordsmith who crafted complex poems for connoisseurs *(sahṛdaya)* who would scarcely be interested in mere colorful tales. Even worse, Kshemėndra's audience would have perceived such as a monotonous breach of poetic propriety *(aucitya)*. As he himself observes:

> *An uncultivated man, who merely cobbles together verses with difficulty, is a lousy poet, aware of only the literal sense of words. Like some newly-arrived, over-awed bumpkin in the depths of the big city, he has no idea what to answer when questioned in an assembly of the learned.*[11]

The offending "didactic" verses, far from being a mere interruption to the all-important narrative, are the focus of Kshemėndra's poetic efforts. It is here that he shows his talent. He lights up these verses with varied and entertaining ornaments of speech *(alaṅkāra)*, often involving learned puns *(śleṣa)* and satirical parallel meanings *(samās'|ôkti)* and above all he is careful to do all of this with the restraint so important to rhetoricians of his time.

Kshemèndra wrote a satire very similar to the "Grace of Guile" early on in his carreer: the *Deś'|ôpadeśa*. This in no way implies that it is an easier or even simpler work. Quite the opposite, like many writers' early work it is replete with learned puns and other rhetorical devices. In eight "lessons" *(upadeśa)* it ridicules wrong-doers, misers, prostitutes, bawds, parasites, and assorted cheats. That work consists of nothing but "didactic" verses. The "Grace of Guile," on the other hand, is arguably didactically superior because Kshemèndra has incorporated brief tales *(dṛṣṭ'|ânta)* to exemplify and reinforce his moral judgements. The result is the lighter and structurally more varied work of a mature and evidently well-established poet at the height of his powers.

Since it is not the narrative development alone that drove Kshemèndra's creative art, we should not be too hasty to judge his work by (for him) irrelevant standards.[12]

What has Kshemèndra himself said about his efforts? Forestalling critics who may charge him with vulgarity, Kshemèndra prefaces one of his satires with a a disclaimer:

> *My labor is in no way meant for those who are tainted even slightly by the symptoms of the disease which is the conceit of sanctimoniousness.*[13]

Like many other satirists Kshemèndra claims that his intentions are entirely praiseworthy:

Someone shamed by laughter will not persist in his wrongs.
To help him, I myself have made this effort.[14]

But it remains questionable if this reflects merely a paternalistic concern with uplifting the lower orders of society.[15] Is his the voice of a Kashmirian moral majority, or a self-appointed minority with moral pretenses? Do we see a learned elite scorning the common people? Are they intended as a taxonomy of fallen characters?[16] Are there sectarian motivations? Who is the "public" for whose instruction he claims to have written the "Grace of Guile"?[17] And not least, how much of it is personal?

The scope for future scholarship is wide.

NILA·KANTHA

Nila·kantha Díkshita (*fl.* 1613–?CE) was born into the family of one the most important figures of sixteenth-century Sanskrit scholarship. As the grand-nephew of Áppaya Díkshita (*fl.* 1553–1625CE) he first studied philosophy *(śāstra)* and literature with his father and eventually became the disciple of his grand-uncle.

Numerous hagiographical accounts agree at least that he was active in the seventeenth century as minister at the court of Tirumalai Náyaka of Maturai.

Although Nila·kantha provides ample information about his ancestral lineage, he never himself mentions by name the prince he served.[18]

His "Mockery of the Kali Age" is a work in 102 *anuṣṭubh* verses that provides a catalogue of fallen characters. It was composed specifically for the amusement of the royal court.[19] As such, it was presumably intended as a warning to his audience.

TEXTUAL CONSTITUTION

For "Bhállata's Hundred Allegories" I have used the *Kāvyamālā* edition, *(gucchaka* IV*)*, Bombay 1899, and the polyglot critical edition by VEDKUMARI GHAI & RAMPRATAP, New Delhi 1985. I have also used the anthologies citing Bhállata's verses.

For the "Grace of Guile" I have prepared a new edition the bare text without apparatus of which is published in this volume, using the following manuscripts: P=Bhandarkar Oriental Research Institute Poona, No. 65, 24 of 1873–74, ff. 21, *Jaina Devanāgarī* dated *saṃvat* 1931. Q=Bhandarkar Oriental Research Institute Poona, No. 66, 373 of 1887–91, ff. 22–34, *sargas* 5–10, *Devanāgarī*, undated. L=India Office Library London, No. 114a, ff. 37, *Devanāgarī*, dated *saṃvat* 1725. Three earlier editions were also consulted: 1. PAṆḌITA DURGĀPRASĀDA & KĀŚĪNĀTHA PĀṆḌURĀṄGA PARAB (1886), 2. E.V.V. RĀGHAVĀCĀRYA & D.G. PADHYE (1961), 3. LAPANICH (1973).

For the "Mockery of the Kali Age" I based my text of the edition of P.-S.FILLIOZAT, IFI 36, Pondichéry 1967, collating it with the lithograph edition by KERAḶAVARMĀ, Trivandrum 1886.

TRANSLATION

The translations offered do not pretend to be poetic. Such attempts seem often doomed to failure, as had already been noted by Kumára·jiva, the early translator of Sanskrit into Chinese(Translated from the "Biography of Kumārajīva" in Hui-chiao's *Biographies of Eminent Monks* by VICTOR H. MAIR & TSU-LIN MEI (1991:382–3)):

> *Once Sanskrit is converted into Chinese, the subtle nuances are lost. Though the general meaning gets across, there is no way to bridge the gap in genre and style. It is like feeding another person with chewed-over rice. Not only is the flavour lost, it will cause the other person to vomit.*

Rather than risking such an outcome by attempting facile reductions to contemporary fashions in English poetry, this translation strives to be an aid so that readers may consult the original themselves and discover whatever poetic beauty there is in the original.

NOTES

1 *Rājataraṅgiṇī* 5.34.

2 *Rājataraṅgiṇī* 5.204.

3 Only four of Kṣemendra's works are dated: [1.] the *Samayamātṛkā* to the first day of the bright lunar fortnight of December–January in the [Laukika] year [41]25 = 1049/50 CE (epilogue 2ab: *saṃvatsare pañcaviṃśe pauṣaśuklādivāsare*). [2.] Somendra writes in his Introduction to Kṣemendra's *Avadānakalpalatā* that it was completed during the Buddha's birth-celebrations in the bright fortnight of April–May of the [Laukika] year [41]27 = 1052 CE (*Avadānakalpalatā* Introduction 16: *saṃvatsare saptaviṃśe vaiśākhasya sitodaye kṛteyaṃ Kalpalatikā Jinajanmamahotsave*). [3.] The *Aucityavicāracarcā* was completed in May–June of the [Laukika] year[41]34 = 1059 CE (*Aucityālaṃkāroddhāra* B.O.R.I ms no. 578/1887–91, colophon: *niṣpannaś cāyaṃ śrīmadAnantarājanarādhirājasamaye– saṃvatsare catustriṃśe jyeṣṭhe śukle 'ṣṭame 'hani / Kāvyaucityavicāro 'yaṃ śiṣyavyutpattaye kṛtaḥ*. [4.] The *Daśāvatāracarita* to October–November of the [Laukika] year [41]41 = 1066 CE (epilogue 5abc: *ekādhike 'bde vihitaś catvāriṃśe sakārtike rājye Kalaśabhūbhartuḥ*). Kṣemendra further tells us that he wrote this work "while enjoying a rest on the summit of the Tripureśvara mountain" (epilogue 3a: *tena śrīTripureśvaraśailaśikhare viśrāntisaṃtoṣinā*), an ancient site of great sanctity near Śrīnagara (see STEIN (1900:192–3)). Secondary literature frequently makes the false assertion that the *Bṛhatkathāmañjarī* is also dated. STERNBACH (1979:1) places it in 1039 CE, then (without explaining the discrepancy) in 1037 CE (1979:10), where it had already been placed by MAHAJAN (1956:i) and SŪRYAKĀNTA (1954:6). This would put the

verifiable beginning of Kṣemendra's literary career back by 10 years, but it is based on no more than a misunderstanding of *Bṛhatkathāmañjarī* 19.37. The verse states merely: *kadā cid eva vipreṇa sa* ***dvādaśyām upoṣitaḥ*** */ prārthito Rāmayaśasā sarasaḥ svacchacetasā*. "At one time, he, full of love, who was **fasting on the twelfth [lunar day]** was requested by the clear-minded Brāhmaṇa Rāmayaśas." Here *dvādaśyām* cannot mean "in the twelfth [Laukika] year," e.g. 4112 = 1037 CE. The *Bṛhatkathāmañjarī* remains undated. We further know that his works were composed in the reign of the Kashmirian kings Ananta (*reg.* 1028–63 CE) and Kalaśa (*reg.* 1063–89 CE).

4 STERNBACH (1979:2–5) lists forty-one works attributed to him, of which twenty are no longer extant. Of these twenty, four titles are however alternates (see STERNBACH (1979:11 footnote 2)), and the *Dānapārijāta* is by a different author called Kṣemendra Mahopādhyāya, hence we arrive at thirty-six works.

5 STERNBACH (1974:81): "His work is often vulgar and it is not an amusing comedy, but an acrid, cheap satire, often in bad taste." STERNBACH (1974:77) does at least concede that: "Perhaps the best of his satiric and didactic works is the *Kalāvilāsa.*"

6 *Bṛhatkathāmañjarī* 19.37.

7 See STERNBACH (1979) for a list of 415 verses quoted in the surviving classical anthologies.

8 *Rājataraṅgiṇī* 1.13: *kavikarmaṇi saty api*.

9 The difficulty, of course, lies in discovering that something is such a preconceived norm in the first place.

10 LAPANICH (1979:9): '. . . the only defect found in the *Kalāvilāsa* is that Kshemêndra intersperses too many didactic verses which interrupt the smooth flow of the didactic story."

11 *Kavikaṇṭhābharaṇa* 5.1: *na hi paricayahīnaḥ kevale kāvyakaṣṭe kukavir abhiniviṣṭaḥ spaṣṭaśabdapraviṣṭaḥ / vibudhasadasi pṛṣṭaḥ kliṣṭadhīr vetti vaktuṃ nava iva nagarāntargahvare ko 'py adhṛṣṭaḥ.* Elaborating on this verse, Ksheméndra demands that a poet must be a cultivated scholar, versed in: logic *(tarka)*, grammar *(vyākaraṇa)*, dramaturgy (Bharata), politics (Cāṇakya), erotics (Vātsyāyana), epic literature (Bhārata), the *Rāmāyaṇa*, the *Mokṣopāya*, (this is the earliest dateable reference to this work), self-knowledge (*ātmajñāna*), metallurgy/chemistry (*dhātuvāda*), gemology (*ratnaparīkṣā*), medicine (*vaidyaka*), astronomy/astrology (*jyautiṣa*), archery (*dhanurveda*), elephant-lore (*gajalakṣaṇa*), equestrian science (*turagalakṣaṇa*), physiognomy (*puruṣalakṣaṇa*), gambling (*dyūta*), and sorcery (*Indrajāla*).

12 This will hardly be news to those familiar with a common type of "criticism" often met in secondary literature on Sanskrit poetry. As Warder & Kunjunni Raja (1986:xliv) remark in their introduction to the *Naiṣadh'/ānanda*: 'Such persons are incapable of grasping the significance of a classical play or of enjoying dramatic poetry. It is shocking that they have condemned this and many other plays, novels and poems without troubling to read them, much worse that such empty arrogance has been set up by others as "authority."'

13 *Deśopadeśa* 3ab: *ye dambhamāyāmayadoṣaleśaliptā na me tān prati ko 'pi yatnaḥ.* These words echo the famous disclaimer of the playwright Bhava·bhuti's *Mālatīmādhava*: *ye nāma ke cid iha naḥ prathayanty avajñāṃ/ jānanti[var: °u] te kim api tān prati naiṣa yatnaḥ.*

14 *Deśopadeśa* 4: *hāsena lajjito 'tyantaṃ na doṣeṣu pravartate / janas tadupakārāya mamāyaṃ svayam udyamaḥ.*

15 Unlike many more well-researched literatures, the study of Sanskrit Kāvya has not yet generated a substantial body of work that could meaningfully contribute to its *Rezeptionsgeschichte.*

16 As BALDISSERA (2000:153) notes: "It is a work that could well compare with Theophrastus' *Characters*."

17 *Kalāvilāsa* 10.43: *lokopadeśaviṣayaḥ*.

18 P-.S. FILLIOZAT (1967) has attempted to reconcile the conflicting hagiographical accounts with other data and provides a fuller account.

19 "Mockery of the Kali Age" 102.

1
BHÁLLATA'S HUNDRED ALLEGORIES

TĀṂ BHAVĀNĪṂ bhav'|ānīta|
kleśa|nāśa|viśāradām,
Śāradāṃ śārad'|âmbhoda|
sita|siṃh'|āsanāṃ numaḥ!

Yuṣmākam ambara|maṇeḥ prathame mayūkhās
te maṅgalaṃ vidadhat' ûdaya|rāga|bhājaḥ
kurvanti ye divasa|janma|mah"|ôtsaveṣu
sindūra|pāṭala|mukhīr iva dik|purandhrīḥ.

Baddhā yad/arpaṇa/rasena vimarda/pūrvam
arthān kathaṃ jhaṭiti tān *prakṛtān* na dadyuḥ?
caurā iv' *âtimṛdavo* mahatāṃ kavīnām
arth'/ântarāṇy api *haṭhād vitaranti* śabdāḥ.

Kāco maṇir maṇiḥ kāco
yeṣāṃ te 'nye hi dehinaḥ.
santi te sudhiyo yeṣāṃ
kācaḥ kāco maṇir maṇiḥ.

Nanv āśraya|sthitir iyaṃ tava, Kālakūṭa!
ken' ôttar'|ôttara|viśiṣṭa|pad" ôpadiṣṭā?
prāg arṇavasya hṛdaye Vṛṣa|lakṣmaṇo 'tha
kaṇṭhe 'dhunā vasasi vāci punaḥ khalānām.

LET US PRAISE Shiva's consort Bhaváni,
skilled at dispelling
the pain of mundane existence,
who as Eloquence,* sits on a lion-throne
as white as autumn clouds!

May the first rays of the sky-jewel,
rising red, bestow their blessing upon you.
They seem to redden* with red minium
the faces of the horizon-goddesses,
in celebration for the birth of the day.

The words of great poets,
chosen with deliberation ⁝ *imprisoned*
to *convey a sentiment* ⁝ *yield*,
why do they not give up
the intended meaning ⁝ *stolen goods* at once?
They *surrender* ⁝ *admit to*
deeper meanings ⁝ *other thefts*
only after *a struggle* ⁝ *torture*,
as if they were *gentle* ⁝ *stealthy* thieves.

A jewel is glass and glass is a jewel
for dumb beasts.*
For the wise
glass is glass and a jewel is a jewel.

Tell me, Venom! Who instigated
this elevation of yours to ever loftier eminence?
First in the heart of the ocean,
then in the throat of bull-bannered Shiva
now you reside in the words of the wicked.*

Draviṇam āpadi, bhūṣaṇam utsave,
śaraṇam ātma|bhaye, niśi dīpakaḥ,
bahu|vidh'|*âbhyupakāra*|bhara|kṣamo
bhavati ko 'pi bhavān iva san|maṇiḥ?

Śrīr viśṛṅkhala|khal'|âbhisārikā
vartmabhir ghana|tamo|malīmasaiḥ
śabda|mātram api soḍhum akṣamā
bhūṣaṇasya guṇinaḥ samutthitam.

Māne n' êcchati, vārayaty upaśame
kṣmām ālikhantyāṃ hriyāṃ
svātantrye parivṛtya tiṣṭhati, karau
vyādhūya dhairyaṃ gate—
tṛṣṇe tvām anubadhnatā phalam iyat|
prāptaṃ janen' âmunā:
yaḥ spṛṣṭo na padā sa eva caraṇau
spraṣṭuṃ na saṃmanyate.

A resource in an emergency, an adornment in festivity,
a refuge in danger, a light in darkness,
helpful ⁝ *pretty* in so many ways,*
can there be another true jewel like you?

The Goddess of Fortune
—a woman shamelessly eloping to her unworthy beau
by paths black with impenetrable darkness—
will not permit even the faintest tinkling
of her stringed girdle.
⁝ *will not heed even a single word*
spoken by the virtuous.

O greed! By casting in my lot with you,
when honor would not permit it,
when restraint forbade it,
when shame scratched lines on the ground,
when free will recoiled, when fortitude left me
as my hands trembled,—
This has been my reward:
He whom I would not touch with my foot
permits me not to touch his feet.

Patatu vāriṇi yātu dig/antaraṃ
viśatu vahnim adho vrajatu kṣitim
ravir asāv iyat" âsya *guṇeṣu* kā
sakala|loka|*camat/kṛtiṣu* kṣatiḥ?

10 Sad|vṛttayaḥ sad|asad|artha|vivekino ye
te paśya kīdṛśam amuṃ samudāharanti
caur'|âsatī|prabhṛtayo bruvate yad asya
tad gṛhyate yadi kṛtaṃ tad ahas|kareṇa.

Pātaḥ pūṣṇo bhavati mahate n' ôpatāpāya, yasmāt
kāle prāpte ka iha na yayur yānti yāsyanti v" āstam?
etāvat tu vyathayatitarāṃ *loka/bāhyais tamobhis*
tasminn eva prakṛti|mahati vyomni labdho 'vakāśaḥ.

Paṅktau viśantu, gaṇitāḥ pratiloma|vṛttyā
pūrve bhaveyur iyat" âpy athavā traperan?
santo 'py asanta iva cet pratibhānti bhānor
bhās" āvṛte nabhasi śīta|mayūkha|mukhyāḥ.

The sun may *sink into the ocean* ⁝ *fall into a puddle*,
may *cross the horizon* ⁝ *run about naked*,
may *be resorbed into fire** ⁝ *tumble into a fire*,
may *descend to the underworld* ⁝ *wallow in the mud*.
Does this in any way diminish his *merits* ⁝ *peculiarities*
which *delight* ⁝ *amuse* the whole world?*

Consider how respectable people, 10
who know truth from falsehood, speak of someone.
If you believe what thieves, prostitutes, and others say,
the day-maker sun has had it.

The sinking of the sun brings no great grief,
for in this world who has not, does not,
or will not depart when their time has come?
Just this is distressing—
darkness ⁝ *the outcaste*,
alien to light ⁝ *black-skinned*,
seizes *its* ⁝ *his* chance in the selfsame inherently vast sky.

The cold-rayed moon and his companions
may *keep noble company* ⁝ *enter in single file*,
reckoned back to front they may be considered leaders.
Despite all this—are they ashamed?
Though they exist it seems as if they do not
when the sky is flooded with the light of the sun.

«Gate tasmin bhānau
tri|bhuvana|samunmeṣa|viraha|
vyathāṃ candro neṣyaty»
anucitam ato nāsty asadṛśam.
idaṃ cetas|tāpaṃ
janayatitarām atra yad amī
pradīpāḥ saṃjātās
timira|hati|baddh'|ôddhata|śikhāḥ.

Sūryād anyatra yac candre
'py arth'|âsaṃsparśi tat kṛtam
kha|dyota iti kīṭasya
nāma tuṣṭena kena cit.

Kīṭa|maṇe! dinam adhunā
taraṇi|kar'|ântarita|cāru|sita|kiraṇam
ghana|santamasa|malīmasa|
daśa|diśi niśi yad virājasi, tad anyat.

Sattv'|ântaḥ|sphuritāya vā kṛta|guṇ'|â-
dhyāropa|tucchāya vā
tasmai kātara|mohanāya mahaso
leśāya mā svasti bhūt
yac chāyā|cchuraṇ'|âruṇena khacatā
khadyota|nāmn" âmunā
kīṭen' āhitayā hi jaṅgama|maṇi|
bhrāntyā viḍambyāmahe.

No thought could be more unworthy or incongruous than:
"Once the sun has set the moon will dispell all panic
as the triple world is lost to view."
It stings the heart even more,
that these lamps should have popped up here,
their sputtering wicks raised to put an end to darkness.

The designation "Sky-illuminator,"
which is a misnomer for anything except the sun,
including even the moon—
Some beguiled man has used it for a firefly.

Firefly! It is day now, 15
the rays of the gentle, pale-beamed moon
are drowned by the rays of the sun.
It is beside the point,
that you gleam in the night
when the ten directions are pitch black
with impenetrable darkness.

We have been fooled by a bug called "glow-worm,"
shining as it sheds a reddish gleam,
to think it is a living jewel.
Cursed be that faint light,*
which flickers in *the organism ∶ the imagination,*
which is trifling as its virtues are another's,
which bedazzles the timid.

Dant'|ânta|kunta|mukha|santata|pāta|ghāta|
saṃtāḍit'|ônnata|girir gaja eva vetti
pañcāsya|pāṇi|pavi|pañjara|pāta|pīḍāṃ
na kroṣṭukaḥ śva|śiśu|huṅkṛti|naṣṭa|ceṣṭaḥ.

Atyunnati|vyasaninaḥ śiraso 'dhun" âiṣa
svasy' âiva cātaka|śiśuḥ praṇayam vidhattām
asy' âitad icchati yadi pratatāsu dikṣu
tāḥ svaccha|śīta|madhurāḥ kva nu nāma n' āpaḥ.

So 'pūrvaḥ rasanā|viparyaya|vidhis
tat karṇayoś cāpalaṃ
dṛṣṭiḥ sā mada|vismṛta|sva|para|dik
kiṃ bhūyas" ôktena vā
itthaṃ niścitavān asi bhramara he
yad *vāraṇo* 'dy' âpy asāv
antaḥ|śūnya|karo niṣevyata iti
bhrātaḥ ka eṣa grahaḥ?

Only an elephant,
  who batters towering cliffs
  with relentless assaults of his spear-pointed tusks,
  knows the pain of being struck
  by a net of thunderbolts which are a lion's paw-swipes—
Not a jackal,
  whose spirit perishes at the yapping of a puppy.*

May now this young *chátaka* bird persuade its own head,
  which is obsessed with lofty ascent.
If it were so inclined,
  where among the many other directions
  would it not find clear, cool, sweet waters?*

This unfamiliar way of turning back the tongue,
  this levity of the ears,
  this delirious glance which has forgotten
  the bounds of "mine" and "other's":
Why say more—Oh bee! you know all this!
My brother, what is this madness?
That even now you dance attendance on
  this *elephant* ⁝ *dolt*
  with his *hollow trunk* ⁝ *empty hand.*

20 Tad vaidagdhyaṃ samucita|payas|
toya|tattvaṃ vivektuṃ
saṃlāpās te sa ca *mṛdu/pada/*
nyāsa/hṛdyo vilāsaḥ—
āstāṃ tāvad, baka! yadi tathā
vetsi kim cic chlath'|âṃsas
tūṣṇīm ev' āsitum api sakhe
tvaṃ kathaṃ me na haṃsaḥ?

Pathi nipatitāṃ śūnye dṛṣṭvā
nirāvaraṇ'|ānanāṃ
nava|dadhi|ghaṭīṃ garv'|ônnaddhaḥ
samuddhura|kandharaḥ
nija|samucitās tās tāś ceṣṭā
vikāra|śat'|ākulo
yadi na kurute kākaḥ kāṇaḥ
kadā nu kariṣyati?

Nṛtyantaḥ śikhino manoharam amī
śrāvyaṃ paṭhantaḥ śukā
vīkṣyante na ta eva khalv iha ruṣā
vāryanta ev' âthavā
pāntha|strī|gṛham iṣṭa|lābha|kathanāl
labdh'|ânvayen' âmunā
sampraty etad anargalaṃ bali|bhujā
māyāvinā bhujyate.

The skill of separating milk from water, 20
those pleasant *tones* : *conversations*,
that grace of *soft footsteps* : *gentle words!*
Never mind about all of that, heron!
If only you knew how to relax your shoulders a bit
  and sit still, my friend,
then why should you not be a swan to me?

Spying an uncovered pot of fresh curd
  fallen by the deserted road—
If the one-eyed* crow,
  puffing himself up with pride,
  stretching out his neck,
  reeling with a hundred urges,
  will not follow his instincts,
  then when will he do so?

No longer can we see those gracefully dancing peacocks,
  and those parrots reciting so sweetly;
  to the contrary, they are angrily chased away.
Now this conjuror crow
  gaining a foothold by a favorable prognostication,
  freely enjoys the house of the absent traveller's wife.

Karabha! rabhasāt
kroṣṭuṃ vāñchasy aho śravaṇa|jvaraḥ!
śaraṇam athav” ân|
ṛjvī dīrghā tav’ âiva śiro|dharā
pṛthu|gala|bil’|ā-
vṛtti|śrānt” ôccariṣyati vāk cirād
iyati samaye
ko jānīte bhaviṣyati kasya kim?

Antaśchidrāṇi bhūyāṃsi
kaṇṭakā bahavo *bahiḥ*
kathaṃ kamala|nālasya
mā bhūvan *bhaṅgurā guṇāḥ?*

Kiṃ dīrgha|dīrgheṣu *guṇeṣu* padma
siteṣv avacchādana|kāraṇaṃ te?
asty eva tān paśyati ced anāryā
trast” êva Lakṣmīr na padaṃ vidhatte.

Na paṅkād udbhūtir
na *jala|saha|vāsa|vyasanitā*
vapur digdhaṃ kāntyā
sthala|nalina ratna|dyuti|muṣā
vyadhāsyad durvedhā
hṛdaya|laghimānaṃ yadi na te
tvam ev’ âiko Lakṣmyāḥ
paramam abhaviṣyaḥ padam iha.

Camel! You're about to bray aloud:
 Ah, what an ear-fever!
Fortunately, your neck is long and crooked,
 so your shriek,
 spent by winding its way
 through your long throat
 will bellow forth after a long delay.
Who knows what might befall whom by then?

Many *holes inside* ⁝ *failings within*,
many *thorns outside* ⁝ *foes without*—
How could *the filaments* ⁝ *virtues*
of the lotus-stalk*
not be *fragile* ⁝ *a sham?*

Why, O lotus, do you conceal 25
 your long *white filaments* ⁝ *pure virtues*?
Its just this. If ignoble Lakshmi saw them
 she might be fearful to tread here.*

O hibiscus,
 your body is tinged with a lustre
 surpassing the radiance of jewels.
 You are not born from a mire,
 you do not *grow in water* ⁝ *befriend fools.*
Had not the wretched creator fashioned you
 with a *flimsy core* ⁝ *ignoble heart:*
You and only you
 would be the abode of Lakshmi in this world.

Uccair uccaratu ciraṃ
cīrī vartmani taruṃ samāruhya;
dig|vyāpini śabda|guṇe
śaṅkhaḥ sambhāvanā|bhūmiḥ.

Śaṅkho 'sthi|śeṣaḥ sphuṭito mṛto vā
procchvāsyate 'ny'|ôcchvasitena satyam.
kiṃ t' ûccaraty eva na so 'sya śabdaḥ
śrāvyo na yo yo na sad|artha|śaṃsī.

Yathā|pallava|puṣpās te
yathā|puṣpa|phala'|rddhayaḥ
yathā|phala'|rddhi|svārohā
hā mātaḥ! kv' âgaman drumāḥ?

30 Sādhv eva tad vidhāv asya
vedhā kliṣṭo na yad vṛthā.
svarūp'|ânanurūpeṇa
candanasya phalena kim?

Grathita eṣa mithaḥ|kṛta|śṛṅkhalair
viṣa|dharair adhiruhya mahā|*jaḍaḥ*
malayajaḥ *sumanobhir* an|āśrito
yad ata eva phalena viyujyate.

The cricket may chirp aloud
perched on a tree on the roadside;
But it is the conch-horn
that is the basis for the notion
that sound pervades all space.

A conch is a skeletal remnant, cracked or dead.
In truth, it blares forth with another's breath.
Yet it emits no sound
that is not attractive
nor that does not praise something worthy.

Alas mother! Where have gone those trees–
whose flowers befitted their shoots,
whose abundance of fruit befitted their flowers
whose elevation befitted the wealth of their fruits?

It is good that the creator did not weary himself in vain 30
as he fashioned the sandalwood tree.
What use would have been an inadequate fruit?

Since this sandalwood tree
is exceedingly *cool* : *ignorant,*
is pinioned with intertwining venomous serpents,*
is not attended by *flowers* : *the wise,*
therefore he bears no fruit.

Candane viṣa|dharān sahāmahe
vastu sundaram aguptimat kutaḥ?
rakṣituṃ vada kim ātma|sauṣṭhavaṃ
sañcitāḥ khadira kaṇṭakās tvayā?

Yat kiñ can' ânucitam apy ucit'|ânubandhi:
kiṃ candanasya na kṛtaṃ kusumaṃ phalaṃ vā?
lajjāmahe bhṛśam upakrama eva yātuṃ
tasy' ântikaṃ parigṛhīta|bṛhat|kuṭhārāḥ.

Labdhaṃ cirād amṛtavat kim amṛtyave syād?
dīrghaṃ rasāyanavad āyur uta pradadyāt?
etat phalaṃ yad ayam adhvaga|śāpa|dagdhaḥ
stabdhaḥ khalaḥ phalati varṣa|śatena tālaḥ.

35 Chinnas tapta|suhṛt sa candana|tarur
yūyaṃ palāyy' āgatā.
bhog'|âbhyāsa|sukhāsikāḥ pratidinaṃ
tā vismṛtās tatra vaḥ?
daṃṣṭrā|koṭi|viṣ'|ôlkayā pratikṛtaṃ
tasya prahartur na cet
kiṃ ten' âiva saha svayaṃ na lavaśo
yātāḥ stha bho bhoginaḥ?

We put up with poisonous serpents on sandalwood trees,
how could anything beautiful be unprotected?
Is it to protect your comeliness, tell us,
O *khádira* tree,* that you bristle so with thorns?

No matter what the impropriety, it can have a positive result:
Why was the sandalwood tree
not given any flowers or fruit at all?
We feel abject shame even to approach it
wielding broad axes.

The fruit that this coarse villain of a palm tree,
burnt by the curses of passing wayfarers,
yields once in a hundred years—
Attained at long last,
does it bestow immortality like ambrosia?
Or does it rejuvenize like an elixir?

Lo serpents! 35
The sandal tree,
a friend to the scorched,
that you went to for shelter has been cut down.
Have you forgotten the comfort
as you *coiled : enjoyed luxuries* there
day by day?
If you will not repay its destroyer
with the flaming poison in your fangs
Why did you not seek ruin along with it?

Saṃtoṣaḥ kim? aśaktatā kim? athavā
tasminn asambhāvanā?
lobho v" āyam? ut' ânavasthitir iyaṃ?
pradveṣa ev' âthavā?
āstāṃ khalv anurūpayā sa|phalayā
puṣpa|śriyā durvidhe!
sambandho 'n|anurūpay" âpi na kṛtaḥ
kiṃ candanasya tvayā?

Kiṃ jāto 'si catuṣ|pathe? ghanatara|
chāyo 'si kiṃ? chāyayā
saṃnaddhaḥ phalito 'si kiṃ? phala|bharaiḥ
pūrṇo 'si kiṃ saṃnataḥ?
he sad|vṛkṣa! sahasva samprati sakhe
śākhā|śikh"|ākarṣaṇa|
kṣobh'|āmoṭana|bhañjanāni janataḥ
svair eva duśceṣṭitaiḥ.

San|*mūlaḥ* prathit'|*ônnatir ghana|lasac|*
chāyaḥ sthitaḥ sat|pathe
sevyaḥ sadbhir it' îdam ākalayatā
tālo 'dhvagen' āśritaḥ
puṃsaḥ śaktir iyaty asau, sa tu phaled
ady' āthavā śvo 'thavā
kāle kv' âpy athavā kadā|cid athavā
n' êty atra Vedhāḥ prabhuḥ

Was it contentedness? Was it inability?
Or was disregard for it?
Or was it greed? Or was it fickleness?
Or even hostility?
Wretched creator! Let's not even talk about
a suitable load of fruit and splendor of flowers!
Why did you not endow the sandalwood tree
even with unsuitable ones?

Ah, good tree! Why were you born at a crossroad?
Why did you have to be rich in shade?
Being rich in shade, why did you bear fruit?
Being laden with burdens fruit,
why did you have to bow down?
Suffer now, for your own misdeeds, my friend,
as people drag, shake,
bend, and break the tips of your branches.

Considering that: *its root* ⁝ *his family* is good,
its height ⁝ *his nobility* is well-known,
its shade is abundant ⁝ *his beauty is intense,*
it stands on a good road ⁝ *he follows right conduct,*
it is frequented by ⁝ *he associates with* the good;
the wayfarer sought the shelter of the palm tree.
This much is in the power of men—
but whether it will bear fruit today, tomorrow,
or at some future time, or never at all, is in God's power.

Tvan|mūle puruṣ'|āyuṣaṃ gatam idam
dehena saṃśuṣyatā
kṣodīyaṃsam api kṣaṇaṃ param ataḥ
śaktiḥ kutaḥ prāṇitum?
tat svasty astu! vivṛdddhim ehi mahatīm!
ady'| âpi kā nas tvarā?
kalyāṇin! phalit" âsi tāla|viṭapin!
putreṣu pautreṣu vā.

«Paśyāmaḥ kim ayaṃ prapatsyata iti»
svalp'|âbhra|siddha|kriyair
darpād dūram upekṣitena *balavat|*
karm'|ēritair mantribhiḥ.
labdh'|ātma|prasareṇa rakṣitum ath' â-
śakyena muktv" *âśaniṃ*
sphītas tādṛg aho *ghanena ripuṇā*
dagdho giri|grāmakaḥ.

Sādh' ûtpāta|ghan'|âugha sādhu! sudhiyā
dhyeyaṃ: «dharāyām idaṃ
ko 'nyaḥ kartum alaṃ?» tav' âiva ghaṭate
karm' ēdṛśaṃ duṣkaram.
sarvasy' âupayikāni yāni kati|cit
kṣetrāṇi tatr' âśaniḥ
sarv'|ânaupayikeṣu dagdha|sikat'|ā-
raṇyeṣv apāṃ vṛṣṭayaḥ.

I have spent my life-span at your foot
withering my body.
How could I go on living
for even the shortest moment beyond this?
So fare thee well!
May you prosper richly!
How could I be in a hurry today?
My benefactor!
may you bear fruit
for my sons
or grandsons.

Thinking: "Let's see if it dares draw near," 40
the haughty *mantra sorcerers ⁝ ministers*
masters of but little cloud magic,
preoccupied with powerful rites ⁝ busy with weighty matters of state, completely ignored
the invincible *hostile cloud ⁝ massed enemy army*
which seized its chance,
released its *thunderbolt ⁝ missiles* and alas!
burnt the thriving mountain village.

Bravo, cloud of doom, bravo! The wise must wonder:
"Who else on earth is capable of this?"
You alone can accomplish this difficult task.
You hurl your thunderbolt on whatever fields
are beneficial to all
and shower rain in scorched deserts
of no use to anybody.

Labdhāyāṃ tṛṣi go|mṛgasya vihagasy'
ânyasya vā kasya cid
vṛṣṭyā syād bhavadīyay" ôpakṛtir ity
āstāṃ davīyasy adaḥ!
asy' âtyantam abhājanasya jalad' ā-
raṇy'|ōṣarasy' âpi kiṃ?
jātā paśya! punaḥ pur" êva paruṣā
s" âiv' âsya dagdhā chaviḥ.

Saṃcintya pān'|ācaman'|ôcitāni
toy'|ântarāṇy asya siseviṣos tvām
nijair na jihreṣi jalair janasya
jaghanya|kāry'|āupayikaiḥ payodhe!

Ā|strī|śiśu|prathita eṣa pipāsitebhyaḥ
saṃrakṣyate 'mbudhir apeyatay" âiva dūrāt.
daṃṣṭrā|karāla|makar'|āli|karālitābhiḥ
kiṃ bhāyayaty aparam ūrmi|paramparābhiḥ?

Sva|māhātmya|ślāghā|
guru|gahana|garjābhir abhitaḥ
kruśitvā kliśnāsi
śruti|kuharam abdhe kim iti naḥ?
ih' âikaś cūḍālo
hy ajani kalaśād yasya sakalaiḥ
pipāsor ambhobhiś
culukam api no bhartum aśakaḥ.

When the *gayal*, or the bird, or any other was thirsty,
your rain gave succor.
Let's completely forget about that for now!
O cloud! What use is it to this utterly worthless
saline wasteland?
Look! Its scorched surface
has become as hostile as it was before.

Hey ocean! Are you not ashamed of your water
used for unclean acts
in front of someone who resorts to you
after doubting
other waters' fitness for drinking and sipping?

It is known even to women and children
that the ocean is shunned as undrinkable by the thirsty.
Why does it menace others
with buffeting waves
terrifying with ranks of *mákaras*
with gaping fanged mouths?

O ocean! Why do you assail our ears, 45
sounding the praises of your own greatness
with a deafening deep roar in all directions?
For, a certain sage was born in this world from a pot.*
When thirsty,
you were unable to fill his cupped hands
with all of your waters.

Sarvāsāṃ tri|jagaty apām iyam asāv
ādhāratā tāvakī
prollāso 'yam ath' âmbudhe! *'mbu|nicaye*
s" êyaṃ *mahā|sattvatā*
sevitvā bahu|*bhaṅga*/bhīṣaṇa|tanuṃ
tvām eva vel"|âcala|
grāva|srotasi pāna|tāpa|kalaho
yat kv' âpi nirvāpyate.

N' *ôdvegaṃ* yadi yāsi yady avahitaḥ
karṇaṃ dadāsi kṣaṇaṃ
tvāṃ pṛcchāmi yad ambudhe kim api tan
niścitya dehy uttaram:
nairāśy'|âtiśay'|âtimātra|nibhṛtair
niḥśvasya yad dṛśyase
tṛṣyadbhiḥ pathikaiḥ kiyat tad adhikaṃ
syād aurvadāhād ataḥ?

Bhidyate 'nupraviśy' āntar yo yathā|rucy upādhinā,
viśuddhiḥ kīdṛśī tasya jaḍasya sphaṭik'|âśmanaḥ?

It is because
you are the foundation of all the water in the triple world.
You *swell with the tide* ⁝ *gladden with your store of water*,
O Ocean!
You *harbor many creatures* ⁝ *are magnanimous*.
Approaching you,
your body terrifying
with many *waves* ⁝ *threatening gestures*
we endure the abuse caused by a burning drink
to be assuaged somewhere
in a rivulet in the mountains at the ends of the earth.

If you won't *swell up* ⁝ *lose your temper*,
and lend me an attentive ear for a moment
let me ask you something, O ocean.
Reflect on it and give me an answer:
How much worse than the submarine fire
is it that you are gazed upon
by thirsty wayfarers
utterly stunned by total despair?

What sort of purity
does the dull crystal possess?
It changes according to the hue
of the thing that is seen through it.*

Cintā|maṇe! «bhuvi na kena cid īśvareṇa
mūrdhnā dhṛto 'ham iti» mā sma sakhe viṣīdaḥ
n' âsty eva hi tvad|adhiropaṇa|puṇya|bīja|
saubhāgya|yogyam iha kasya cid uttam'|âṅgam.

50 Saṃvittir asty, atha guṇāḥ pratibhānti loke,
tad dhi praśastam iha kasya kim ucyatāṃ vā?
nanv evam eva sumaṇe! *luṭa* yāvad|āyus.
tvaṃ me jagat|prasahan'|âika|kathā|śarīram.

Cintā|maṇes tṛṇa|maṇeś ca kṛtaṃ vidhātrā
ken' ôbhayor api maṇitvam adaḥ samānam?
n' âiko 'rthitāni dadad arthi|janāya khinno
gṛhṇañ jarat|tṛṇa|lavaṃ tu na lajjate 'nyaḥ

O wishgranting gem! "No king on earth
  bears me on his head."
My friend, do not despair at this thought.
For in this world,
  nobody's head is worthy of the blessing
  won by the seed of meritorious deeds
  justifying your investiture.

50

There must be recognition
  before people can appreciate virtues.
So,
  is anything of anybody ever praised in this world?
  Pray tell!
O good jewel! This being so,
  please *shine* : *endure* for as long as you are alive.
You are for me the sole embodiment
  of the rumor that the world can be endured.

What kind of creator made the common jewelness
of the wishgranting jewel and the electric tourmaline?*
The one never tires in fulfilling the wishes of the suppliant;
the other is not ashamed to accept a bit of old straw.

Dūre kasya cid eṣa, ko 'py akṛta|dhīr
n' âiv' âsya vetty antaraṃ,
mānī ko 'pi na yācate, mṛgayate
ko 'py alpam alp'|āśayaḥ,
itthaṃ prārthita|dāna|durvyasanino
n' âudārya|rekh"|ôjjvalā
jāt" ânaipuṇa|dustareṣu nikaṣa|
sthāneṣu cintā|maṇeḥ.

Par'|ârthe yaḥ *pīḍām* anubhavati bhaṅge 'pi *madhuro*
yadīyaḥ sarveṣām iha khalu *vikāro* 'py abhimataḥ.
na samprāpto vṛddhiṃ sa yadi bhṛśam akṣetra|patitaḥ,
kim ikṣor doṣo 'sau na punar a|guṇāyā maru|bhuvaḥ?

Āmrāḥ kiṃ phala|bhāra|namra|śiraso?
ramyā kim ūṣma|cchidaḥ
sa|cchāyāḥ kadalī|drumāḥ surabhayaḥ?
kiṃ puṣpitāś campakāḥ?
etās tā niravagrah'|ôgra|karabh'|ô-
llīḍh'|ârdha|rūḍhāḥ punaḥ
śamyo. bhrāmyasi mūḍha! nirmaruti kiṃ
mithy" âiva martuṃ marau?

It is remote for one,
another cannot perceive its essence,
an arrogant man does not entreat it,
the shallow minded man asks for trifles.
Consequently,
  the glint of the wishgranting jewel's generosity,
  it being addicted to giving what is asked for,
  has not appeared in places of trial
  inaccessible without skill.

It endures *pressing* ⁝ *torment* for the benefit of others,
and remains *sweet* ⁝ *kind* even when broken,
its *refined produce* ⁝ *good work* is without fail welcomed
  by everyone in this world.
If it fails to prosper,
  falling woefully astray on fallow ground:
Is this the fault of the sugar-cane
  and not of the worthless wasteland?

Are there mango trees,
  bowing their heads with burdens of fruits?
Are there fragrant, shady plantains
  to dispel the heat?
Are there blossoming *chámpaka* trees?
Here there are *shami* hardwoods,
  straggly for being chewed by fierce wild camels.
Fool! Why, in vain,
  are you straying to your death in this windless desert?

55 Ājanmanaḥ kuśalam aṇv api re kujanman
pāṃso! tvayā yadi kṛtaṃ vada tat tvam eva!
utthāpito 'sy anala|sārathinā yad|arthaṃ
duṣṭena tat kuru, kalaṅkaya viśvam etat.

Niḥsārāḥ sutarāṃ laghu|prakṛtayo
yogyā na kārye kva cic
chuṣyanto 'dya jarat|tṛṇ'|ādy|avayavāḥ
prāptāḥ svatantreṇa ye
antaḥ|sāra|parāṅ|mukhena dhig aho!
te māruten' âmunā
paśy' âtyanta|calena sadma mahatām
ākāśam āropitā.

Ye jātyā laghavaḥ, sad" âiva gaṇanāṃ
yātā na ye kutra cit,
padbhyām eva vimarditāḥ pratidinaṃ,
bhūmau nilīnāś ciram,
utkṣiptāś capal'|āśayena marutā,
paśy' ântarikṣe 'dhunā
tuṅgānām upari|sthitiṃ kṣiti|bhṛtāṃ
kurvanty amī pāṃsavaḥ.

Fie upon you, lowborn dust! Have you ever accomplished 55
any good since your birth? Tell me!
Bring to pass that for which this evil wind,
   the charioteer of fire,
   has raised you up:
Befoul the world.

Altogether hollow, inherently flimsy,
   useless for any task—
Woe, alas! Look! Today the wilful, volatile wind
   turning away from the *mountains ∶ men of worth*
has raised up
   such bits of dry, withered straw as were at hand
   into the sky, the abode of the great.

Inherently low,
never taken into any kind of account,
ground underfoot every day,
clinging to the ground for a long time—
Behold! Now, blown up by the unsteady wind,
these motes of dust soar in the sky,
   above the towering, earth-supporting mountains.

Re dandaśūka! yad ayogyam ap' *Īśvaras* tvām
vātsalyato *nayati nūpura|dhāma* satyam;
āvarjit'|âli|kula|jhaṃ|kṛti|mūrcchitāni
kiṃ śiñjitāni bhavataḥ kṣamam eva kartum?

Maulau san|maṇayo gṛhaṃ giri|guhā
    tyāgitvam ātma|tvaco
  niryatn'|ôpanataiś ca vṛttir anilair
    ekatra cary" ēdṛśī.
anyatr' ân|ṛju vartma vāg dvi|rasanā
    dṛṣṭau viṣaṃ dṛśyate
  yā dik tām anu dīpako jvalati. bho
    bhogin, sakhe! kiṃ nv idam?

60 Kallola|vellita|dṛṣat|paruṣa|prahārai
ratnāny amūni makar'|ālaya! m" âvamaṃsthāḥ;
kiṃ kaustubhena vihito bhavato na nāma
yācñā|prasārita|karaḥ Puruṣottamo 'pi?

Fie upon you, serpent!
It is true that, though you are unworthy,
Shiva : *the king*, forsooth,
affectionately
  adorns with you his ankles : *led you to his feet*.
Do you have the skill to susurrate,
outrivalling the rapturous humming of swarms of bees?

Friend snake! Why all this?
  You wear excellent gems on your crest,
  live in a mountain cave,
  and relinquish your own skin.
  You live off air, available without effort.
On the one hand, you behave like this.
On the other hand,
  your path is crooked,
  your tongue is forked,
  your glance is poison,
  a light gleams in whatever direction you glare.

O Ocean! Do not mistreat these jewels 60
with sharp blows of boulders rolling in the waves.
Did not the *káustubha* jewel
  bring even Vishnu to you
his hand held out to beg?

Bhūyāṃsy asya mukhāni nāma vidit" âi-
v' āste mahā|prāṇatā
Kadrvāḥ sat|prasavo 'yam atra kupite
cintyaṃ yath" êdaṃ jagat
trailoky'|âdbhutam īdṛśaṃ tu caritaṃ
Śeṣasya yen' âpi sā
pronmṛjy' êva nivartitā viṣa|dhara|
jñāteya|durvṛttitā.

Varṣe samasta ev' âikaḥ
ślāghyaḥ ko 'py eṣa vāsaraḥ
janair mahattayā nīto
yo na pūrvair na c' âparaḥ.

Ābaddha|kṛtrima|saṭā|jaṭil'|âṃsa|bhittir
āropito mṛga|pateḥ padavīṃ yadi śvā
matt'|êbha|kumbha|taṭa|pāṭana|lampaṭasya
nādaṃ kariṣyati kathaṃ hariṇ'|âdhipasya?

The world-serpent Shesha's heads are numerous,
his great power is renowned,
he is noble progeny of Kadru.
When he is angry the world is in peril.
Such are his exploits, the marvel of the triple world,
  that his offense of belonging to snake-kind
  seems wiped away.

Glorious is that wonderful day,
even if it be just one in the whole year,
spent in greatness, not enjoyed
by those who have gone before
nor by those who will come.

If a dog, festooned with a fake mane on his shoulders,
is put in place of a lion, king of beasts,
how can he roar like the lord of animals,
impatient to rend asunder the frontal lobes
  of a rutting tusker?

Kim idam ucitaṃ *śuddheḥ*? śliṣṭaṃ *sva/pakṣa/samunnateḥ*?
phala|pariṇater yuktaṃ? prāptaṃ *guṇa*|praṇayasya vā?
kṣaṇam upagataḥ karṇ'|ôpāntaṃ parasya, puraḥ sthitān
viśikha! nipatan krūraṃ dūrān nṛśaṃsa nihaṃsi yat

65 Amī ye dṛśyante nanu subhaga|rūpāḥ, sa|phalatā
bhavaty eṣāṃ yasya kṣaṇam upagatānāṃ viṣayatām
nirāloke loke katham idam aho! cakṣur adhunā
samaṃ jātaṃ sarvair? na samam athav" ânyair avayavaiḥ?

Āhūteṣu vihaṅgameṣu maśako
    n' āyān puro vāryate
  madhye|vāridhi vā vasaṃs tṛṇa|maṇir
    dhatte maṇīnāṃ rucam
kha|dyoto 'pi na kampate pracalituṃ
    madhye 'pi tejasvināṃ
  dhik sāmānyam acetanaṃ prabhum iv' â-
    n|āmṛṣṭa|tattv'|ântaram.

Does it befit your *accuracy* : *purity*?
Is it related to the *position of your fletching* : *promotion*
of your people?
Does it the behove of your *preparation* : *past karma,*
or does it befit your attachment to *the bow-string* : *virtue?*
O *arrow* : *shaveling!* That,
for an instant you reach the ear of the chief,
fly forth and cruelly strike down from afar
those who stand before you, o ruthless one.

These attractive forms that are seen 65
surely, they become fruitful
when they fleetingly become the objects of the eye.
Now, when the world is lightless,
alas! How is it that this eye has
just become the same as all the other organs?
Or rather they are not the same.*

When birds are summoned,
a mosquito who appears is not warded off.
A tourmaline* placed in the depths of the ocean
takes on the lustre of jewels.
A glow-worm fears not to move among the luminaries.
Curses upon similarity,
inconsiderate of actual differences.

Hema|kāra! sudhiye namo 'stu te!
dustareṣu bahuśaḥ parīkṣitum
kāñcan'|ābharaṇam aśmanā samaṃ
yat tvay" âivam adhiropyate tulām.

Vṛtta eva sa ghaṭo 'ndha|kūpa yas
tvat|prasādam api netum akṣamah
mudritaṃ tv adhama|ceṣṭitaṃ tvayā
tan|mukh'|âmbu|kaṇikāḥ pratīcchatā.

Tṛṇa|maṇer manujasya ca tattvataḥ
kim ubhayor vipul'|āśayat" ôcyate
tanu|tṛṇ'|âgra|lav'|âvayavair yayor
avasite grahaṇa|pratipādane.

70 Śata|padī sati pāda|śate kṣamā
yadi na goṣ|padam apy ativartitum
kim iyatā dvi|padasya Hanumato
jala|nidhi|kramaṇe vivadāmahe?

Na *guru/vaṃśa/parigraha*|śauṇḍatā
na ca *mahā/guṇa/saṃgrahaṇ'*|ādaraḥ
phala/vidhāna/kath" âpi na *mārgaṇe*
kim iha *lubdhaka/bāla*|gṛhe 'dhunā?

Goldsmith! Wise man, hail to you!
For to ascertain repeatedly what is undetermined
you place on your scales
ornaments of gold and weighing stones as equals.

O blind well! The pot has returned
unable to win your favor.
But you have sealed your low deed
by taking the droplets of water from its mouth.

In truth, what can one say about the liberality
of both the tourmaline and of man?
Their giving and taking extends only to
fragmentary bits of fine straw-tips.

If a centipede, equipped with a hundred feet, 70
is unable to cross a small puddle,
should we, on account of this,
dispute two-legged Hanuman's leap across the ocean?

In the house of the *young hunter* ⁝ *avaricious simpleton*
there is
no devotion *to selecting long bamboo* ⁝ *in discerning noble lineages,*
no zeal in *twining cords* ⁝ *accumulating exalted virtues*
no *sign of fixing the tips on arrows* ⁝ *hint of rewarding the needy*;
why linger here?

Tanu|tṛṇ'|âgra|dhṛtena hṛtaś ciraṃ
ka iva tena na mauktika|śaṅkayā
sa jala|bindur aho! viparīta|dṛg
jagad idaṃ, vayam atra sa|cetanāḥ.

Budhyāmahe na bahudh" âpi vikalpayantaḥ
kair nāmabhir vyapadiśema mahā|matīṃs tān
yeṣām aśeṣa|bhuvan'|ābharaṇasya hemnas
tattvaṃ vivektum upalāḥ paramaṃ pramāṇam

Saṃrakṣituṃ kṛṣim akāri kṛṣī|valena
paśy' ātmanaḥ pratikṛtis tṛṇa|pūruṣo 'yam
stabdhasya niṣkriyatay" âsta|bhiyo 'sya nūnam
aśnanti go|mṛga|gaṇāḥ pura eva sasyam

Kasy' ânimeṣa|nayane vidite div'|âuko|
lokād ṛte, jagati te api vai gṛhītvā
piṇḍa|prasārita|mukhena time kim etad
dṛṣṭaṃ na bāliśa viśad baḍiśaṃ tvay" ântaḥ?

Is there anyone, who is not taken in for a long time
by this thing
balanced on the tip of a slender blade of grass
wondering if it might be a pearl?
Ah! it is a droplet of water.
The world perceives it falsely.
I am aware of it.

I do not know, even after much reflection,
by what names I should call those great-minded persons
who use a stone as the ultimate proof
to discern the true value of gold,
the ornament of the entire world.

Look at this straw scarecrow made by the ploughman
in his own image to guard the field.
Now, freed from fear
by the *stillness of this propped up thing* ⁝ *lack of action of this arrogant man*
herds of deer feed on wheat right in front of it.

Who has unwinking eyes 75
except the heaven-dwelling gods?
Endowed with these on earth, O stupid fish,
why did you not detect the hook entering within
as your mouth opened for a morsel?

Puṃstvād api pravicaled yadi, yady *adho* 'pi
yāyād, yadi *praṇayane na mahān* api syāt,
abhyuddharet tad api viśvam it' īdṛś" îyaṃ
ken' âpi dik prakaṭitā *Puruṣottamena*

Sv|alp'|āśayaḥ sva|kula|śilpa|vikalpam eva
yaḥ kalpayan skhalati kāca|vaṇik piśācaḥ
grastaḥ sa kaustubha|maṇ'|îndra|sapatna|ratna|
niryatna|gumphanaka|vaikaṭik'|ērṣyay" ântaḥ

Tat|pratyarthitayā vṛto, na tu kṛtaḥ
    samyak svatantro bhayāt
«svasthas tān na nipātayed» iti yathā|
    kāmaṃ na samposịtaḥ
saṃśuṣyan pṛṣadaṃśa eṣa kurutāṃ
    mūka|sthito 'py atra kiṃ
gehe kiṃ bahunā? 'dhunā gṛha|pateś
    caurāś caranty ākhavaḥ.

Even if one *strays from manliness* ⁝ *becomes a woman,*
even if one *loses status* ⁝ *delves into the netherworld,*
even if one *humbles oneself when begged* ⁝ *becomes*
a dwarf to beg
nevertheless one can rescue the world
this way was shown by a certain *king* ⁝ *Vishnu.*

This petty-minded demon of a glass-merchant
who blunders even while practising
the highly specialised art of his family
has become consumed with jealousy towards the jeweller
who can effortlessly string together
gems akin to the Káustubha, king of jewels.

It was taken in because it was inimical to them,
but it was not given free scope.
Thinking: "If it is content
it will not hunt them down," it was not fed its fill.
What can that scrawny cat, become a mute, do here?
Why say more?
Now the rats scurry about in the master's house.

Evaṃ cet *sa/rasa*|svabhāva|mahimā
jāḍyaṃ kim etādṛśaṃ?
yady eṣā ca nisargataḥ *saralatā*
kiṃ *granthimatt"* ēdṛśī?
mūlaṃ cec *chuci«* paṅkaja|śrutir» iyaṃ
kasmād? *guṇā* yady amī
kiṃ *chidrāṇi*? sakhe mṛṇāla bhavatas
tattvaṃ na manyāmahe!

80 Ye digdhv" êva kṛtā viṣeṇa, *kusṛtir*
yeṣāṃ kiyad gaṇyate
lokaṃ hantum anāgasaṃ dvi|rasanā,
randhreṣu ye *jāgrati*
vyālās te 'pi *dadhaty* amī sad|asator
mūḍhā *maṇīn mūrdhabhir*
n' âucityād guṇa|śalināṃ kva cid api
bhraṃśo 'sty alaṃ cintayā!

If such is the greatness
of your inherent *sweetness* ⁝ *worth*, why this
coolness ⁝ *imbecility*?
If such is your spontaneous *straightness* ⁝ *forthrightness*,
why this *knottiness* ⁝ *perversion*?
If your *root* ⁝ *origin* is *pure* ⁝ *noble*,
why this appelation "mud-born"?
If these be *fibres* ⁝ *virtues*,
why these *holes* ⁝ *defects*?
O lotus-stalk! My friend, I cannot figure you out!

Those who were created seemingly smeared 80
with venom,
whose *sinuous movements* ⁝ *misdeeds*
are beyond reckoning,
who have a forked tongue to slay the innocent,
who *lurk in holes* ⁝ *are fault-finders*,
—these serpents
though ignorant of good and bad
bear jewels in their hoods ⁝ *place a worthy man in charge.*
Nowhere do the virtuous fall from propriety.
Stop worrying!

Aho strīṇāṃ krauryaṃ!
    hata|rajani! dhik tvām! atiśaṭhe!
vṛthā prakrānt" êyaṃ
    timira|kabarī|mokṣa|kusṛtiḥ
avaktavye pāte
    jana|nayana|nāthasya śaśinaḥ
kṛtaṃ snehasy' ânto-
    citam udadhi|mukhyair nanu jaḍaiḥ

Aho gehe|nardī
    divasa|vijigīṣā|jvara|rujā
pradīpaḥ sva|sthāne
    glapayati mṛṣ" âmūn *avayavān*
udātta|svacchand'|ā-
    kramaṇa|hṛta|viśvasya tamasaḥ?
parispandaṃ draṣṭuṃ
    mukham api ca kiṃ soḍham amunā?

Nām' apy anya|taror nimīlitam abhūt
    tat tāvad unmīlitaṃ
prasthāne skhalataḥ sva|vartmani vidher
    apy udgṛhītaḥ karaḥ
lokaś c' âyam a|dṛṣṭa|darśana|bhuvaḥ
    dṛg+vaiśasān mocito
yuktaṃ kāṣṭhika lūnavān yad asi tām
    āmr'|ālim ākālikīm.

Lo! the cruelty of women!
Wretched night! Fie upon you! Utter villainess!
Vainly you attempt this trick of releasing
the fillet of your hair.
Even the inert ocean & co. did what befitted
the end of their love
during the indescribable sinking of the moon,
lord of the people's eyes.

Oho! The lamp, a defiant hero at home,
ablaze with the fever of conquering the day,
vainly soils its *parts* ⁝ *family members*.
Could it bear to behold
even the *face* ⁝ *beginning* of the darkness
that deprives the world of
its complete freedom of action?

Even the name of other trees was obscured
while it was exalted.
The hand of God who had stumbled
on his path was checked,
the world was spared the eye-distress
born from an unknown sight,
—you were right, O woodcutter, to cut down
the mango grove flowering out of season.

Vāt'|āhāratayā jagad viṣa|dharair āśvāsya niḥśeṣitaṃ
te grastāḥ punar abhra|toya|kaṇikā|tīvra|vratair barhibhiḥ
te 'pi krūra|camūru|carma|vasanair nītāḥ kṣayaṃ lubdhakair
dambhasya sphuritaṃ vidann api jano jālmo guṇān īhate

85 Ūḍhā yena mahā|dhuraḥ su|viṣame
mārge sad" âikākinā
soḍho yena kadā cid eva na nije
goṣṭhe 'nya|śauṇḍa|dhvaniḥ
āsīd yas tu gavāṃ gaṇasya tilakas
tasy' âiva sampraty aho!
dhik kaṣṭaṃ dhavalasya jāta|jaraso
goḥ paṇyam udghoṣyate

Asthān'|ôdyoga|duḥkhaṃ
jahihi! na hi nabhaḥ paṅgu|saṃcāra|yogyaṃ.
sv'|āyāsāy' âiva sādho
tava śalabha! jav'|âbhyāsa|durvāsan" êyam
te Devasy' âpy acintyāś
caṭulita|bhuvan'|ābhoga|vel"|âvahelā
mūl'|ôtkhāt'|ânumārg'|
āgata|giri|guravas Tārkṣya|pakṣ'|âgra|vātāḥ.

By feeding on air, snakes won
the world's confidence, and wrought havoc.
They, in turn, were devoured by peacocks, who observe
the severe vow of feeding on drops of rainwater.
They, in turn, are slaughtered by hunters clad
in the coarse skin of *chamúru* deer.
Though perceiving this obvious hypocrisy,
a wretched person still craves such virtues.

He who all alone bore a great burden 85
on the uneven road,
who never tolerated another's proud bellow in his pen,
who was the ornament of oxenkind,
now that the white ox has grown old,
what shame! His price is proclaimed aloud.

Abandon your misplaced effort!
The sky is no place for the lame to roam.
My good locust!
Your harmful inclination of flitting about
will only exhaust you.
Even the god Vishnu cannot conceive of the gusts
of wind, streaming from Gáruda's wing-tips
which effortlessly shake the bound sof the world,
and are heavily laden with mountains torn
from their roots in his path.

Candreṇ' âiva taraṅga|bhaṅgi|mukharaṃ
saṃvardhyamān'|âmbhaso
dadyur jīvitam eva kiṃ giri|saric
srotāṃsi yady ambudheḥ
teṣv eva pratisaṃvidhāna|vikalaṃ
paśyatsu sākṣiṣv iva
drāg darp'|ôddhuram āgateṣv api na sa
kṣīyeta yady anyathā.

Kil' âika|culukena yo munir apāram abdhiṃ papau
sahasram api ghasmaro 'vikṛtam eṣa teṣāṃ pibet
na sambhavati kiṃ tv idaṃ bata vikāsi|dhāmnā vinā?
sad apy asad iva sthitaṃ sphuritam anta ojasvinām.

Grāvāṇo 'tra vibhūṣaṇaṃ tri|jagato,
maryādayā sthīyate
nanv atr' âiva vidhuḥ sthito hi vibudhāḥ
sambhūya pūrṇ'|āśiṣaḥ
śete c' ôdgata|nābhi|padma|vilasad|
brahm" êha Devaḥ svayaṃ
daivād eti *jaḍaḥ sva/kukṣi/bhṛtaye*
so 'py ambudhir nimnatām

If the moon alone imbues life, garrulous
with fleeting waves,
to the ocean, swelling its waters,
then how could the mountain streams do so?
If this were not true,
then it would not be diminished
as they rush to it
headlong with a swagger,
to look on like bystanders,
helpless to render assistance.

The sage* who long ago drank the boundless ocean
with one handful,
voracious,* he could without harm
drink a thousand of them.
But, surely, this would not be possible without
a radiant brilliance?
Though it exists, it seems not to,
blazing within the powerful.

There are *rocks* ∶ *jewels* in it,
it is the ornament of the triple world,
it stays within its bounds.
Indeed, the moon dwells in it alone,
it fulfilled the gods' desires,
Vishnu himself sleeps upon it,
Brahma manifest on the lotus sprouting from his navel.
Fate decrees that even the *water* ∶ *ignorant* ocean,*
sinks low to fill *his belly* ∶ *his submarine caves*.

90 Anīrṣyā śrotāro! mama vacasi ced vacmi tad ahaṃ
sva|pakṣād bhetavyaṃ na tu bahu vipakṣāt prabhavataḥ!
tamasy ākrānt'|āśe kiyad api hi tejo 'vayavinaḥ!
sva|śaktyā bhānty ete divasa|kṛti saty eva na punaḥ.

Etat tasya mukhāt kiyat kamalinī|
patre kaṇaṃ vāriṇo
yan muktā|maṇir ity amaṃsta sa jaḍaḥ.
śṛṇv anyad asmād api:
aṅguly|agra|laghu|kriyā|pravilayiny
ādīyamāne śanaiḥ
«kutr' ôḍḍīya|gato mam' êty» anudinaṃ
nidrāti n' ântaḥ|śucā.

Āste 'tr' âiva sarasy, aho bata kiyān
saṃtoṣa|pakṣa|graho!
haṃsasy' âsya manāṅ na dhāvati manaḥ
śrī|dhāmni padme kva cit.
«supto 'dy' âpi na budhyate tad itarāṃs
tāvat pratīkṣāmahe!»
velām ity udaraṃ|priyā madhu|lihaḥ
soḍhuṃ kṣaṇaṃ na kṣamāḥ

O listeners! If you will bear with me, I will speak. 90
Fear one's own side, not the powerful foe!
How the stars shine
when the horizon is invaded by darkness!
When the sun shines,
they cannot shine by their own power.

It is no big deal
that the fool mistook the water drop
  on the lotus leaf for a pearl.
Hear more about him:
As he gently picked it up
  it dissolved by the slight motion of his fingertip.
"Where has it flown to?"
Now, every day, he cannot sleep with inner grief.

He dwells here in this lake.
Ah! how gratifying!
The swan's mind does not hanker even slightly
after the lotus, the abode of Lakshmi.
Saying: "It's asleep, even now it's still not awake!
  Let's go wait on someone else first!"
The gluttonous bees cannot bear
a delay of even a moment.

Bhekena kvaṇatā sa|roṣa|paruṣaṃ
yat kṛṣṇa|sarp'|ānane
dātuṃ gaṇḍa|capetam ujjhita|bhiyā
hastaḥ samullāsitaḥ
yac c' âdho|mukham akṣiṇī pidadhatā
nāgena tatra sthitaṃ
tat sarvaṃ viṣa|mantriṇo bhagavataḥ
kasy' âpi līlāyitam

Mṛtyor āsyam iv' ātataṃ dhanur idaṃ
c' āśīviṣ'|ābhāḥ śarāḥ
śikṣā s'' âpi jit'|ârjuna|prabhṛtikā
sarvatra nimnā gátiḥ
antaḥ|krauryam aho śaṭhasya madhuraṃ
hā hāri *geyaṃ* mukhe
vyādhasy' âsya yathā bhaviṣyati tathā
manye vanaṃ nir|mṛgam

95 Ko 'yaṃ bhrānti|prakāras
tava pavana padaṃ loka|pād'|āhatīnāṃ
tejasvi|vrāta|sevye
nabhasi nayasi yat pāṃsu|pūraṃ pratiṣṭhām
yasminn utthāpyamāne
jana|nayana|path'|ôpadravas tāvad āstāṃ.
ken' ôpāyena sādhyo
vapuṣi kaluṣatā|doṣa eṣa tvay' âiva

That an angrily croaking frog,
without fear, should raise its hand
to deliver a slap
in the face of a black cobra,
and that the serpent should remain there
lowering its face
closing its eyes
all this is the play of some powerful snake-sorcerer.

This strung bow is like the gaping mouth of Death,
and the arrows are like venomous snakes
his marksmanship exceeds that of Arjuna & co,
his movement is always stealthy.
Lo! the cruelty within the cunning hunter and, alas!
the sweet, captivating *song* : *praise* in his mouth.
With this I fear the forest will be emptied of animals.

What a blunder you are committing, o wind, 95
when you raise up the abundant dust,
crushed underfoot by the whole world
to prominence in the sky,
worthy of the company of a host of luminaries!
Let's not even mention that the vision of the people
is impaired when it is raised up.
What remedy is there to rid this stain of filth
from your body?

Ete te vijigīṣavo nṛpa|gṛha|
dvār'|ârpit'|âvekṣaṇāḥ
kṣipyante vasu|yācan"|āhita|dhiyaḥ
kop'|ôddhatair vetribhiḥ
arthebhyo viṣay'|ôpabhoga|virasair
n' âkāri yair ādaras
te tiṣṭhanti manasvinaḥ sura|sarit|
tīre manohāriṇi.

Vātā vāntu kadamba|reṇu|śabalā
nṛtyantu sarpa|dviṣaḥ
s'|ôtsāhā nava|toya|bhāra|guravo
muñcantu nādaṃ ghanāḥ
magnāṃ kānta|viyoga|duḥkha|dahane
māṃ vīkṣya dīn'|ānanāṃ
vidyut kiṃ sphurasi tvam apy akaruṇe
strītve 'pi tulye sati

Prāṇā yena samarpitās tava, *balād* yen' âivam *utthāpitaḥ skandhe* yena ciraṃ *dhṛto* 'si, *vidadhe* yas te *saparyām* api tasy' ânta|smita|mātrakeṇa janayañ jīv'|âpahāraṃ kṣaṇād. bhrātaḥ! pratyupakāriṇāṃ dhuri paraṃ vetāla|līlāyase!

These ambitious men,
  fixing their eyes to the royal gate,
  intent on begging for wealth
are scattered by gatekeepers flying up in a rage.
The wise, made averse to wealth
by their shunning of worldly enjoyments,
rest on the delightful banks of the heavenly river.

The breezes waft, speckled with *kadámba* pollen,
peacocks, the foes of serpents, dance,
threatening clouds, laden with fresh water, thunder.
Seeing me, looking melancholy,
sinking in the fire of separation from my beloved
O lightning! Why are you flashing forth, merciless one, are we not both women?

He who gave you *life* ⁝ *hope*,
who *helped you stand up* ⁝ *powerfully promoted you*
who *carried you on his shoulders* ⁝ *retained you in*
  the army for a long time,
who *adored you* ⁝ *gave you respect*,
in an instant, with no more than
  a secret smile you take his life.
Brother! You are the epitome of the grateful
behaving thoroughly like a vampire!*

Rajjvā diśaḥ pravitatāḥ salilaṃ viṣeṇa
khātā mahī huta|bhujā jvalitā van'|ântāḥ
vyādhāḥ padāny anusaranti gṛhīta|cāpāḥ
kaṃ deśam āśrayatu yūtha|patir mṛgāṇām

100 «Ayaṃ vārām eko nilaya iti, ratn'|ākara iti»
śrito 'smābhis tṛṣṇā|taralita|manobhir jala|nidhiḥ
ka evaṃ jānīte nija|kara|puṭī|koṭara|gataṃ
kṣaṇād enaṃ tāmyat|timi|nikaram āpāsyati muniḥ

Viśālaṃ śālmalyā nayana|subhagam vīkṣya kusumaṃ
śukasy' āsīd buddhiḥ: «phalam api bhaved asya sadṛśam!»
cir'|āsīnaṃ tasmiṃś ca phalam api daivāt pariṇataṃ
vipāke tūlo 'ntaḥ sapadi marutā so 'py apahṛtaḥ.

Sarva|prajā|hita|kṛte Puruṣottamasya
vāse, samasta|vibudha|prathit'|êṣṭa|siddhau
candr'|âṃśu|vṛnda|vitata|dyutimaty amuṣmin
he kālakūṭa! tava janma kathaṃ payodhau?

The quarters are fenced off with ropes,
the water is impassable with poison,
the earth is dug up, the brushwood is set ablaze,
hunters, bows in hand, are hard on his heels;
whither can the chief of the herd flee?

Thinking: "This is the sole store of water, 100
the mine of jewels!"
I approached the ocean, my heart aquiver with thirst.
Who could have known that the sage Agástya
would drink it down in a flash
  from his hollow cupped hands
  along with its teeming shoals of fish.

Espying the large, eye-delighting flower
  of the silk-cotton tree
the parrot thought: "It's fruit will be comparable!"
It sat on it for a long time and as luck would have it
  a fruit grew.
When it was ripe
there was cotton inside
and even that was blown away by the wind.

The dwelling place of Vishnu,
  benefactor of all,
the granter of countless wishes to all of the gods,
dazzlingly radiant with bundles of moon-beams,
–Ah! Kala·kuta poison,
how could you be born from that ocean?

Phalita|ghana|viṭapa|vighaṭita|
paṭu|dina|kara|mahasi lasati kalpa|tarau
chāy"|ârthī kaḥ paśur api
bhavati jarad|vīrudhāṃ praṇayī.

In the presence of a wishgranting tree,
skilled at dispelling the blaze of the sun with
its dense canopy of fruit-bearing boughs
is there even a dumb beast seeking shade,
that would be attracted to
a withered shrub?

KSHEMÉNDRA: THE GRACE OF GUILE 1. SANCTIMONIOUSNESS

1.1 Asti *viśālaṃ kamalā|lalita|*
pariṣvaṅga|maṅgal'|āyatanam
Śrī|pati|vakṣaḥ|sthalam iva
ratn'|ôjjvalam ujjvalaṃ nagaram.

Maṇi|bhū|bimbita|muktā|
pralamba|nivahena yatra Śeṣ'|âhiḥ
bhavanāni bibharti sadā
bahudh" ātmānaṃ vibhajy' âikaḥ.

Vighno 'bhisārikāṇāṃ
bhavana|gaṇaḥ sphāṭika|prabhā|vikaṭaḥ
yatra virājati Rajanī|
timira|paṭa|prakaṭa|luṇṭhākaḥ.

Yatra Trinayana|nayana|
jvalana|jvāl"|āvalī|śalabha|vṛttiḥ
jīvati Mānasa|janmā
śaśi|vadanā|vadana|kānti|pīyūṣaiḥ.

1.5 Rati|lulita|lalita|lalanā|
klama|jala|lava|vāhino muhur yatra
ślatha|keśa|kusuma|parimala|
vāsita|dehā vahanty anilāḥ.

THERE IS *a vast, magnificent city* 1.1
with mansions blessed
by the refining touch of wealth,
dazzling with riches.
It resembles the *expansive* chest of Shri's consort Vishnu—
the happy mainstay of Lakshmi's graceful embrace,
*resplendent with the Káustubha jewel.**

A city where the world-serpent Shesha*
tirelessly seems to prop up the palaces,
—refracting himself manifold though he is one—
by the opulence of dangling strings of pearls
reflected in jewelled floors.

Where gleam serried mansions,
glaring with crystalline radiance:*
brazen thieves of lady Night's dark veil,
—a dilemma for women stealing to their lovers.

Where the God of love,*
who is prone to behave like a moth
drawn towards the wisps of flame
shooting from Shiva's third eye,
is nurtured by the nectar of loveliness
in the countenance of moon-faced ladies.

Where steadily there waft breezes, 1.5
laden with droplets of perspiration
from the fatigue of ravishing, uninhibited women
exhausted by love-play,
and perfumed by the fragrance of the blossoms
in their loosened hair.

Nava|bisa|kisalaya|kavalana|
kaṣāya|kala|haṃsa|kala|ravo yatra
kamala|vaneṣu prasarati
Lakṣmyā iva nūpur'|ārāvaḥ.

Nṛtyan|mugdha|mayūrā|
marakata|dhārā|gṛh'|āvalī satatam
s'|êndr'|āyudha|ghana|nivahā
prāvṛṇ mūrt" êva yatr' āste.

Śaśi|kiraṇa|prāvaraṇa|
sphāṭika|harmyeṣu hariṇa|śāv'|âkṣyaḥ
yatra vibhānti sudh"|âmbudhi|
dugdha|taraṅg'|ôdgatā iv' âpsarasaḥ.

Tatr' âbhūd abhibhūta|
prabhūta|māyā|nikāya|śata|dhūrtaḥ
sakala|kalā|nilayānāṃ
dhuryaḥ śrī|Mūladev'|ākhyaḥ.

1.10 Nānā|dig|deś'|āgata|
dhūrtair upajīvyamāna|mati|vibhavaḥ
sa *prāpa vipula/saṃpadam*
ātma|guṇaiś cakra|vart" îva.

Bhukt'|ôttaraṃ sa|hṛdayaiḥ
āsthānī|saṃsthitaṃ kadā cit tam
abhyetya sārtha|vāho
datta|mah"|ârh'|ôpahāra|maṇi|caṣakaḥ
Praṇato Hiraṇyaguptaḥ
sahitaḥ putreṇa Candraguptena
prāpt'|āsana|satkāraḥ
provāca muhūrta|viśrāntaḥ.

Where the melodious cry of wild geese, warm in timbre
because their beaks are filled
with shoots and fresh sprouts,
spreads through the lotus-ponds,
as if it were the tinkling of Lakshmi's anklets.

Where the rainy season seems to linger on
with a host of rainbows and clouds,
embodied in a row of emerald fountains,*
and dancing, tame peacocks.

Where ladies, with eyes like those of young does,
shine forth on crystalline pavilions
cloaked in moonlight,
like nymphs* born from the churned waves
of the ocean of nectar.

There dwelt the foremost repository of all guile: a cunning man named Mula·deva* who had mastered a hundred
categories of unsurpassed deceptions. Villains, depending 1.10
for their livelihood on the prowess of his intellect, flocked to him from remote lands.* He *received enormous wealth*, just as an universal emperor *exults in glory* by his inherent virtues.

One day, after he had dined and was seated in his audience hall with men of refined taste,* a caravan-leader approached him and offered him a jewel-inlaid chalice as a priceless gift. The bowing Hiránya·gupta, accompanied by his son Chandra·gupta, received a seat and due hospitality, and after a brief rest, broke the silence:

«Ayi! paricaya|sa|pratibhā
tava purato mādṛśām iyaṃ vāṇī
grāmy'|âṅgan" êva nagare
na tathā pragalbhyam āyāti.

Pihita|Bṛhaspati|dhiṣaṇo
ruciraḥ prajñā|marīci|nicayas te
tigm'|âṃśor iva saha|jaḥ
proṣita|timirāḥ karoty āśāḥ.

1.15 Ā|janm'|ârjita|bahu|vidha|
maṇi|mauktika|kanaka|pūrṇa|koṣasya
eko mam' âiṣa sūnuḥ
saṃjātaḥ paścime vayasi.

Moha|sthānaṃ bālyaṃ
yauvanam api madana|mānas'|ônmādam
anil'|âvalola|nalinī|
dala|jala|capalāś ca vitta|cayāḥ.

Hāriṇyo hariṇa|dṛśaḥ
satataṃ bhog'|âbja|madhu|karī|dhūrtāḥ.
patitā paraṃpar" âiṣā
doṣāṇāṃ mama sutasy' âsya.

Dhūrta|kara|kandukānāṃ
vāra|vadhū|caraṇa|nūpura|maṇīnām
dhanika|gṛh'|ôtpannānāṃ
muktir nāsty eva mugdhānām.

"Alas! Before you, this my voice,
which assumes the brazenness of familiarity,
dares not become too audacious,
as though it were a village girl in the city.

The magnitude of your *illuminating* rays of wisdom,
*harboring the sagacity of Brihas·pati,**
gives hope dispelling blindness;
As though it were a *dazzling* brother of the sun,
who eclipses the planet Jupiter
and frees the points of the compass from darkness.

Since my birth I have hoarded a treasury 1.15
brimming with many kinds of gems, pearls and gold.
Now, in the eve of my life
a single son has been born to me.

Infancy is a period of folly,
youth is a mental derangement wrought by love,
and the survival of accumulated wealth
is as uncertain as droplets of water
on the petals of water-lilies,
quivering in the breeze.*

Ravishing, doe-eyed damsels
are ever malicious like female bees
concealed in the lotus of enjoyment.
This chain of misadventures has befallen my son here.

Truly, there is no release for balls in the hands of cheats,*
for gems set in the anklets of prostitutes,
and for the naive scions of wealthy houses.

Ajñāta|deśa|kālāś
    capala|mukhāḥ paṅgavo 'pi sa|plutayaḥ
nava|vihagā iva mugdhā
    bhakṣyante dhūrta|mārjāraiḥ.

1.20 Āśrita|jana|tanayo 'yaṃ
    tava vidvan! nija|sut'|âdhikaḥ satyam:
na yathā prayāti nāśaṃ
    tath" âsya buddhiṃ prayaccha parām.»

Iti vinaya|namra|śirasā
    tena vaco yuktam uktam avadhārya
tam uvāca Mūladevaḥ
    prīti|prasara|prasārit'|ôṣṭh'|âgraḥ:
«Āstām eṣa sutas te
    mama bhavane nija iva. prayatna|paraḥ
jñāsyati may" ôpadiṣṭaṃ
    śanakaiḥ sakalaṃ kalā|hṛdayam.»
Iti tasya śāsanena
    sva|sutaṃ niḥkṣipya tad|gṛhe matimān
natvā taṃ s'|ârtha|yatiḥ
    prayayau nija|mandiraṃ muditaḥ.

Śithilita/kara/pracāro
    dhūsara/kāntir nirambaras taraṇiḥ
abhavad alakṣyaḥ śanakaiḥ
    dhūrtair iva nirjitaḥ kitavaḥ.

The untutored are like fledgling birds,
chattering on, incautious of time and place,
hopping about though they are yet unable to walk,
preyed on by swindler-cats.

Wise master! This son of your petitioner 1.20
who is verily more than another son of yours:
grant him your supreme wisdom
so that he does not perish!"

Acknowledging that he had pleaded his case diffidently, with his head bowed in humility, Mula·deva addressed him, the boundary of his lips giving way to a flood of goodwill:

"This son of yours may stay in my home as though he were my own. With diligence, he will gradually come to understand the complete heart of guile, in which I will instruct him."

The wise caravan-master consigned his son to Mula·deva's house as instructed, bowed to him and, delighted, departed to his own mansion.

The sun *gradually faded from sight,*
with the radiance of its beams dwindling,
gleaming duskily without a clear outline,
Just like a gambler *with an ashen complexion,*
whose hand-control has become slack,
who has lost even his clothes,
eventually loses a fortune, plundered by cheats.

1.25 Astam|ite divasa|kare
timira|bhara|dvirada|saṃsaktā
sindūra|paṭala|pāṭala|
kāntir iv' âgre babhau sandhyā.

Tyakt" âpi pratidivasaṃ
divasa|dyutir anujagāma divasa|karam
anurakt" âpi na sandhyā
hṛdayaṃ jānāti kaḥ strīṇām.

Gagan'|âṅgaṇa|kamala|vane
sandhyā|rāge gate śanaiḥ kv' âpi
aprāpta|pad'|ākulitaṃ
babhrāma ravi|bhramaṃ timiram.

Tigm'|âṃśu|viraha|mohaiḥ
timirair iva mīlitā babhūva mahī
tīvro janasya hi sadā
yātaḥ khalu vallabho bhavati.

Rajanī rarāja sitatara|
tāraka|muktā|kalāpa|kṛta|śobhā
śabara|ramaṇ" îva paricita|
timira|mayūra|cchad'|ābharaṇā.

When the day-maker had set, 1.25
a half-light shone on the summit
of the Western horizon-mountain,
as though it were the ruddy glow of a coat of red minium
adhering to the elephant that was darkness.*

Although she is deserted every day,
Daylight-splendor follows the Day-maker sun.
Twilight does not, though she is his beloved.*
Who can understand the hearts of women?

When the impassioned flush of Twilight
had gently faded away
into the lotus-pond of the courtyard of the firmament,
her paramour Darkness,
mistakenly fearing this heralded the arrival
of her husband the Sun,
flounced about without gaining a secure foothold.

The earth seemed to become obscured by gloom,
unconscious because of her separation
from the scorching-rayed sun.
For someone who is constant and fiery
is cherished as a lover.

The night was magnificent
like a forest-dwelling *shábara* maiden,
made lovely with pearl necklaces
strung with whiter than white stars,
adorned with a peacock-cloak
made of intense darkness.

1.30 Atha pathika|vadhū|dahanaḥ
śanakair udabhūn niśā|kar'|ālokaḥ
kumuda|prabodha|dūto
vyasana|guruś cakravākīṇām.

Manmatha|sit'|ātapatraṃ
dig|vanitā|sphaṭika|darpaṇo vimalaḥ
virarāja rajani|ramaṇī
sita|tilako yāminī|nāthaḥ.

Nija|kara|mṛṇāla|vallī
valaya|vilāsī lalāsa sita|kāntiḥ
gagana|taṭinī|taṭ'|ânte
rajani|karo rāja|haṃsa iva.

Śyāmā śuśubhe śaśinā
tayā mano|bhūr madh'|ûtsavas tena
mada/mudita|mānasānāṃ
ten' âpi mṛgī|dṛśāṃ līlā.

Dhūrtāḥ samṛddhi|sacivā
vicchāyāṃ padminīṃ parityajya
phullāni viviśur alayaḥ
s'|ānandāḥ kumuda|vṛndāni.

Then, slowly, the light of the night-maker* rose up, 1.30
scorching the wives of those travelling afar,
a herald for the awakening of the night-blooming lilies,
a teacher of separation to the *chakra·vaki** birds.

The lord of the night gleamed,
a white parasol for the God of love,
a crystal mirror for the ladies of the compass points,*
a white forehead-mark
on the beautiful damsel darkness.

The night-maker beamed with a pale beauty
like a flamingo on the verge of the banks
of the celestial river Mandákini,*
shimmering within an aura
of the encircling filaments of his own rays.

The dark night was made beautiful by the moon,
love by the night,
the spring festival by love,
and the charms of fawn-eyed girls,
their hearts *merry with wine : thrilled with passion,*
by the spring festival.*

Being libertines, mere fair-weather friends,
bees deserted the lackluster lotus,
and, in ecstasy,
fell upon the blossoming clusters of night-lilies.

1.35 Jyotsnā|bhasma|smerā
sulalita|śaśi|śakala|peśala|kapālā
tār"|âsthi|paṭala|hārā
śuśubhe kāpālin" îva niśā.

Tasmin prauḍha|niśā|kara|
kiraṇa|prakara|prakāśit'|âśeṣe
nija|maṇi|bhavan'|ôdyāne
nirvartita|bhāvanā|samādhānaḥ
sphaṭik'|āsan'|ôpaviṣṭaḥ
saha Śaśinā nirvibhāga|mitreṇa
Kandali|mukhyaiḥ śiṣyaiḥ
saṃsevita|pāda|pīṭh'|ântaḥ.

Provāca Mūladevo
vīkṣya ciraṃ s'|ârtha|vāha|sutam agre
kurvan daśana|mayūkhaiḥ
lajjā|līnām iva jyotsnām.

«Śṛṇu putra vañcakānāṃ
sakala|kalā|hṛdaya|sāram ati|kuṭilam
jñāte bhavanti yasmin
kṣaṇa|ruci|capalāḥ śriyo 'py acalāḥ.

1.40 Eko 'smin bhava|gahane
tṛṇa|pallava|valaya|jāla|saṃchannaḥ
kūpaḥ patanti yasmin
mugdha|kuraṅgā nirālambe.

The night was radiant 1.35
like a female skull-bearing ascetic,*
shining with ash made of moonlight,
with a graceful skull-bowl
made of the pleasing lunar crescent,
with a necklace of bone-sections made of stars.

When the myriad rays
of the full moon had become altogether visible
in the inner garden of his jewelled mansion,
Mula·deva,
serenely composed after arising from his contemplations,
settled on a crystal seat
with his inseparable companion Shashin.
His disciples headed by Kándali
attended at the side of his foot-stool.

After gazing at the caravan-leader's son who waited before him for a long time, Mula·deva spoke, making the moonlight disappear with shame, as it were, with the light-rays shining from his teeth.

"Hear, my son, the extremely crooked heart-essence of all of the guile of swindlers. When this is grasped, wealth, normally fleeting like a momentary flash, becomes stable.

In this thicket of existence there is a pit, 1.40
concealed by a web of grass, shoots and vines,
into whose bottomless void fall innocent deer.

So 'yaṃ *nidhāna|kumbho*
dambho nāma svabhāva|gambhīraḥ
kuṭilaiḥ kuhaka|bhujaṃgaiḥ
saṃvṛta|vadanaḥ sthito loke.

Māyā|rahasya|mantraḥ
cintā|maṇir īpsit'|ârthānām
dambhaḥ prabhāva|kārī
dhūrtānāṃ Śrī|vaśī|karaṇam.

Matsyasy' êv' âpsu sadā
dambhasya jñāyate gatiḥ kena?
yasya na karau na caraṇau
na śiro durlakṣya ev' âsau.

Mantra|balena bhujaṃgā
mugdha|kuraṅgāś ca kūṭa|yantreṇa
sthala|jālena vihaṅgā
gṛhyante mānavāś ca dambhena.

1.45 Jana|hṛdaya|vipralambho
māyā|sthambho jagaj|jay'|ārambhaḥ
jayati sad"|ânupalambho
nirgata|Daṃbhodayo dambhaḥ.

This is the *treasure-pot ⁝ funerary-urn**
called "sanctimoniousness,"
inherently unfathomable.
In this world its opening is veiled
by coiling villain-serpents.

For villains, sanctimoniousness is a secret magic spell,
a wish-fulfilling gem for all they crave, an empowerment,
a means to subjugate the Goddess of fortune.

Who can fathom the path of sanctimoniousness,
which is like that of a fish
perpetually submerged under water?
It is indeed difficult to make out the movements
of that which has no hands, no feet, no head.

Snakes are captured by the power of mantras,
trusting deer by a concealed trap,
birds by a net on the ground,
people by sanctimoniousness.

Sanctimoniousness is triumphant, 1.45
dismaying people's hearts,
a paralysis induced by delusion overwhelming the world
⁝ a pillar of deceit
erected to commemorate world-domination,
a perpetual unawareness,
an incarnation of Dambhódbhava.*

Satat'|āvarta|bhrānte
duḥsaha|māyā|sahasra|kuṭil'|âre
mūlaṃ dambho nābhiḥ
vipulatare cakrikā|cakre.

Nayana|nimīlana|mūlaḥ
sucira|snān'|ârdra|cūla|jala|siktaḥ
dambha|taruḥ śuci|kusumaḥ
†bahu|sukha†śākhā|śataiḥ phalitaḥ.

Vrata|niyamair baka|dambhaḥ
saṃvṛta|niyamaiś ca kūrma|jo dambhaḥ
nibhṛta|gati|nayana|niyamaiḥ
ghoro mārjāra|jo dambhaḥ.

Baka|dambho dambha|patiḥ
dambha|nar'|êndraś ca kūrma|jo dambhaḥ
mārjāra|dambha eṣa
prāpto dambheṣu cakravartitvam.

1.50 Nīca|nakha|śmaśru|kacaś cūlī
jūṭī pralamba|kūrco vā
bahu|mṛttikā|piśācaḥ
parimita|bhāṣī prapanna|pādatraḥ;

Sanctimoniousness is the base,
the hub in a vast wheel of circular reasoning,*
which has a thousand bent spokes
of unbearable absurdities,
which rolls astray whirling around incessantly.

With shut eyes for roots,
irrigated with water
dripping from hair moist from lengthy ritual ablutions,
the tree of sanctimoniousness
bears ritual purity for flowers
and yields fruit
with †upraised arms† for hundreds of branches.*

Through the penance of observing vows
arises the smugness of the heron,
through the penance of withdrawal,
the smugness peculiar to the tortoise,
through the penance of fixing the eyes impassively
on the path,
the terrifying smugness peculiar to cats.*

Heron-smugness is a chieftain among false pieties,
the smugness peculiar to the tortoise is a king,
but the smugness of cats has assumed imperial sovereignty.

A man* with trimmed nails, beard and hair, 1.50
a crested man, a man with matted locks, a long-beard,
a man obsessed with smearing himself with much clay,
a tight-lipped man, a man in boots;

Sthūla|granthi|pavitraka|
    pṛṣṭh'|ârpita|hema|vallīkaḥ
kakṣ'|ârpita|paṭa|pallava|
    ruddha|bhujo bhāṇḍa|hasta iva;
Aṅguli|bhaṅga|vikalpana|
    vividha|vivāda|pravṛtta|pāṇḍityaḥ
japa|capal'|âuṣṭhaḥ sajane
    dhyāna|paro nagara|rāja|rathyāsu;
S'|âbhinay'|âñcita|culukaiḥ
    ācamanaiḥ sucira|majjanais tīrthe
sīt|kāra|danta|vīṇā|
    vedita|hemanta|duḥsaha|snānaḥ;
Snigdh'|êtara|nikhil'|âṅga|
    prakaṭita|sārvadika|mṛttikā|snānaḥ
vistīrṇa|tilaka|carcā
    sūcita|sarv'|ôpacāra|Sura|pūjaḥ;
1.55 Śirasā bibharti kusumaṃ
    vinipatitāṃ kāka|dṛṣṭim iva—
evaṃ|rūpaḥ puruṣo
    yo yaḥ sa sa dāmbhiko jñeyaḥ.

A man who has affixed a _hema·valli_*
on top of his large-knotted sacred thread,
a man who looks like he were holding
a casket in his hand,
because his arm is immobilised
by the border of his robe* tucked into his armpit;
A man displaying his erudition by various squabbles,*
by dithering and by gesticulated denials,
a man whose lips are animated with muttered prayers
in crowds,
a man absorbed in meditation
on the main streets of the city;
A man at a sacred ford
advertising the hardship of his ritual bath in mid-winter
with chattering teeth and hissing,
submerging himself interminably,
ritually rinsing his mouth
with hands bent into cupped hollows
in a dramatic gesture;
A man whose incessant dirt-baths
are betrayed by the scoured roughness of his entire body,
a man whose worship of the Gods
with unabridged ceremonies
can be deduced from the enormous mark
plastered on his forehead;
A man who wears a flower on his head 1.55
which looks like a crow's eye* bobbing from side to side,
— any man of this sort must be recognised as a charlatan.

Nir|guṇa|loka|praṇataḥ
    sa|guṇa|stabdhaḥ sva|bandhu|vidveṣī
para|jana|karuṇā|bandhuḥ
    kīrty|ārthī dāṃbhiko dhūrtaḥ.

Kāry'|ôpayoga|kāle
    praṇata|śirāś cāṭu|śata|kārī
sa|bhrū|bhaṅgo maunī
    kṛta|kāryo dāmbhikaḥ krūraḥ.

Stambhita|Vibudha|samṛddhiḥ
    daityo Diti|jo 'bhavat purā Jambhaḥ.
Dambhaḥ so 'yaṃ nivasati
    bhūmi|tale bhūta|deheṣu.

Śuci|dambhaḥ śama|dambhaḥ
    snātaka|dambhaḥ samādhi|dambhaś ca
niḥspṛha|dambhasya tulāṃ
    yānti tu n' âite śat'|âṃśena.

The charlatan is a villain who pays homage to the worthless,
who is arrogant to the worthy,
who is hostile to his own relatives,
who acts like a compassionate relative to strangers,
he is a man who craves fame.*

When he needs help in some undertaking,
the cruel charlatan bows his head
and ingratiates himself with a hundred flatteries.
But he frowns and remains silent
once his immediate goal is achieved.

Long ago, there was a titan called Jambha,* the son of Diti,
who had thwarted the Gods' prosperity.
On the surface of the earth
he now dwells in the hearts of living beings
as sanctimoniousness.

The sanctimoniousness of purity,
the sanctimoniousness of quietism,
the sanctimoniousness of the *snátaka,**
and the sanctimoniousness of exalted meditation:
These are not even equal to the hundredth part
of the sanctimoniousness of aloofness.

1.60 *Śauc'/âśauca/vivādī*
mṛt/kṣaya/kārī sva/bāndhav'/âsparśī
śuci|dambhena jano 'yaṃ
Viśvāmitratvam āyāti.

Saṃhata|bahuvidha/*sattvo*
nikṣepa|draviṇa|vāri|bahu|tṛṣṇaḥ
satatam ahiṃsā|dambho
vaḍav"|âgniḥ sarva|bhakṣo 'yam.

Khalvāṭaḥ sthūla|vapuḥ
śuṣka|tanur muni|samāna|rūpo vā
śāṭaka|veṣṭita|śīrṣaḥ
caity'|ônnata|śikhara|duḥkhiko v" âpi.

Affected by the sanctimoniousness of purity 1.60
a person
quibbles about what is pure and what is impure,
*squanders cleansing clay,**
does not touch his own relatives,
*becomes an enemy to all and sundry,**
⁝ *he contests the distinction*
*between the pure and the impure,**
builds an earthen penance-hut,
*becomes different from his own kin**
and thus becomes a veritable Vishva·mitra.

The sanctimoniousness of non-violence is a ceaseless,
all-devouring submarine fire,
which has destroyed all manner of *creatures* ⁝ *treasures*,
which thirsts for water in the form of deposited wealth.

The Snátaka can be a bald man,
a fat man,
a man with a shrivelled body,
or a man resembling a sage,
a man with a cloth wound around his head,
or a man in agony
because his lofty crest
protrudes like a funeral mound.

Muṇḍo jaṭilo nagnaḥ
chatrī daṇḍī kaṣāya/cīrī vā
bhasma/smera/śarīro
diśi diśi bhogī vijṛmbhate dambhaḥ.

Lobhaḥ pit" âti|vṛddho
janani Māyā sah'|ôdaraḥ kūṭaḥ
kuṭil'|ākṛtiś ca gṛhiṇī
putro dambhasya huṃkāraḥ.

1.65 Bhagavān purā Svayaṃbhūḥ
kṛtvā bhuvanāni bhūta|sargaṃ ca
virata|vyāpāratayā
suciraṃ cint"|ânvitas tasthau.
Dṛṣṭvā sa martya|loke
divya|dṛśā mānuṣān nirālambān
ārjava|yoga|viśeṣād
aprāpta|dhan'|ādi|saṃbhogān,
Mīlita|nayanaḥ kṣipraṃ
sthitvā māyā|maye samādhāne
asṛjan nṛṇāṃ vibhūtyai
Dambhaṃ saṃbhāvan"|ādhāram.

The sanctimoniousness of exalted contemplation
is a gaping serpent,
which proliferates in all lands.
It might be *blunt[-nosed]* ⁝ *a shaveling ascetic,*
twisted around itself ⁝ *a matted-hair ascetic,*
unmarked ⁝ *a naked ascetic*,
hooded ⁝ *a parasol-bearer,*
stiff ⁝ *a staff-bearer,*
red-banded ⁝ *a red-robe,*
or with a body *as white as ash* ⁝ *stark with white ash;**

Greed is the ancient father of sanctimoniousness,
Maya is his mother,
falsehood is his uterine brother,
deformity is his wife,
and the sneer *Hum!* is his son.*

Long ago, the blessed Self-born Brahma created the worlds and species of living creatures. Thereafter he remained for a long time in contemplation, desisting from all activity. With his divine eye he saw that the self-reliant people in the world of the mortals had not appropriated the pleasures of wealth etc., because of their peculiar adherence to forthrightness. Closing his eyes he immersed himself immediately in a profound meditation imbued with the power of creative illusion. He brought forth Dambha as a receptacle of esteem, to ensure the prosperity of men. 1.65

Bibhrāṇaḥ kuśa|pūlīṃ
pustaka|bhāraṃ kamaṇḍaluṃ śūnyam
nija|hṛdaya|kuṭila|śṛṅgaṃ
daṇḍaṃ kṛṣṇ'|âjinaṃ khanitraṃ ca;

Sthūlatara|kuśa|pavitraka|
lāñchita|karṇaḥ pavitra|pāṇiś ca
suvyakta|muṇḍa|mastaka|
saṃveṣṭita|cūla|mūla|sita|kusumaḥ;

1.70 Kāṣṭha|stabdha|grīvo
japa|capal'|ôṣṭhaḥ samādhi|līn'|âkṣaḥ
rudr'|âkṣa|valaya|hasto
mṛt|paripūrṇāṃ vahan mahā|pātrīm;

Nayan'|âñcalaiḥ sa|kopaiḥ
bhṛ|kuṭī|huṃ|kāra|vadana|saṃjñābhiḥ
bahuvidha|kadarthanābhiḥ
kathit'|âkhila|hṛdaya|vāñchito maunī;

Rakṣan para|saṃsparśaṃ
śauc"|ārthī Brahma|loke 'pi
Dambhaḥ puro 'sya tasthau
utthita ev' āsan'|ākāṅkṣī.

Taṃ dṛṣṭvā Parameṣṭhī
līlā|kṛta|sakala|sarga|vargo 'pi
gaurava|vismaya|harṣaiḥ
nispand'|ândolitas tasthau.

Bearing a bundle* of purifying *kusha* grass,
a burden of scriptures,* an empty water-pot,
an antelope horn* as twisted as his own heart,
the skin of a black antelope and a hoe;

He had stuffed thick bunches of sacred grass*
behind his ears
wore a sacrificer's ritual-ring* on his hand,
and the root of his topknot was encircled by white flowers
on his starkly clean-shaven head;

His neck was stiff like a plank,* 1.70
his lips restless with muttered prayers,
his eyes deadened by yogic trance,
a *rudráksha* rosary wrapped around his hand,
holding a large bowl of purifying clay;

Mute, yet revealing all of the cravings lurking in his heart
with angry side glances, with grimaces,
grunting and frowning,
and by all kinds of irritations;

Wary of touching others;
requiring cleansing even
in the paradise-world of Brahma,
Dambha stood before the Creator, expecting a seat.

Seeing him, the Creator,
although he had with ease begotten all orders of creation,
was shaken with shivers,
brought on by a thrill of great incredulity.

Ākalpena sumahatā
sahas" âsya vaśīkṛtāḥ paraṃ tena
Saptarṣayo 'pi tasmai
praṇatās tasthuḥ kṛt'|âñjalayaḥ.

1.75 Tasy' âti|tīvra|niyamād
graste 'gastye 'ti|vismayen' êva
alpa|tapo|vrata|lajjā|
kuñcita|pṛṣṭhe Vasiṣṭhe ca;

Ati|sarala|nija|muni|vrata|
parigata|kutse ca kūṇite Kautse,
ḍambara|rahit'|ātma|tapo|
nirādare Nārade vihite;

Nija|jānu|saṃdhi|śikhare
Jamadagnau magna|vadane ca,
traste Viśvāmitre,
valita|gale Gālave, Bhṛgau bhagne;

Sucir'|ôtthitam ati|kopād
āsana|kamale niviṣṭa|dṛṣṭiṃ ca
śūla|protam iv' âgre
niḥspandam amanda|garva|guru|gātram.

The Seven Sages, too,
powerfully compelled by Dambha's great pomp,
stood bowing, their hands folded in supplication.

While Agástya seemed to be devoured* by astonishment 1.75
with Dambha's extremely severe abstentions,
while Vasíshtha hunched his back in shame
at his own meagre store of austerities;*

While Kautsa shrank as if a slur had been cast
on his own very simple vow of silence,*
while Nárada was made to feel contempt
for his own penances which lacked ostentation;*

While Jamad·agni buried his face
in the peaks of his own knee-caps,*
while Vishva·mitra trembled in fear,*
while Gálava's neck rolled about,
while Bhrigu was crushed;*

The four-faced Creator-god realized
that Dambha had been standing all the while,
and that he had furiously fixed his gaze
upon Brahma's lotus-throne.
He stood motionless as if impaled,
his limbs torpid with avid arrogance.

Jñātvā tam āsan'|ârthinam
avadad devaś Catur|mukhaḥ prītyā
visṛjan nija|daśana|rucā
vihasann iva vāhanaṃ haṃsaṃ:

1.80 «Upaviśa putra mam' âṅke.
niyamena mahīyas" âti|citreṇa
arho 'si guṇa|gaṇ'|ôdgata|
gaurava|saṃvādin" ânena.»

Ity|ukto Viśvasṛjā
tasy' âṅkam aśaṅkayā sa|saṃkocaḥ
abhyukṣya vāri|muṣṭyā
kṛcchreṇ' ôpāviśad Dambhaḥ.

Dambha uvāca:
«n' ôccair vācyam avaśyaṃ!
yadi vācyaṃ hasta|padmena
ācchādya vaktra|randhraṃ,
spṛṣṭo na syāṃ yath" āsya|vāt'|âṃśaiḥ.»

Tat tasya śaucam atulaṃ
dṛṣṭvā harṣa|smita|prabhā|śubhraḥ
«Dambho 's' îti!» jagāda
Prajāpatiś choṭikāṃ dattvā.

Realizing that he wanted to sit down,
Brahma spoke to him with a smile,
as though creating his vehicle, the wild white goose,
with the dazzle from his own teeth:

"My son, be seated on my lap. 1.80
You are worthy because your stupendous
and substantial self-restraint
accords with an earnestness born from a host of virtues."

Addressed in this way by the All-creator,
Dambha, unhesitatingly, and with revulsion,
sprinkled his lap with a handful of water
and sat down with a show of discomfort.

Dambha said:
"You really must not speak so loud!
If you have to speak,
then cover your mouth with your lotus-hand,
so that I will not be touched
by the particles in the breath
streaming from your mouth."*

Then, seeing his incomparable purity,
the Creator Praja·pati,
radiant with the lustre of his joyful smile,
snapped his fingers and said:
"You must be *Dambha* ⁝ *phoney*!

«Uttiṣṭha sakala|jala|nidhi|
    parikhā|maṇi|mekhalāṃ mahīm akhilām
avatīrya bhuṅkṣva bhogān
    vibudhair api tattvato na vijñātaḥ.»

1.85 Ity ādarād visṛṣṭo
    vidhinā saṃsāra|sāgara|gatānām
kaṇṭhe śilāṃ nibadhnan
    martyānām avatatāra mahīm.

Atha martya|lokam etya
    bhrāntvā Dambho vanāni nagarāṇi
viniveśya Gauḍa|viṣaye
    nija|jaya|ketuṃ jagāma diśaḥ.

Vacane Bāhlīkānāṃ
    vrata|niyame Prācya|dākṣiṇātyānāṃ
adhikāre Kīrāṇāṃ
    Dambhaḥ sarvatra Gauḍānām.

Ete Dambha|sahāyāḥ
    pratigraha|śrāddha|siddha|cūrṇena
kurvanti ye prabhāte
    yatas tato bhasmanā tilakam.

Tūrṇaṃ *sahasra|bhāgaiḥ*
    bhuvana|tale *saṃvibhajya* bhūtāni
mūrtaḥ satataṃ nivasati
    Dambho vadane 'dhikaraṇa|bhaṭṭānām.

Arise and descend to the earth,
encompassed by the jewel-girdle of the oceans,
and enjoy pleasures,
your true nature unrecognised even by the wise."

Duly and respectfully dismissed, 1.85
he descended to earth,
tying a stone to the necks of mortals
doomed in the ocean.

Arriving in the world of mortals,
Dambha ranged through forests and cities.
He planted his triumphal banner in Bengal
and advanced in every direction.

Dambha lives in the speech of people in Balkh,
in the South-easterners' observance of vows of penance,
in the authorities of Kashmir,
and everywhere in Bengal.

Those who make their forehead marks
with ash obtained from whatever source,
a magic powder
at funerary ceremonies involving donations,
are Dambha's helpers.

Dambha quickly *isolated* ⁝ *devastated**
the living beings on the surface of the earth
in thousands of different classes ⁝ *with a thousand taxes*,
and physically embodied himself
in the faces of those in charge.

1.90 Guru|hṛdayam aviśād agre
pālaka|hṛdayaṃ tapasvi|hṛdayaṃ ca
kuṭilaṃ niyogi|hṛdayaṃ
dīkṣita|hṛdayaṃ svayaṃ Dambhaḥ.

Tad anu ca gaṇaka|cikitsaka|
sevaka|vaṇijāṃ sa|hema|kārāṇām
naṭa|bhaṭa|gāyaka|vācaka|
cakra|carāṇāṃ ca hṛdayāni.

Aṃśaiḥ praviśya hṛdayaṃ
vividha|vikāraiḥ samasta|jantūnām
Dambho viveśa paścād
antaram api pakṣi|vṛkṣāṇām.

Matsy'|ârthī carati tapaḥ
suciraṃ niḥspanda eka|pādena
tīrtheṣu baka|tapasvī
tena vihaṅgān gato Dambhaḥ.

Vipula|jaṭā|valkalinaḥ
śīt'|ātapa|vṛṣṭi|kaṣṭitāḥ satatam
vṛkṣā phal'|ârthino yad
Dambhasya vijṛmbhitaṃ tad api.

1.95 Evaṃ vicāraṇīyaḥ
sarva|gataḥ sarva|hṛt sadā Dambhaḥ.
jñāte tasmin vividhe
viphalā māyāvināṃ māyā.

Dambha himself first of all entered 1.90
the hearts of religious teachers,*
then the twisted hearts of provincial governors,*
the hearts of ascetics,
the hearts of commissioners,
and the hearts of initiates.*

Then he passed into the hearts of astrologers,
physicians, servants, merchants,
goldsmiths, actors, mercenaries,
singers, story-tellers, and jugglers.

Distributing himself, assuming many guises,
Dambha entered the hearts of all walking creatures,
then he even entered into birds and trees.*

The heron-ascetic struts about in sacred fords,
hungering for fish*
motionless on one leg;
through him Dambha reached the birds.

That trees should have many tangled roots
and be clad in bark,*
be ever battered by cold, heat and rain,
in the hope of bearing fruit,
that too, is the influence of Dambha.*

Therefore one must always be wary of Dambha 1.95
who has permeated everything, who destroys everything.
Once he is known in his diverse forms,
the spell of conjurors is broken.*

Dambha|vikāraḥ purato
vañcaka|cakrasya kalpa|vṛkṣo 'yam.
Vāmana|dambhena purā
Hariṇā trailokyam ākrāntam.

iti mahā|kavi|śrī|Kṣemendra|viracite
Kalā|vilāse
dambh'|ākhyānaṃ nāma
prathamaḥ sargaḥ.

This diversity of Dambha is a wish-granting tree*
before the realm of deceivers.
Long ago, Hari vanquished the three worlds
by the sanctimoniousness of the Dwarf-incarnation.*

The first canto,
named the description of sanctimoniousness
in the "Grace of Guile"
composed by
the great poet Ksheméndra.

THE GRACE OF GUILE
2. GREED

LOBHAḤ SADĀ vicintyo
lubdhebhyaḥ sarvato bhayaṃ dṛṣṭam
kāry'|âkārya|vicāro
lobha|visaṃjñasya n' âsty eva.

Māyāvi|niyama|vibhrama|
nihnava|vaicitrya|kūṭa|kapaṭānām
*sañcaya|durga|*piśācaḥ
sarva|saho mūla|kāraṇaṃ lobhaḥ.

Sattva|praśama|tapobhiḥ
sattva|dhanaiḥ śāstra|vedibhir vijitaḥ
lobho 'vaṭaṃ praviṣṭaḥ
kuṭilaṃ hṛdayaṃ kirāṭānām.

Kraya|vikraya|kūṭa|tulā|
lāghava|niḥkṣepa|rakṣaṇa|vyājaiḥ
ete hi divasa|caurā
muṣṇanti mudā janaṃ vaṇijaḥ.

2.5 Hṛtvā dhanaṃ janānāṃ
dinam akhilaṃ vividha|kūṭa|māyābhiḥ
vitarati gṛhe kirāṭaḥ
kaṣṭena varāṭika|tritayam.

BEWARE of avarice,—
the threat of the avaricious is evident everywhere.
Someone oblivious with greed
does not care what is right or wrong.

Avarice,
a *vicious obsession of hoarding* : *fiend lurking in a*
fortified treasury
is capable of anything,
is the root cause
of *frauds and deceits* : *camouflaged vaults,*
of all kinds *of prevarications* : *obstructions,*
conflations : *blind corners*
and *false agreements* : *magical boundaries.**

Defeated by knowers of sacred scripture,
rich in virilty,
virtuous, tranquil and penitent,
avarice crept into its den:
the crooked heart of merchants.

Merchants, indeed, are daylight-robbers,*
they delight in robbing people
by ploys such as witholding deposits,
using too light weights,
and sleight of hand while buying and selling.

All day long 2.5
the merchant relieves his customers of their money
with all kinds of scams and tricks.
But he frets to hand over three cowries
to support his household.*

Ākhyāyik"|ânurāgī
vrajati sadā puṇya|pustakaṃ śrotum.
daṣṭa iva kṛṣṇa|sarpaiḥ
palāyate dāna|dharmebhyaḥ.

Dvādaśyāṃ pitṛ|divase
saṃkramaṇe soma|sūryayor grahaṇe
suciraṃ snānaṃ kurute,
na dadāti kapardikām ekām.

Dattvā diśi diśi dṛṣṭiṃ
yācaka/cakito 'vaguṇṭhanaṃ kṛtvā
caura iva *kuṭila/cārī*
palāyate vikaṭa/rathyābhiḥ.

Na dadāti prativacanaṃ
vikraya|kāle śaṭho vaṇiṅ maunī.
nikṣepa|pāṇi|puruṣaṃ
dṛṣṭvā saṃbhāṣaṇāṃ kurute.

2.10 Uttiṣṭhati namati vaṇik
pṛcchati kuśalaṃ dadāty avasthānaṃ
niḥkṣepa|pāṇim āptaṃ
dṛṣṭvā dharmyāḥ kathāḥ kurute.
Kaś cid vadati tam etya:
«draviṇaṃ nikṣipya hanta gant" âsmi,
bhrātaḥ! paraṃ prabhāte
viṣṭi|dinaṃ kiṃ karomy adya?»

Fond of tales,*
he always runs along to hear the recitation
of pious books.
But he flees, as though bitten by black cobras,
from the duty of alms-giving.

On the twelfth lunar day,
on the day sacred to the ancestors,
during the solar transits,
during eclipses of the sun and moon,
he takes a long bath and does not donate* a single cowrie.

Just like a thief
he *scans the directions* : *keeps a lookout,*
he is *alarmed by beggars* : *startled by questioners,*
he hides himself behind *a veil* : *disguise,*
he *makes detours* : *behaves suspiciously*
and *runs off down wide streets* : *escapes by secret paths.*

The mean merchant keeps mum, he gives no reply to bargainers at the time of selling. Only when he has spotted a man with a deposit* in his hand does he strike up a conversation.

2.10 He gets up and bows down as soon as he has seen someone respectable with a deposit in his hand, asks about his wellbeing, offers a seat, and starts telling pious stories.

Someone comes to him and says: "Hullo! I will go abroad after depositing my money with you, brother! But this morning it happens to be the astrologically ominous vishti·kárana.* Shall I do so today?"

Tac chrutvā vikasita|dṛg
vadati sa mithy" âiva nāṭayan khedam
kārye prasārit'|âkṣaḥ
punaḥ punaḥ pārśvam avalokya:
«Tvad|adhīnaṃ sthānam idaṃ,
kiṃ tu ciraṃ nyāsa|pālanaṃ kaṭhinam,
viṣamau ca deśa|kālau.
sādho tava hanta dāso 'ham.
Bhadrā na dūṣit" âiṣā
nikṣepa|kṣema|kāriṇī śastā
ity|anubhūtaṃ śataśaḥ
kārya|jñais tvaṃ tu jānāsi.
2.15 Viṣṭi|dine kim api purā
nyastaṃ ken' âpi mitreṇa
tūrṇaṃ punar etya śanair
nītaṃ kṣemeṇa kuśalena.»
Ity|ādi mugdha|buddher
asamañjasa|varṇanaṃ rahaḥ kṛtvā
gṛhṇāti kanaka|nikaraṃ
nṛtyaṃs tat|tan|manorath'|ôpāyam.
Tat|saṃcūrṇana|jātaiḥ
kraya|vikraya|lābha|rāśibhir anantaiḥ
bhāṇḍa|pratibhāṇḍa|cayaiḥ
upahasati dhan'|âdhināthaṃ saḥ.

Pūrṇāḥ kadarya|vaṇijāṃ
niḥsaṃbhogā nidhāna|dhana|kumbhāḥ
sīdanti kuca|taṭā iva
duḥkha|phalā bāla|vidhavānām.

On hearing this with widening eyes he pretends to be bothered. His eyes wander to his business, he glances sideways again and again, and says:

"This establishment is at your service, my good man, but it will be a nuisance to look after your deposit for long, time and place are adverse. Alas! I am your servant. This half-day of *bhadra** is not unfavorable; it is taught that it ensures the safety of a deposit. But as you know, this has been confirmed hundreds of times by those knowledgeable in business. Some time ago a friend of mine deposited something 2.15
on a *vishti* day. He returned quickly and gradually withdrew it safe and sound."

After he has thus talked nonsense to the simple-minded man in confidence, he dances as he relieves him of the hoard of gold, the means to all of his desires.

With incalculable profit from buying and selling that ground-down gold, with piles of goods for barter, he laughs in mockery at the God of wealth.

The treasure-vats of miserly merchants,
brimming with stored wealth,
waste away ⁝ sink down
  without being put to good use,
  bringing sorrow,
  just as do the breasts
  of youthful widows.

Dān'|ôpabhoga|virahita|
hiraṇya|rakṣā|kṛta|kṣaṇāḥ satatam
saṃsāra|jīrṇa|mandira|
viṣama|mahā|mūṣakā vaṇijaḥ.

2.20 *Aṭati samutkaṭa|veṣṭita|*
vikaṭa|paṭī|sphuṭa|phaṭ'|āṭopaḥ
kuṭilaṃ kañcuka|nicitaḥ
pura|pati|nāmā nidhi|vyālaḥ.

Atha puruṣaḥ sa dig|antaṃ
bhrāntvā ken' âpi daiva|yogena
naṣṭa|dhano jana|rahitaḥ
prāptaḥ sucirān nijaṃ deśam.
Pṛcchati kam api saśaṅkaḥ:
«sa kirāṭaḥ kva nu gato mahā|sattvaḥ?»
tam upetya vadati kaś cit:
«tasy' âdya sakhe vibhūtir any" âiva!
Vividha|nav'|âṃśuka|mṛga|mada|
candana|karpūra|marica|pūga|phalaiḥ
khaṭikā|hastaḥ sa sadā
gaṇayati koṭīr muhūrtena.
Asmin Meru|viśāle
vara|bhavane rucira|bhitti|kṛta|citre
pura|patin" âpy anuyāto
vasati sukhaṃ sa hi mahā|jano nagare.»

2.25 Śrutv" âitad atula|vismaya|
lolita|mauliḥ sa tad|gṛhaṃ gatvā
dvāri sthagitas tiṣṭhati
niṣpratibho jīrṇa|karpaṭaḥ suciram.

Merchants are revolting fat rats*
infesting the dilapidated mansion that is *samsára.**
Ever biding their time,
they stash away gold
out of reach from enjoyment or charity.

As a serpent guarding a treasure 2.20
bearing the title 'lord of the city,'
he *goes about hunched over* : *slithers about windingly,*
swathed in a robe : *covered in scaly skin,*
puffed up with a plainly visible hood
made of garish cloth wound high into a crest.

Doomed by fate, that man who had deposited his money strayed to the ends of the earth. He lost his money and his people and returned to his own land only after a lengthy absence.

Full of apprehension, he asked someone: "Where has that sagacious merchant gone?" Somebody approached him and said: "My friend, nowadays, his circumstances are quite different! Holding a piece of chalk in his hand, he ceaselessly calculates crores per hour* by dealing with all kinds of new fabrics, musk-perfume, sandalwood, camphor, black pepper, and betel-nuts. He lives in style in the city, in yonder exquisite palace, towering like Mount Meru, its bright walls adorned with frescos. Even the governor of the city defers to him."

When he heard this he went to the merchant's house, 2.25
his head reeling with utter amazement. Stunned, he stood for a long time at the door, at a loss what to do, dressed in worn-out rags.

Taṃ tuṅga|bhavana|valabhī|
jāl'|ântarato vaṇik parijñāya
n' ôcchvasiti naṣṭa|cetaḥ
tāḍita iva mūrdhni vajreṇa.
Upasṛtya manda|mandaṃ
katham api saṃprāpta|nirjan'|âvasaraḥ
taṃ yācate sa puruṣaḥ
sva|draviṇaṃ prakaṭit'|âbhijñaḥ.
Taṃ vadati so 'nya|dṛṣṭiḥ
sa|bhrū|bhaṅgaṃ vidhūta|hast'|âgraḥ:
«vañcaka|vacanaḥ pāpo
vṛtti|kṣīṇaḥ kuto 'yam āyātaḥ?
Kas tvaṃ? kasya suto vā?
darśanam api na smarāmi, kiṃ kathanaiḥ?
ahaha kadā kutra kathaṃ?
vada! kasya kim arpitaṃ kena?
2.30 Paśyata kaṣṭham aniṣṭaḥ
kali|kālaḥ kīdṛśo 'yam āyātaḥ!
matto 'rtham eṣa vāñchati
loko jānāti vā sarvam.
Haragupta|kule 'smākaṃ
nikṣepa|grahaṇam apy asaṃbhāvyam,
kiṃ punar apahnav'|ôdgata|
ghora|mahā|pātaka|sparśaḥ?
Tad api sa tad"|âbhiśaṃsī
saṃtyājyo 'yaṃ janaḥ kathaṃ mahatām?
kathaya dinaṃ! tad|divase
likhitaṃ sarvaṃ, svayaṃ paśya!
Vṛddho 'haṃ, nyasta|bharaḥ
putre, sa hi vetti likhitaṃ me.»

The merchant recognized him through the lattice-window in the pinnacle of his lofty mansion and his mind went numb, his breath ceased, he felt as if a thunderbolt had struck him on his head.

Hesitantly, the man approached him, when he managed to find an uncrowded opportunity. He refreshed his memory, and asked for his money.

The merchant averted his eyes, frowned, shook his fingers and said to him:

"Where has this evil wretch without any livelihood come from, spouting falsehoods?

Who are you?

Whose son?

I do not remember ever seeing you:

How could I have talked with you?

Huh? When? Where? How?

Speak up!

Who gave what to whom?

Woe! Behold! What has it come to in this accursed, dark 2.30
age. This lunatic demands money, or else the public will hear all about it. In our Hara·gupta* family even accepting a deposit is unheard of, never mind the insinuation of the perfidious, capital offence resulting from calumny.

But on the other hand, how can the great simply ignore a man who insults with such an accusation? Say what day it was! Everything was recorded on that day. See for yourself!

I am old. I have passed on the burden of management to my son. He knows for sure what I have written." With this

iti tena vinaṣṭa|dhṛtiḥ
sa visṛṣṭas tat|sut'|ântikaṃ prāptaḥ.
«Tāto jānāti!» «sa me putro
jānāti likhitam akhilaṃ yat!»
iti tasya bhavati suciraṃ
gat'|āgataṃ kandukasy' êva.

2.35 Rāja|kula|dvāra|gate
tasmin prāyopaveś'|ârthe
sahate narapati|kopaṃ
tyajati kirāṭo na rūpakasy' âṃśam.
Paripīḍitaḥ sa rājñā
vividhair api yātanā|śastraiḥ
«mama haste nikṣiptaṃ
kiṃ cin nāst' îti» vakty eva.

Aurvā iv' âti|lubdhā
bhavanti dhana|lavaṇa|vāri|bahu|tṛṣṇāḥ
tṛṇa|lavam iva nija|dehaṃ
tyajanti leśaṃ na vittasya.

Devaṃ dhan'|âdhināthaṃ
Vaiśravaṇaṃ sakala|saṃpadāṃ nilayam
Śukraḥ provāca purā
vitt'|ârthī bāla|mitram abhyetya:
«Pūrṇaḥ, sakhe, tav' âyaṃ
vibhavo vijit'|âmar'|âsur'|āiśvaryaḥ
harṣaṃ vidadhāti paraṃ
suhṛdāṃ śokaṃ ca śatrūṇām.

the merchant showed him the door. Faltering in determination, he went to see the son.

"Father knows!"

"My son knows all that I have recorded!"

In this manner he went to and fro like a ball, interminably.

When he reached the gate* of the royal court and started 2.35
a solemn fast of starvation,* the merchant suffered the king's wrath, yet he did not give up a fraction of the money.

Even though the king had him tormented with all kinds of instruments of torture, all he would say was: "Nothing was handed over to me!"

The excessively avaricious
are like submarine fires thirsting
for the salt-water that is wealth.
They will give up their own bodies
as though they were bits of straw,
but not even a little bit of money.

Long ago,* Shukra,* in need of money, approached his boyhood-friend Vaishrávana, the God of wealth, the fund of all affluence, and spoke:

"My friend! Your abundant glory, surpassing in majesty the Gods and titans, gives utter joy to your friends and grief to your enemies.

2.40 Tvayi suhṛdi vitta|Nāthe
niḥsvo 'haṃ bahu|kuṭumba|saṃbhāraḥ
sama|duḥkha|sukhaṃ mitraṃ
svādhīnatay" ôditaṃ praśaṃsanti.

Yaśasi vihit'|ādarāṇām
arthibhir upajīvyamāna|vibhavānām
abhijāta|vaṃśa|jānāṃ
suhṛd|upayogyāḥ śriyo mahatām.

Upanatam atipuṇya|cayaiḥ
saṃpūrṇaṃ rakṣitaṃ ca yatnena
saṃpadi vipadi trāṇaṃ
bhavati nidhānaṃ ca mitraṃ ca.»

Ity|uktaḥ sa|praṇayaṃ
Daity'|ācāryeṇa nirjane Dhanadaḥ
tam uvāca vicintya ciraṃ
saṃruddhaḥ sneha|lobhābhyām:

«Jānāmi bāla|mitraṃ
tvām aham atyanta|saṃbhṛta|sneham.
kiṃ tu na jīvita|jīvaṃ
draviṇa|lavaṃ tyaktum īśo 'smi.

2.45 Sneh'|ârthī bandhu|janaḥ,
kāryair bahubhir bhavanti mitrāṇi,
dārāḥ sutāś ca sulabhā,
dhanam ekaṃ durlabhaṃ loke.

Ati|sāhasam ati|duṣkaram
aty|āścaryaṃ ca dānam arthānām.
yo' pi dadāti śarīraṃ
na dadāti sa vitta|leśam api.»

While you, my friend, are the God of wealth, I, penni- 2.40
less, am burdened with a huge family. A friend, constant in happiness and hardship, who has achieved financial independence, is acclaimed.

It is quite in order for friends to avail themselves of the wealth of the great, who are earnest about their reputation, upon whose magnanimity the needy depend, who are born in illustrious lineages.

A plentiful treasure-trove and a friend are both won by amassing stockpiles of exceptional merits. In prosperity they are safeguarded with care, and in adversity they afford protection."

Thus, in all sincerity, the preceptor of the Daityas confided in him in private. The God of wealth pondered this for a long while, torn between affection and avarice, and finally said to him:

"I remember you as my boyhood companion with affection beyond all measure.* But I cannot afford to give up even a minuscule sum of money, the essence of life.*

A kinsman is someone who demands affection, 2.45
friends can be made by all kinds of favors,
wives and sons are easy to come by,—
it is wealth alone
that is difficult to win in this world.

Giving away money is extremely rash,
is beset with difficulties,
is a most startling feat.
Even someone who is ready to give up his own body
could not give up even a paltry amount of money."

Ity|āśā|parihāraiḥ
pratyākhyāto Dhan'|âdhināthena
bhagna|mukho lulita|matiḥ
lajjā|vakro yayau Śukraḥ.
Sa vicintya gṛhe suciraṃ
sacivaiḥ saha māyayā mahā|yogī
hartuṃ draviṇam aśeṣaṃ
viveśa hṛdayaṃ Dhan'|ēśasya.
Śukr'|āviṣṭa|śarīro
Vaiśravaṇaḥ sakalam adbhuta|tyāgaḥ
tat|kṛta|saṅketebhyaḥ
pradadau vittaṃ dvi|jātibhyaḥ.
2.50 Kauberaṃ dhanam akhilaṃ
hṛtvā yāte 'tha dānav'|ācārye
suciraṃ Dhan'|âdhināthaḥ
śuśoca vijñāya tāṃ māyām.
Hasta|nyasta|lalāṭaḥ
saha Śaṅkha|Mukunda|Kunda|Padm'|ādyaiḥ
saṃcintya Śukra|vikṛtiṃ
sa jagād' ôṣṇaṃ viniḥśvasya:
«Suhṛdā marma|jñena
vyājān māyāvin" âti|lubdhena
dhūrtena vañcito 'haṃ
Daity'|āśraya|durjayena Śukreṇa.
Adhunā dravya|vihīnas
tṛṇa|lava|laghutāṃ kṣaṇena saṃprāptaḥ
kathayāmi kasya duḥkhaṃ?
karomi kiṃ vā? kva gacchāmi?

Repudiated by the God of wealth, Shukra departed with a haggard face, his hopes dashed. His mind was reeling, and he was bent low with shame.

Back at home, he plotted with his counsellors for a long time. Then the great yogi magically possessed* the heart of the God of wealth in order to deprive him of all of his money. With his body possessed by Shukra, Vaishrávana became startlingly generous and gave all of his wealth to brahmins who were in league with Shukra.

After he had relieved Kubéra of all of his wealth, the 2.50
preceptor of the Daityas withdrew. The God of wealth then perceived the scheme and grieved for a long time.

He put his head in his hands and brooded over Shukra's sorcery with Shankha, Mukúnda, Kunda, Padma etc.* He lamented with a hot sigh:

"I have been duped by a thoroughly avaricious sorcerer masquerading as a friend. The evil Shukra knows my weaknesses, and he is unassailable since he has the support of the *daityas*.

Now, bereft of wealth, I have all of a sudden become as insignificant as piece of straw. To whom can I confide my grief? What can I do? Where can I go?

Dhana|rahitaṃ tyajati jano,
jana|rahitaṃ paribhavāḥ samāyānti.
paribhūtasya śarīraṃ
vyasana|vikāro mahā|bhāraḥ.

2.55 Dayiteṣu śarīravatāṃ
bata Dharma|lat"|ālavāleṣu
draviṇeṣu jīviteṣu ca
sarvaṃ yāti prayāteṣu.

Vidvān subhago mānī
viśruta|karmā kul'|ônnataḥ śūraḥ
vittena bhavati sarvo,
vitta|vihīnas tu sad|guṇo 'py aguṇaḥ.»

Iti duḥsaha|dhana|viraha|
kleś'|ānala|śoṣit'|āśayo Dhana|paḥ
suciraṃ vimṛṣya sacivair
devaṃ Śarvaṃ yayau śaraṇam.
Prāk|pratipanno 'tha sakhā
viśva|śaraṇyo Maheśvaras tena
vijñapto nija|vṛttaṃ
dūtaṃ visasarja Śukrāya.

Dūt'|āhūtaṃ sahasā
prāptaṃ Śukraṃ dhana|prabhā|śukram
añjali|viracita|mukuṭaṃ
provāca puraḥ|sthitaṃ Purajit:

2.60 «Mitram ayaṃ Draviṇa|patiḥ
bhavatā bata! vañcitaḥ kṛta|jñena
mitra|drohe prasarati
na hi nāma janaḥ kṛta|ghno 'pi.
Agaṇita|yaśasā tyakta|

Retainers desert a man stripped of wealth.
Without attendants, a man is shown contempt.
The body of a disgraced man becomes a heavy burden,
a pernicious blight.

Alas! When riches or life, 2.55
cherished by embodied beings,
irrigation basins for the vine of the Law,
are lost, all is lost.

A man with money becomes all:
wise, handsome, respected, renowned, noble, valorous;
but without money,
even a virtuous man becomes infamous."

The God of wealth, his hopes parched by the fire which was the unbearable misery of losing his wealth, deliberated with his counsellors for a long time, then sought refuge with the God Shiva. Long ago he had gained a friend in Shiva, a refuge accessible to everyone. Appraised of events, Shiva sent a personal envoy to Shukra.

Summoned by the envoy, Shukra presented himself at once, dazzling with the splendor of wealth, with a crown made of his hands folded in reverence. Shiva, the destroyer of the citadel, spoke to him as he stood before him:

"Dear me! Though fully conscious of your obligations, 2.60
you have cheated this friend of yours, the God of wealth. Not even a selfish ingrate goes as far as harming a friend. My good man! Who has ever deceived an affectionate friend, innocent and trusting, as you have, heedless of your reputation, straying from your station?

sthitinā sādho tvayā yathā kena
snigdhe suhṛdi nirāgasi
viśvaste vañcanā kriyate?

Etat kiṃ śruta|sadṛśaṃ
tvad|vrata|yogyaṃ kul'|ânurūpaṃ vā
kṛtavān asi yat sumate
paribhūta|guṇ'|ôdayaṃ karma?

Kim ayaṃ sunay'|âbhyāsaḥ
praśamo vā guru|jan'|ôpadeśo vā
mati|vibhavaḥ saha|jo vā
vañcakatāṃ yena yāto 'si?

Kasya na dayitaṃ vittaṃ?
cittaṃ hriyate na kasya vittena?
kiṃ tu yaśo|dhana|lubdhā
vāñchanti na duṣkṛtair arthān.

2.65 Mā mā malinaya vimalaṃ
bhṛgu|kulam akhilaṃ malena lobhena.
lobha|jala|do hi śatruḥ
viśada|yaśo|rāja|haṃsānām.

Tyaktvā kīrtim anantām
anil'|ākula|jala|lav'|ôpamān arthān
gṛhṇāti yaḥ sa madhye
dhūrtānāṃ kīdṛśo dhūrtaḥ?

Utsṛjya sādhu|vṛttaṃ
kutila|dhiyā vañcitaḥ paro yena
ātm" âiva mūḍha|matinā
hata|sukṛto vañcitas tena.

Does this befit your learning, is it compatible with the vows you observe, is it in keeping with your lineage, wise man, that you have done a deed springing from a disregard of virtue?

Was it perhaps your adherence to prudent conduct, or your practice of tranquility, or the instruction of your teachers, or your inborn high-mindedness, that led you to become a fraud?

To whom is wealth not dear? Who is not fascinated by wealth? But those who long for the wealth of a good reputation do not aspire to gain riches by illicit means. Do not! Do 2.65
not besmirch the entire, unsullied lineage of Bhrigu with the stain of avarice! For the cloud of avarice is the enemy of the swans of untainted repute.

What a villain among villains is he
who throws away immortal fame and prefers riches,
which are like droplets of water
blown about by the wind?

He who strays from good conduct
and with wily cunning deceives another,
that simpleton deceives only himself,
wiping out meritorious deeds done in the past.

Nipatita|dūṣita|yaśasāṃ
    nava|kisalaya|komalā prakṛty" âiva
apavāda|viṣa|tar'|ûtthaiḥ
    āmodair mūrchitā lakṣmīḥ.

Na hi nāma saj|janānāṃ
    śuddha|yaśaḥ sphaṭika|darpaṇo vimalaḥ
paribhava|duḥkhita|janatā|
    niśvāsair malinatām eti.

2.70 Asamañjasam atimalinaṃ
    mohād vyaktiṃ samāgataṃ karma,
tasya viśuddhiḥ kriyatāṃ
    para|vitta|samarpaṇen' âiva.
Apavāda|dhūli|dhūsaram
    amala|yaśo mṛjyatāṃ sva|hastena!
asmad|vacanaṃ kriyatāṃ!
    para|dhanam utsṛjyatām etat!»
Ity|uktaḥ s'|ânunayaṃ
    tri|bhuvana|guruṇ" âpi Deva|devena
para|dhana|nibaddha|tṛṣṇaḥ
    provāca kṛt'|âñjaliḥ Śukraḥ:
«Bhagavan, bhavataḥ śāsanam
    amar'|êndra|kirīṭa|koṭi|viśrāntam
laṅghayati ko nu mohād
    daurgatyaṃ sattva|hāri yadi na syāt?
Yasya kṣīṇasya gṛhe
    bhṛtyā dārāḥ sutāś ca sīdanti
kāry'|âkārya|vicāro
    draviṇ'|ādāneṣu kas tasya?

For those who have fallen
  and whose reputation has become tarnished,
good fortune,
  which is by nature delicate
  like a freshly sprouted tendril,
wilts with the fumes
  given off by the toxic tree of infamy.*

For indeed, the pure repute of the virtuous,
is a veritable stainless crystal mirror,
that does not become tarnished
  by the sighs of people anguished by humiliation.

2.70 Make amends for this unbecoming, despicable deed, perpetrated out of folly, by simply returning the money belonging to another.

Wipe clean with your own hand your pure reputation, soiled by the dust of condemnation! Do what we say! Relinquish the money belonging to another!"

Even though he was thus spoken to in conciliatory tones by the God of gods, Shiva, the teacher of the triple world, Shukra, resolute in his craving for another's wealth, folded his hands and spoke:

"Blessed one! Who would foolishly dare transgress your command which rests on the myriad crowns of the foremost Gods, were it not that destitution had robbed his good sense?

What deliberation of right or wrong in the procuring of money can there be for a wretch in whose house his retainers, wives and sons languish in despair?

2.75 Mitram ayaṃ Dhana|nātho
vipadi trāṇaṃ vicintitaḥ satatam.
vṛddhiṃ yātaḥ sumahān
āśā|bandhaś ca me hṛdaye.
Abhyetya yācito 'pi
tyaktvā lajjāṃ mayā vigata|lajjaḥ
cicched' âiṣa mam' āśāṃ
sahasā pratiṣedha|śastreṇa.
Tena prahṛtam aśastraṃ
dāho 'nagniś ca nirviṣaṃ maraṇam
vihitaṃ śaṭhena mohād
āśā|bhaṅghaḥ kṛto yena.
Tasmān mam' âiṣa śatruḥ
sukṛta|samaṃ śatru|vañcan" âpāpam.
riktasya nirapavādo
vyājen' ôpārjito 'py arthaḥ.
Aṇu dhanam api na
tyājyaṃ mama bhavatā jñāpite satyam
vittam jīvitam agryaṃ.
jīvita|hānir dhana|tyāgaḥ.»
2.80 Iti bhāṣamānam asakṛd
Daitya|guruṃ prārthitaṃ punar bahuśaḥ
kavalī|cakāra sahasā
pratiṣedha|ruṣā Virūpākṣaḥ.
Jaṭhar'|ântare Purāreḥ
pralay'|ānala|vipula|bhīṣaṇ'|ābhoge
prakvāthyamāna|kāyaḥ
Śukraś cukrośa s'|ākrośaḥ.

I had always considered the God of wealth as my friend, and a shelter in adversity. A great expectation had grown strong in my heart. 2.75

Even though I approached him and begged him, swallowing my pride, he, unabashed, brusquely severed my hope with the blade of rejection.

That miscreant ignorantly shattered my hopes, wounded me without a weapon, burnt me without fire, brought death without venom.

Therefore he is my foe. Deceiving an enemy is equivalent to a good deed, and not a sin. The wealth of an indigent man, even if won by guile, is beyond reproach.

I need not give up even an atom of wealth when you yourself have rightly just said that *fame : wealth* is the vital spark. Giving up wealth is to lay down one's life."*

The teacher of the Daityas kept on prevaricating in this 2.80
way despite many repeated appeals. Angry at his obstinacy, the three-eyed Shiva suddenly swallowed him down.

Shukra shrieked and cursed as his body stewed in the terrifying cavern suffused with the world-ending fire inside the belly of Shiva.

«Tyaja dhanam!» iti Viṣamadṛśā
punaḥ punaḥ prerito 'vadac Chukra:ḥ
«nidhanaṃ mam' âstu bhagavan
Dhanada|dhanaṃ n' ânujānāmi.»

Atha dhāraṇā|pravṛddha|
jvalana|jvālā|sahasra|vikarāle
Śukraś cukrośa bhṛśaṃ
ghora|gabhīre Har'|ôdare patitaḥ.

Tam uvāca Deva|devaḥ:
«tyaja durgraha|dagdha para|vittam!
asminn udara|mah"|ôdadhi|
vaḍav"|âgnau mā gamaḥ pralayam.»

2.85 So 'vadad: «ati|śaya|tāpa|
sphuṭit'|âsthi|vasā|pravāha|bahal'|âgnau
varam iha maraṇaṃ śreyo
draviṇa|kaṇaṃ na tyajāmi s'|ôcchvāsaḥ.»

Punar api ghoratar'|ôdgata|
kāl'|ânala|dhāraṇ"|ânale jvalati
Śukraś cakre Devyāḥ
stotraṃ kṣaṇa|leśa|śeṣ'|āyuḥ.

Stotra|pad'|ārādhitayā
Gauryā praṇaya|prasādite Rudre
tad|vacasā labdha|dhṛtiḥ
śukra|dvāreṇa niryayau Śukraḥ.

Evaṃ sva|bhāva|lubdhāḥ
tīvratarāṃ yātanām api sahante
na tu saṃtyajanti vittaṃ
kauṭilyam iv' âdhamāḥ sahajam.

"Yield the money!" Again and again Shiva urged him. Shukra said: "Let me die, Blessed one! I will not give back the money of the God of wealth."

Then Shukra plummeted downwards into the horrifying depths of Shiva's bowels, horrendous with thousands of seething flames intensified by his yogic fixation,* and wailed aloud.

The God of gods said to him: "Stubborn wretch! Give up the money of another! Don't perish in the submarine fire in my stomach-ocean!"

Shukra replied: "I prefer death here in this conflagration 2.85
fanned up with the marrow-fat streaming from my bones cracking asunder by the extreme heat. I will not surrender any money as long as I breathe."

As the flames of Shiva's yogic fixation and the ferocious world-ending fire flared up yet more, Shukra, with the last remaining moments of his life, composed a hymn to the Goddess.

Then Gauri, propitiated by the words of his hymn, affectionately appeased Shiva, and Shukra regained his stability by Shiva's command and came forth as Shiva's semen.

So, those avaricious by nature endure even savage torture without giving up money, just as lowborn wretches cannot give up their inbred dishonesty.

Tasmāl lobha|samutthā
kapaṭa|kalā kuṭila|vartinī māyā
lubdha|hṛdayeṣu nivasati.
n' âlubdho vañcanāṃ kurute.

iti mahā|kavi|śrī|Kṣemendra|viracite
Kalā|vilāse
lobha|varṇanaṃ nāma
dvitīyaḥ sargaḥ.

Therefore, the art of fraud, born from avarice, a delusion which moves crookedly, dwells in the hearts of the greedy. A man who is not greedy does not cheat.

The second canto,
named the description of avarice,
in the "Grace of Guile" composed by
the great poet Ksheméndra.

THE GRACE OF GUILE
3. LUST

KĀMAḤ kamanīyatayā
kim api nikāmam* karoti sammoham.
viṣam iva madhunā sahitaṃ
madhuratayā jīvanaṃ harati.

Ete hi *kāma|kalitāḥ*
parimala|līn'|āli|valaya|huṃkāraiḥ
sūcita|dānāḥ kariṇo
badhyante kṣipram *abalābhiḥ.*

Pād'|āghātaṃ *daśana|*
cchedy'|âṅkuśa|ghaṭana|nigaḍa|saṃrodhān
viṣaya|muṣitaḥ kar'|îndraḥ
kiṃ na *smara|vañcitaḥ* sahate?

Dīrgha|vyasana|niruddho
bhrū|bhaṅg'|ājñā|vidheyatāṃ yātaḥ
viṣaya|vivaśo manuṣyaḥ
keli|śikhaṇḍ" îva nartyate strībhiḥ.

SENSUALITY, BY ITS ALLURE,
somehow manages to make infatuation desirable.
It destroys life by its sweetness,
like a poison taken with honey.

For *elephants* ⁝ *men,*
maddened by passion ⁝ *incited to lust*,
with their rut-fluid betrayed by the buzzing of encircling bee-swarms attracted by its fragrance
⁝ *by the tinkling sounds of perfumed bracelets arrayed in rows, and who bring suitably lavish gifts,*
are quickly *bound by their hind-legs* ⁝ *embraced by women.**

Does not a mighty *elephant* ⁝ *lover*,
deprived of his open range ⁝ *blinded by sensual pleasures,*
tricked by affection ⁝ *duped by Cupid,*
endure being kicked,*
let itself be shorn of its tusks ⁝ *endure bites,*
driven with a goad ⁝ *nail scratches,*
and *fettered with iron chains* ⁝ *entwining in erotic gymnastics?**

Women make a man,
rendered impotent by severe vices,
tamed to obey commands given by raised eye-brows,
overpowered by sensual pleasures,
dance like a pet peacock.

3.5 *Rakt'/ākarṣaṇa/saktā*
māyābhir moha/timira/rajanīṣu
nāryaḥ piśācikā iva
haranti hṛdayāni mugdhānām.

Rāgi|mṛga|vāgurāṇāṃ
hṛdaya|dvipa|bandha|śṛṅkhal'|âughānām
vyasana|nava|vallarīṇāṃ
strīṇāṃ na hi mucyate vaśa|gaḥ.

Saṃsāra|citra|māyāṃ
Śambara|Māyāṃ Viṣṇu|māyāṃ ca
yo jānāti jit'|ātmā
so 'pi na jānāti yoṣitāṃ māyām.

Kusuma|sukumāra|dehā
vajra|śilā|kaṭhina|hṛdaya|sadbhāvāḥ
janayanti kasya n' ântaḥ
vicitra|caritāḥ striyo moham?

Women, intent on attracting impassioned men 3.5
on nights dark with infatuation,
steal the hearts of the simple-minded with cunning,
just like demonesses,
: *intent on drinking blood,*
seize the hearts of their innocent victims
*with sorcery on nights dark with witchcraft.**

There is no escape for those under the sway of women,
for they are snares
for the deer that are impassioned men,
they are a throng of chain-fetters
for the elephant that is the heart,
they are the thriving tangle-weed that is addiction.

Even a self-realised person,
who understands the strange delusion of transmigration,
the sorcery of Shámbara,
and Vishnu's Maya,
cannot grasp the deception of women.

With bodies as delicate as flowers,
with hearts tough like slabs of diamond,
whom do women, with their bizarre behavior,
not trouble deep within?

Anurakta|jana|viraktā
namr'|ôtsiktā virakta|rāgiṇyaḥ
vañcaka|vacan'|āsaktā
nāryo 'sadbhāva|bhāṣiṇyaḥ.

3.10 Jātaḥ sa eva loke
bahu|jana|dṛṣṭā vilāsa|kuśal'|âṅgī
dhairya|dhvaṃsa|patākā
yasya na patnī prabhur gehe.

Vijitasya mada|vikāraiḥ
strībhir mūkasya naṣṭa|saṃjñasya
gṛha|dhūli|paṭalam akhilam
vadane nikṣipyate bhartuḥ.

Kṛtak'|âparisphuṭ'|âkṣara|
kāma|kalābhiḥ sva|bhāva|mugdh" êva
tilakāya candra|bimbaṃ
mugdha|patiṃ yācate prauḍhā.

Svaira|vihāra|gat'|āgata|
khinnāyās tīrtha|darśana|vyājaiḥ
bhartā vilāsa|vijitaḥ
caraṇau mṛdnāti capalāyāḥ.

Women are hostile to those who show affection,
contemptuous of the subservient,
infatuated with the indifferent,
full of regard for the words of fraudsters,
and inclined to lie.

Only that man becomes master of his house, 3.10
  who has a wife who is not frequented by many people,
  whose limbs are not good at flirting gestures,
  who is not a banner to the ruin of fortitude.

Women empty the whole dustbin
of household rubbish*
  into the face of their husband who,
  stupefied by infatuation,
  remains dumb and witless.

In a loving, sweet tone with artificially indistinct syllables,
the bossy matron,
  as though she were a naturally artless girl,
begs her dim husband
  for the moon-disk as her forehead-ornament.

The fickle woman exhausts herself
by coming and going to amuse herself at will
with her lovers
  under the pretext of going to see sacred fords.
Her husband, taken in by her affected coyness,
  then massages her feet.

Nayana|vikārair anyaṃ
vacanair anyaṃ viceṣṭitair anyam
ramayati suraten' ânyaṃ
strī bahu|rūpā sva|bhāvena.

3.15 Nija|pati|capala|kuraṅgī
para|taru|bhṛṅgī sva|bhāva|mātaṅgī
mithyā|vibhrama|bhaṅgī
kuṭila|bhujaṅgī nijā kasya?

«Bahu|vidha|taruṇa|nirargala|
saṃbhoga|sukh'|ârtha|bhoginī veśyā
dhany" êti» vadanti sadā
s'|ôcchvāsā nirjane nāryaḥ.

Capalā tiṣṭhati harmye
gāyati rathy"|âvalokinī svairam
dhāvaty akāraṇaṃ vā
hasati sphaṭik'|âśma|māl" êva.

«Paśur iva vaktuṃ kartuṃ
kiṃ cid ayaṃ mama patir na jānāti»
uktv" êti gṛhe sva|janaṃ
puruṣa|vyāpāram aṅganā kurute.

Pratyutthānaṃ kurute
vyavahāra|gat'|āgataiḥ svayaṃ yāti
uccair vadati ca gehe
gṛhiṇī jīvan|mṛtasy' êva.

She loves one man by flirting with her eyes,
another with her words,
another with her gestures,
another physically—-a woman inherently has many forms.*

A female antelope inconstant to her mate, 3.15
a female bee on another's tree,
an outcaste by nature,
a wave of false coquetry,
a crooked serpent
—whose is she?

When alone, women always sigh, saying:
"Fortunate is a courtesan,
enjoying the pleasure of free union with many youths!"*

She is unpredictable: either she remains in her mansion,
  sings and at will casts an eye on the street below,
or she runs or laughs for no reason,
  seemingly garlanded with a rosary of rock-crystal.

"Like a brute,
this husband of mine does not know how to say or do anything,"
saying this to her servants in the house,
the woman takes over the man's business.*

The wife,
  whose husband may as well be dead while still alive,
welcomes visitors,
goes herself for routine business,
and raises her voice in the house.

3.20 Īrṣyālu|vṛddha|bhāryā
sevaka|patnī niyogi|kāntā vā
kāru|kuśīlava|nārī
lubdha|vadhūḥ sārthavāha|vanitā vā;
Goṣṭhī|viharaṇa|śīlā
taruṇa|jane vatsalā prakṛty" âiva
para|guṇa|gaṇane saktā
nija|pati|doṣ'|âbhidhāyinī satatam;
Alpa|dhanā bahu|bhogā
rūpavatī vikṛta|rūpa|bhāryā vā
mugdha|vadhūḥ sakala|kalā
mānavatī nīca|saṃgam'|ôdvignā;
Dyūta|madhu|pāna|nityā
dīrgha|kathā|gīta|rāgiṇī|kuśalā
bahu|puṃś|calī|vayasyā
śūra|jane prakṛti|pakṣa|pāt" âiva;
Tyakta|gṛha|vyāpārā
bahu|vidha|veṣā nirargala|tyāgā
pratyuttara|sa|pratibhā
satya|vihīnā sva|bhāva|nirlajjā;
3.25 Kuśal'|ânāmaya|vārtā|
praśna|parā prīti|peśal'|ālāpā
vijane vividha|krīḍā|

The wife of a jealous old man, 3.20
the wife of a servant,
or the spouse of a commissioner,*
the woman of an artisan or a performer,
the wife of a lecher,*
the wife of a caravan-leader;
A woman accustomed to frequenting congregations,
a woman by nature fond of young people,
a woman addicted to recounting the virtues of other men,
a woman who incessantly lists the faults of her own husband;
A poor woman who spends much,
a beautiful woman or the wife of a misshapen man,
the wife of a naive man,
a woman proud of her skill in all of the arts,
a woman excited by associating with lowly people;
A woman who is always gambling and drinking,
a woman accomplished in singing musical modes,
songs and telling drawn out tales,
a woman whose companions have many affairs,
a woman who instinctively is partial to intrepid men;
A woman who neglects her household duties,
a woman with a large wardrobe of garments,
a woman free to leave the house,
a woman who gives audacious answers,
a woman without honesty,
an inherently shameless woman;
A woman given to queries about welfare, 3.25
health and gossip,
a woman whose speech is tender with affection,
a woman who is publicly a loyal Sávitri* but in secret,

ḍambara|śauṇḍā prakāśa|Sāvitrī;
Kratu|tīrtha|sura|niketana|
gaṇaka|bhiṣag|bandhu|geha|gamana|parā
bhojana|pāna|bahu|vyaya|
yāg'|ôtsava|kāriṇī sva|tantr" êva;
Bhikṣuka|tāpasa|bhaktā
sva|jana|vimuktā mano|ram'|āsaktā
darśana|dīkṣā|raktā
dayita|viraktā samādhi|saṃyuktā;
Goṣṭhī|rañjana|mitrā
vacana|vicitrā sa|śabda|pādatrā
gala|dhṛta|yāga|pavitrā
vijñeyā naṣṭa|cāritrā.

Satat'|ânurakta|doṣā
mohita|janatā bahu|grahāś capalāḥ
saṃdhyāḥ striyaḥ
piśācyo *rakta|cchāyā|harāḥ* krūrāḥ.

  is addicted to an entanglement
  of all kinds of amorous sports;
A woman keen to visit sacrifices,
  sacred fords, temples, astrologers,
  physicians, and relatives,
a woman who, as though she were independent,
  arranges festivals of ceremonial offerings
  with great expense for drink and food;
A woman devoted to monks and ascetics,
a woman abandoned by her kinsfolk,
a woman attached to pleasant things,
a woman desiring to see icons and have initiations,
a woman separated from her lover,
  but with him in meditation;
A woman whose friends divert themselves
  with social functions,
a woman who entertains with her words,
a woman with clattering shoes,
or a woman with sacrificial grass around her neck,
—such like must be known as a woman of loose conduct.

Women are twilight-skies,
  are ever fond of vices : *ever reddening the night,*
  delude people : *delight people,*
  take many men : *are full of planets,*
  are inconstant : *last but a short while*;
they are cruel demonesses
  beautiful with red cheeks : *drawn by the life-glow of blood.*

3.30 Kasya na vāhana|yogyā
mugdha|dhiyas tuccha|śāsane lagnāḥ
ṣaṃḍhatayā praśama|rucaḥ
capalāsu strīṣu ye dāntāḥ?

Śṛṅgāra|śaurya|kathanam
asamañjasa|dāna|varṇanā vividhāḥ
etāvad eva tāsām
amantra|yantraṃ vaśī|karaṇam.

Kali|kāla|timira|rajanī|
rajani|carīṇāṃ sahasra|māyānām
strīṇāṃ nṛśaṃsa|caritaiḥ
kasya na saṃjāyate kampaḥ?

Nirjita|dhana|pati|vibhavo
babhūva bhuvi viśruto vaṇiṅ|nāthaḥ
Dhanadatto nāma purā
ratnānām āśrayaḥ payodhir iva.

Tasy' âbhavad vibhūtiḥ
mūrt" êva Mano|bhuvaḥ sulalit'|âṅgī
tanayā nayana|vilāsaiḥ
vijit'|āśā Vasumatī nāma.

3.35 Pradadau sa tām aputraḥ
putra|pade vinihitāṃ priyāṃ putrīṃ
vaṇije vibhava|kul'|ôdaya|
tulyāya Samudra|dattāya.

Ramamāṇaḥ sa tayā saha
hariṇ"|âkṣyā śvaśura|mandire suciram
prayayau kadā cid agre
dvīp'|āyātasya sārthasya.

For whom might naive men,— 3.30
obedient to the slightest whim of women,
who have lost their dignity
because they have become emasculated,
who are subdued among women,—
not serve as beasts of burden?

Bragging of audacity in love,
and various boasts of gifts to unworthy people,*
this is sufficient to captivate* women
without using mantras or yantras.

Who does not tremble at the cruel deeds of women,
who are night-stalkers
on nights dark like the age of discord,
who know thousands of sorceries?

Once, there was a world-famous merchant-prince called Dhana·datta who surpassed the God of wealth with his splendor. Like the sea, he was a repository of gemstones.

He had a voluptuous daughter called Vásumati, the magnificence of the God of love embodied, as it were. With the playful movements of her eyes she had conquered the points of the compass.

Being sonless, he appointed his cherished daughter as heir 3.35
in place of a son, and gave her in marriage to the merchant Samúdra·datta, her equal in wealth and noble lineage.

For a long time Samúdra·datta remained in his father-in-law's palace, enjoying the pleasures of love with the doe-eyed maiden. Then, the time came when he set out at the head of a trade caravan which had arrived from a foreign island.

Patyau yāte taruṇī
janaka|gṛhe harmya|śikharam ārūḍhā
vilalāsa vilāsa|mahī|
keli|vilolā sakhībhiḥ sā.

Saudhe Manmatha|rūpaṃ
pṛthu|nayanā pathi dadarśa puruṣaṃ sā
yaṃ dṛṣṭv" âiva gat" âsyāḥ
kv' âpi dhṛtiḥ kumati|kupit" êva.

Sā tena capala|nayanā
sahasā muṣit" êva hārita|vicārā
adhyavasāy'|âśaktā nitarāṃ
saṃvaraṇe smara|vikārasya.

3.40 «Śīlaṃ pālaya capale!
mā pātaya nimnag eva kula|kūlam»
iti tām avadad iv' ôccaiḥ
kamp'|ākula|mukhara|mekhalā suciram.

Sā kṛtvā vidita|kathāṃ
rahasi sakhīm ānindruāya taṃ taruṇam.
calitaṃ hi kāminīnāṃ
dhartuṃ śaknoti kaś cittam?

Kāmaṃ kāma|vikāsaiḥ
surata|vilāsaiḥ sunarma|parihāsaiḥ
sahaja|prema|nivāsaiḥ
mumude sā svairiṇī tena.

Atha kṛta|nija|dhana|kṛtyaḥ
tvaritaṃ dayitā|vilokan'|ôtkaṇṭhaḥ
aviśat Samudradattaḥ
śvaśur'|āvāsaṃ mah"|ārambhaḥ.

While her husband was abroad, the young lady ascended to the spires of her father's palace and diverted herself by playing games on the amusement-terraces* with her friends.

While she was among the spires, the large-eyed lady espied on the road a man, as beautiful as the God of love. No sooner had she seen him, than her self-control slipped away, as though angered by her improper thoughts.

The lady with tremulous eyes, deprived of her discernment, seemed as if she had been forcibly robbed by him, and was incapable of mustering enough purpose of mind to conceal the changes love had wrought in her.

Her girdle, tinkling because it was shaken by tremors, 3.40
seemed ever to call out to her in shrill tones:
"Hold on to your morals!
Do not drag down the limits of your family!"

In secret, she confided the affair to her friend and ordered: "Bring me that young man!" For, who can grasp the volatile mind of impassioned women?

The uninhibited woman made love with him to her heart's content, with rising passion, with playful gestures during intercourse, with wit and humor, and with love-nests chosen at fancy.*

Samúdra·datta, with great haste, settled his financial affairs, and, longing to see his beloved wife, he rushed home to his father-in-law's residence.

Vipula|mah"|ôtsava|līlā|
vyagra|janair bhoga|saṃpadāṃ nicayaiḥ
ati|vāhya dinaṃ dayitā
sahitaḥ śayyā|gṛhe sa yayau.

3.45 Viracita|varatara|śayane
baddha|vitāne manorama|sthāne
jṛmbhita|saurabha|dhūpe
sura|gṛha|rūpe pradīpta|maṇi|dīpe.

Tatra sa madhu|kara|vilulita|*
locana|kamalāṃ priyāṃ samādāya
mada|gaja iva nava|nalinīṃ
bheje rati|lālasaḥ śayyām.

S" âpi *hṛday'|ântara|sthita|*
para|puruṣa|dhyāna|baddha|lakṣ" âiva
tasthau nimīlit'|âkṣī
dhyāna|parā yogin" îva ciram.

Āliṅgana|paricumbana|
nīvi|vimokṣeṣu bahutar'|ôcchvāsā
patyau saṅkucit'|āṅgī
sasmāra tam eva śīla|haram.

Praṇaya|kupit" êti matvā
mugdha|patis tāṃ Samudradatto 'pi
praṇipatya cāṭu|kāraiḥ
kim api yayāce prasādāya.

3.50 Para|puruṣa|rāgiṇīnāṃ
vimukhīnāṃ praṇaya|kopa|vāmānām
puruṣa|paśavo vimūḍhā
rajyante yoṣitām adhikam.

The day was spent with people revelling in the merriment of a huge festival, and with an exuberance of exquisite entertainments. Then he retired with his beloved wife to the sleeping-quarters.

They were furnished with an impeccable bed, covered 3.45
with a canopy, delightfully appointed, suffused with fragrant incense, as beautiful as a palace of the Gods, and provided with gleaming jewel-inlaid lamps.

There, he took hold of his beloved, whose eye-lotuses were tremulous with flitting bee-pupils and, eager for love-making, he went to bed, just as a rutting elephant enters a pond full of fresh lilies.

Her thoughts, on the other hand, *centered on that other man who dwelt in her heart. She remained indifferent* with her eyes shut for a long time like a Yógini deep in meditation, *who has fixed as the goal of her meditation the supreme soul which abides in the innermost heart.*

Time and again she sighed while he embraced her, kissed her and undid her garments. She shrank from her husband and remembered only him who had robbed her virtue.*

Her naive husband Samúdra·datta thought her to be coquettishly feigning anger.* He fell at her feet and tried hard to mollify her with honeyed words.

For dim-witted man-beasts are even more fascinated by 3.50
women infatuated with other men, who are standoffish and obstinate with feigned anger.

Kiṃ kriyate kāmo 'yaṃ
    para|gata|kāmaḥ sva|tantra|kāmaś ca?
bata Śaśa|dhara|raktāyām
    Saṃdhyāyāṃ Bhāskaro rāgī.

Gūḍh'|ôpavana|nikuñje
    nyastaṃ sā vallabhaṃ sa|saṃketam
saṃcintya ciraṃ sva|patiṃ
    viṣam iva saṃmūrchitā mene.
Nidrā|mudrita|nayane
    praṇaya|śrānte Samudradatte sā
utthāya racita|veṣā
    śanakair gaman'|ônmukhī tasthau.
Cauraḥ kṣaṇe 'tha tasmin
    madhu|matta|jane praviśya tad|bhavanam
gaman'|ônmukhām apaśyan
    mukhar'|ābharaṇām alakṣyas tām.

3.55 *Atr' ântare śaś'|âṅkaḥ*
    śanakaiḥ Sura|rāja|vallabhāṃ kakubham
cakita iv' āśu cakampe
    mīlita|tārāṃ samāliṅgya.

How can love manage to be both
  aimed at dependency on another
  and also aimed at being independent?
Alas! The Sun loves lady Twilight
  who loves the hare-marked Moon.*

For a long time she fantasized about her lover who lay waiting in a concealed bower in a grove as agreed, and swooning, she thought of her husband as venom.

At last, when Samúdra·datta's eyes were sealed by sleep, exhausted as he was by his attemps to placate her, she arose, quietly put on her garments, and paused, ready to leave.

Now, at that very moment, a thief entered the building while the people were intoxicated with wine. Unnoticed, he watched her as she stood there anxious to depart, tinkling with ornaments.

Just then, the hare-marked moon, 3.55
which had slowly risen into the eastern quarter,
  twinkling with stars,
suddenly flickered with a flash, as it were.*
⁝ The moon,
slowly embracing the lady of the eastern quarter,
  beloved by the king of Gods,
who had shut her eyes,
suddenly trembled,
  exhilarated, as it were.

Saṃkocita|kamalāyāḥ
kumuda|vijṛmbhā|virājamānāyāḥ
prasasāra Tuhina|kiraṇo
Yāminyāḥ kapaṭa|hāsa iva.

Ravi|paritāpa|śrāntāṃ
vīkṣya Divaṃ prasarad|indu|s'|ānandām
jahasur iva kumuda|vṛndaiḥ
ali|kula|jhaṅkāra|nirbharā vāpyaḥ.

Jagrāha rajani|ramaṇī
śaśi|kara|hṛta|timira|kañcuk'|āvaraṇā
lajj"|ânvit" êva purataḥ
kumud'|āmod'|ākul'|âli|paṭala|paṭam.

Supta|jane 'tha niś"|ârdhe
candr'|āloke'pi vimalatāṃ yāte
tamas' îva nirviśaṅkā
sā śanakair upavanaṃ prayayau.

The cold-rayed Moon came forth
as though he were pretending to be
the laughter of the Night,
who drew back her pale red lotus-lips,
and who was bright
with wide open night-lily-teeth.

On seeing the sky,
exhausted by the scorching heat of the sun,
rejoice at the rising of the moon,
: On seeing lady Div,
worn out by the passionate ardor of Ravi,
rejoice as he reaches his climax,
the ponds, seemed to laugh, as it were,
with clusters of night-lilies,
boisterous with the drone of bee-swarms.

The beautiful lady night,
her veiling bodice of darkness
pulled off by the rays* of the moon,
seemingly abashed,
veiled herself in a cloak of swarms of bees
excited by the scent of night-lilies.

Then, when everyone was asleep at midnight, the undaunted lady quietly went to the grove in a *darkness of immorality,** as it were, even though the moon was bright.

3.60 Atha sā viveśa vivaśā
viṣama|śara|ploṣitā nij'|ôpavanam
channaṃ bhūṣaṇa|lobhād
anuyātā vismitena caureṇa.

Tatra dadarśa vibhūṣitam
ujjvala|lalit'|âṃśukaṃ lasat|kusumam
śaṅkā|janakaṃ vipine
pakṣibhir upalakṣitaṃ dayitam.
Hṛdaya|dayitā|viyoga|
jvalana|jvāl'|āvalī|taptam
diṅ|mukha|vilasita|rucinā
caṇdreṇa kar'|ânalair dagdham.
Cira|saṅketa|sthityā
mukt'|āśaṃ priyatamā|punar|milane
vṛkṣ'|ālambita|vallī|
valay'|ālambena vigalita|prāṇam.
Taṃ dṛṣṭv" âiva vilīnā
vilapantī vyasana|śoka|saṃtrāsaiḥ
nipapāta vallar" îva
kvaṇad|ali|valay'|ākulā tanvī.
3.65 Saṃmoha|mīlit'|ākṣī
suciraṃ sthitvā mahīṃ samāliṅgya
śanakair avāpta|jīvā
vilalāpa laghu|svaraiḥ svairam.

The impulsive woman, 3.60
burnt by the God of love
who bears an uneven number of arrows,
entered the familiar grove,
secretly followed by the astonished thief
out of greed for her ornaments
: like a hunted animal wounded by terrible arrows,
*she entered her grove wishing to die,**
secretly followed by the gleeful hunter
greedy for trophies.

There she beheld her lover. He wore ornaments, was clothed in a shimmering, sumptuous robe, he gleamed with flowers, ominous in the thicket, he was advertised by birds.

He had been scorched by the banks of blazing flames of separation from his heart's beloved, and blistered by the moon, whose splendor illuminated the quarters, with fires which were his rays.

After waiting for a long time at the rendez-vous, he had given up hope of ever meeting his beloved again. His life had drained away as he hanged himself in the noose of a vine dangling from a tree.

When she saw him, the slender lady faltered, and weeping with shivers of grief at the tragedy, she fell to the ground like a vine overrun by swarms of humming bees.

Her eyes closed in oblivion, she lay there for a long time, 3.65
embracing the earth. Then, slowly regaining consciousness, she sobbed without holding back with feeble tones.

«Hā hā! nayan'|ānanda!
kva nu te pūrṇ'|êndu|sundaraṃ vadanam?
drakṣyāmi manda|bhāgyā
kim idaṃ? kv' âhaṃ kva me kāntaḥ!»
Iti taruṇa|karuṇam abalā
vilapya pāśaṃ vimucya yatnena
aṅke dhṛtv" âsya mukhaṃ
cucumba jīvaṃ kṣipant" îva.
Sā tasya vadana|kamalaṃ
nija|vadane mohitā kṛtvā
tāmbūla|garbham akarot
†prakaṭita|sākāra|rāg" êva.†
Atha tasyāḥ kusum'|ôtkara|
mṛga|mada|dhūp'|ādi|saurabh'|āhūtaḥ
āviśya śava|śarīraṃ
nāsāṃ ciccheda vetālaḥ.
3.70 Sā prāpya cāpal'|ôcitam
anaya|phalaṃ chinna|nāsikā gatvā
bhavanaṃ praviśya
bhartus tāraṃ «hāh" êti» cukrośa.
Pratibuddhe sakala|jane
nāda|traste Samudradatte ca
«sā nāsikā mṛt" êyaṃ
bhartrā chinn" êti» cakranda.
śvaśur'|ādi|bandhu|vargaiḥ
pṛṣṭaḥ kupitaiḥ Samudradatto'pi
vikrītaḥ para|deśe
mūka iv' ōce na kiṃ cid api.

"Alas! Alas! O delight of my eyes! Where now is your face, handsome like the full moon? Will I, hapless woman, see it again? What a gulf between between me and my lover!"

The frail woman lamented tenderly and pitifully. She struggled to release the noose, held his face in her lap and kissed him as though she were transferring life back into him.

Dazed, she pressed her own mouth against his mouth-lotus and transferred betelnut into it, †as though to demonstrate the depth of her love†.

Now a Vetála was summoned by the fragrance of the piles of flowers, musk-incense and the like. He entered the corpse and bit off her nose.*

Reaping retribution for her misconduct appropriate to 3.70
her insolence, she escaped with a severed nose.* She entered the house of her husband and shrieked aloud: "Alas! Alas!"

When everyone had been awakend, and Samúdra·datta was frightened by the noise, she wailed: "My nose is ruined, cut off by my husband!"

When her angry kinsmen, headed by the father-in-law questioned Samúdra·datta, he said nothing at all, as though he were a dumb person being sold in a foreign land.*

Atha c' âsya saṃprabhāte
bandhubhir āvedite nṛpa|sabhāyām
tatr' âbhūn nṛpa|kopo
bahu|dhana|daṇḍaḥ Samudradattasya.

Cauro 'pi nikhila|vṛttaṃ
pratyakṣam avekṣya vismay'|āviṣṭaḥ
āvedya bhūpa|purataḥ
prāpya ca valay'|ādi|satkāram;

3.75 Udyāne śava|vadane
tasyās tāṃ nāsikāṃ ca saṃdarśya
niṣkāraṇa|suhṛd|ucitāṃ
śuddhiṃ vidadhe Samudradattasya.

Ity etāḥ kuṭilatarāḥ
krūr'|ācārā gata|trapāś capalāḥ
yo nāma vetti vāmāḥ
sa strībhir n' âiva vañcyate matimān.

iti mahā|kavi|śrī|Kṣemendra|viracite
Kalā|vilāse
kāma|varṇanaṃ nāma
tritīyaḥ sargaḥ.

So, in the morning her kinsmen reported the crime in the royal court. The king's wrath fell upon Samúdra·datta and he was fined a huge sum of money.

Now the thief who had witnessed the whole affair was stricken with wonder. He reported it before the king, and on receiving a reward of a bracelet and such like,

He pointed out her nose in the mouth of the corpse in the grove. Thus he exonerated Samúdra·datta as it would have befitted a friend with no ulterior motive. 3.75

The wise man,
who truly understands such beautiful ladies
to be exceedingly crooked,
cruel in conduct, shameless and fickle,
is not deceived by women.*

The third canto,
named the depiction of lust,
in the "Grace of Guile" composed by
the great poet Ksheméndra.

THE GRACE OF GUILE
4. UNFAITHFULNESS

TATR' ÂPI veśa|yoṣāḥ
kuṭilatarāḥ kūṭa|rāga|hṛta|lokāḥ
kapaṭa|caritena yāsāṃ|
Vaiśravaṇaḥ pravaṇatām eti.

Hāriṇyaś caṭulatarā
bahula|taraṅgāś ca nimna|gāminyaḥ
nadya iva jaladhi|madhye
veśyā|hṛdaye kalāś catuḥ|ṣaṣṭiḥ.

Veśa|kalā nṛtya|kalā
gīta|kalā vakra|vīkṣaṇa|kalā ca
kāmi|parijñāna|kalā
grahaṇa|kalā mitra|vañcana|kalā ca;
Pāna|kalā keli|kalā
surata|kal"|āliṅgan'|ântara|kalā ca
īrṣyā|kali|keli|kalā
rudita|kalā kopa|saṃkṣaya|kalā ca;
4.5 Cumbana|nakha|danta|kalā
nirlajj"|āvega|saṃbhrama|kalā ca
virah'|âsaha|rāga|kalā
kāma|pratiṣedha|niścaya|kalā ca;
Sveda|klama|kampa|kalā
punar|ekānta|prasādhana|kalā
netra|nimīlana|niḥsaha|
nispanda|kalā mṛt'|ôpama|kalā ca;

AMONG THEM, courtesans are the most perfidious.*
they ravish the world with feigned love,
to whom, by treacherous machinations,
even the God of wealth becomes a generous donor.

In the heart of courtesans
are sixty-four *arts* ⁝ *motions*;*
they are *ravishing* ⁝ *destructive*, *fickle* ⁝ *heave*,
capricious ⁝ *abound in waves*,
and *consort with mean characters* ⁝ *flow downwards*;
just as there are currents
in the ocean.*

The art of couture,
the art of dancing,
the art of singing, the art of sidelong glances,
the art of recognising lustful men,
the art of ensnaring, the art of deceiving friends;
The art of cocktail-making, the art of amorous sport,
the art of intercourse, the art of various embraces,
the arts of playful jealousy and quarrel,
the art of crying, the art of dissipating anger;
The arts of kissing, scratching and biting,* 4.5
the arts of being shameless, aroused, and ardent,
the art of passion which cannot endure separation,
the art of resolving to frustrate passion;
The arts of perspiring, fatigue and trembling,
the art of frequently freshening up in private,
the arts of shutting the eyes,
the art of appearing powerless and motionless,
the art of appearing dead;

Nija|jananī|kalaha|kalā
sad|gṛha|gaman'|êkṣaṇ'|ôtsava|kalā ca
sarvasv'|āharaṇa|kalā
yācñā|kali|kalā caura|pārthiva|kalā ca;
Gaurava|śaithilya|kalā
niṣkāraṇa|doṣa|bhāṣaṇa|kalā ca
śūla|kal"|âbhyaṅga|kalā|
nidr"|âkṣi|rajasvalāvara|kalā ca;
Rūkṣa|kalā tīkṣṇa|kalā|
gala|hasta|gṛh'|ârgal'|ârpaṇa|kalā ca
saṃtyakta|kāmuk'|āhṛti|
darśana|yātrā|stuti|kalā ca;

4.10 Tīrth'|ôpavana|sur'|ālaya|
viharaṇa|helā|kalā graha|kalā ca
vaśy"|āuṣadha|mantra|kalā|
vṛṣya|kalā keśa|rañjana|kalā ca;
Bhikṣuka|tāpasa|bahu|vidha|
puṇya|kalā dvīpa|darśana|kalā ca
khinnā|kalā|tri|ṣaṣṭyā
paryante kuṭṭinī|kalā veśyā.

The art of brawling with her own mother,
the art of glad eyes when visiting her house,
the art of stealing everything,
the arts of being a king among thieves,
  and a hero among scroungers;
The arts of indifference and cumbrousness,
and the art of slandering without cause,
the art of acute pain,
the art of applying unguents,
the arts of sleepy eyes
  and being at the lowest ebb of menstruation;*
The art of being unkind,
the art of vehemence,
the art of locking,
the art of fastening her house's door-bolt
the art of throttling,
the arts of calling back jilted lovers
  and going to see deities, pilgrimages, and hymns of praise;
The arts of being frivoulous 4.10
  while roaming about sacred fords, pleasure groves,
  and temples,
the art of demonic possession,
the art of drugs and mantras used for subjugation,
the art of sexual stimulation,
the art of dyeing hair to disguise the age;
the art of knowing the many merits
  of Buddhist monks and ascetics,
the art of visiting refuges,
and the sixty-third art being decrepitude
the courtesan ends up becoming a procuress.

Ajñāta|nāma|varṇeṣu
ātm" âpi yay" ârpyate dhan'|âṃśena
tasyā api sad|bhāvaṃ
mṛgayante megha|saṅkāśam.

Nikhila|jana|vañcan'|ârjitam
akhila|dhanaṃ rāga|dagdha|hṛdayānām
khādati guṇa|gaṇa|bhagno
nagno hīno 'thavā kaś cit.

Nīcas turag'|āroho
hasti|pakaḥ khalataro 'thavā śilpī
vañcita|sakala|janānāṃ
tāsām api vallabho bhavati.

4.15 Rājā Vikramasiṃho
balavadbhir bhūmipaiḥ purā vijitaḥ
mānī yayau vidarbhān
Guṇa|yaśasā mantriṇā sahitaḥ.
Tatra sa veśyā|bhavanaṃ
praviśya bhuvi viśrutāṃ Vilāsavatīm
bheje gaṇikāṃ bahu|dhana|
bhojyām aty|alpa|vibhavo 'pi.
Taṃ rāja|lakṣaṇ'|ôcitam
ā|jānu|bhujaṃ vilokya pṛthu|sattvam
vividha|maṇi|kanaka|koṣaṃ
cakre sā tad|vyay'|ādhīnam.
Sahajam anurāgam adbhutam
aucityaṃ vīkṣya bhū|patis tasyāḥ
vismaya|vivaśaḥ premṇā
jagāda vijane mah"|āmātyam.

She who, for a little money,
hands herself over to men whose name and caste is unkown,*
—her reality, which resembles that of clouds,
is still a matter of enquiry.

All of the money of men
whose hearts have been burnt by desire,
that she gained from deceiving everyone,
is eaten up by some depraved character,
a naked mendicant,
who has eradicated a host of virtues,
or even better someone lowborn.

A base man, a horseman,
an elephant-driver, or a villainous craftsman,
becomes the beloved of these courtesans
who have deceived all people.*

Long ago, king Víkrama·simha was defeated by powerful 4.15
enemy monarchs. Indignant, he went to Vidárbha with his minister Guna·yashas.*

There, he entered a brothel and, although in reduced circumstances, frequented the famous courtesan Vilásavati, enjoyed by men of great wealth.

Perceiving him to be a man of great vigor, with arms reaching down to his knees,* evidence confirming his royal constitution, she put a treasury of gold and all variety of jewels at his disposal.

Seeing her innate affection and remarkable decorum, the king, unsettled with astonishment, affectionately spoke to his chief minister in private:

«Citram idaṃ bahu vittaṃ
kṣapayati veśy" âpi mat|kṛte tṛṇavat.
prīti|padavīṃ visṛṣṭo
veśyānāṃ dhana|nibandhano rāgaḥ.

4.20 Mithyā dhana|lava|lobhād
anurāgaṃ darśayanti bandhakyaḥ.
tad api dhanaṃ visṛjati yā
kas tasyāḥ premṇi saṃdehaḥ?»

Iti vacanaṃ bhūmi|pateḥ
śrutvā mantrī vihasya s'|āsūyaḥ
tam uvāca «kasya rājan
veśyā|carite 'sti viśvāsaḥ?

Etāḥ satya|vihīnā
dhana|lava|līnāḥ sukha|kṣaṇ'|ādhīnāḥ
veśyā viśanti hṛdayaṃ
mukha|madhurā nirvicārāṇām.

Prathama|samāgama|sukha|dā
madhye vyasana|pravāsa|kāriṇyaḥ
paryante duḥkha|phalāḥ
puṃsām āśāś ca veśyāś ca.

Adyāpi Hari|Harādibhiḥ
Amarair api tattvato na vijñātāḥ
bhrama/vibhrama/bahu/mohā
veśyāḥ saṃsāra|māyāś ca.»

4.25 Iti saciva|vaco nṛ|patiḥ
śrutvā kṛtvā ca saṃvidaṃ tena
mithyā|mṛtam ātmānaṃ
cakre veśyā|parīkṣāyai.

"This is strange! Though she is a courtesan, she spares no expense for my sake, as though money were straw. The passion of courtesans depends on money, has forsaken the path of love.

Harlots display affection falsely out of greed for a little money. But she relinquishes that very money, so what doubt could there be about her love?" 4.20

When he heard these words of the king, the minister laughed and scornfully said to him: "O king! Who can trust the dealings of a courtesan?

Courtesans are dishonest, they cling to scraps of wealth, rely on a moment of pleasure, and, uttering sweet cries, penetrate the hearts of injudicious men.

Men's aspirations and courtesans are akin: They give pleasure at the first encounter, in the intervening period they cause calamity and exile, in the end they bear fruits of misery.

Until this very day, even the Gods headed by Hari and Hara have not really managed to understand either the illusion of transmigration or courtesans, *full of confusions, deceptive appearances and fallacies : full of infatuation, coquetry and giddiness."*

The king listened to the minister's speech, and agreed on the ruse of pretending to be dead in order to test the courtesan.* 4.25

Tasmin kuṇapa|śarīre
vinyaste mantriṇā citā|vahnau
sahas" âiva Vilāsavatī
vahni|bhuvaṃ bhūṣitā prayayau.

Tāṃ prabala|jvalit'|ôjjvala|
jvalana|jvālā|nipāta|s'|āvegām
dorbhyām āliṅgya nṛpo
«jīvām' îty» abhyadhān muditaḥ.

Tat tasyāḥ prema dṛḍhaṃ
satyaṃ ca vicārya saṃbhṛta|snehaḥ
rājā nininda mantriṇam
asakṛd veśyā|guṇ'|âbhimukhaḥ.

Atha veśyā|dhana|saṃcayam
ātm'|ādhīnaṃ mahī|patir vipulam
ādāya gaja|turaṃgama|
bhaṭa|vikaṭām ādade senām.

4.30 *Sambhṛta|vipula|bal'|âughaiḥ*
jitvā vasudh"|âdhipān sa bhū|pālaḥ
nijam āsasāda maṇḍalam
indur iv' ānanda|kṛt pūrṇaḥ.

Sarv'|ântaḥ|pura|kāntā|
mūrdhni kṛtvā bhū|bhujā Vilāsavatī
śuśubhe Śrīr iva cāmara|
pavan'|ākulit'|âlakā tanvī.

S" âtha kadā cin nara|patim
ek'|ânte viracit'|âñjaliḥ praṇatā
ūce «nātha mayā tvaṃ
kalpa|taruḥ sevitaḥ svayaṃ dāsyā.

When the minister laid his corpse on the funeral pyre, Vilásavati, immediately rushed to the cremation ground, wearing her ornaments.*

As she was about to hurl herself headlong into the blazing conflagration which flared up with fierce flames, the king clasped her in his arms, and joyfully announced: "I live!"*

Then, convinced that her love was firm and true, the thoroughly infatuated king scolded the minister not once, being committed to the virtues of the courtesan.

Now, the king, using the amassed wealth of the courtesan put at his disposal, built up a mighty army of elephants, horses, and warriors.*

The king *conquered the rulers of the earth with an inundation of his well-equipped, vast forces* and regained his own realm, spreading delight like the moon, *who outmatches the mountains by raising up huge, powerful tidal floods.* 4.30

The king installed Vilásavati at the head of the whole harem; the slender lady, her locks fanned by a light wind from Yak-tail whisks,* shone like Lakshmi.

Then, one day, when they were alone, she folded her hands, bowed to the king, and said: "O lord, I have served you as my wish-granting tree, abasing myself as a slave.

Yadi nāma kutra cid ahaṃ
    yātā te hetutāṃ vibho lakṣmyāḥ
tan mama saphalām āśām
    arhasi kartuṃ prasādena.

Puṇya|phala|prāpyānāṃ
    hṛta|para|rajasāṃ sva|bhāva|vimalānām
tīrthānām iva mahatāṃ
    na hi nāma samāgamo viphalaḥ.

4.35 Abhavan mama ko'pi yuvā
    dayito dhana|jīvit'|âdhikaḥ preyān.
baddhaḥ sa Vidarbha|pure
    daiva|vaśāc cora|rūpeṇa.

Tan|muktaye mayā tvaṃ
    śaktataraḥ sevito mahī|nātha.
adhunā kriyatām ucitaṃ
    sattvasya kulasya śauryasya.»

Iti vañcanām avāpto
    vismita iva tad|vaco nṛpaḥ śrutvā
suciraṃ vilokya vasudhāṃ
    sasmār'âmātya|vacanaṃ saḥ.

Atha tāṃ tath" âiva rājā pari|
    sāntvya vidarbha|bhū|bhujaṃ jitvā
bandhana|mukten' âsyāḥ
    caureṇa samāgamaṃ cakre.

Ity evaṃ bahu|hṛdayā
    bahu|jihvā bahu|karāś ca bahu|māyāḥ
tattvena sattva|rahitāḥ
    ko jānāti sphuṭaṃ veśyāḥ?

If, in any way, O great one, I have contributed to your fortune, then you should oblige me by fulfilling my hope.

An encounter with the great, *who can be reached as the reward of merit, who are not tainted with the defilements of others, who are inherently pure*, is like an encounter with sacred fords : *which are suitable to attain great merit, which have destroyed the greatest sins, which are by nature pellucid*– it cannot be unprofitable.

I had a certain young lover, more dear to me than money 4.35
or life. As fate would have it, he is imprisoned in the city of Vidarbha as a thief.

Great king! I have served you according to my abilities in order to free him. Now do what befits your character, your lineage and your valour!"

When the king realised that he had been cheated he was as if dumbfounded. He stared at the ground for a long time and recalled the words of his minister.

Then the king nevertheless consoled her. He vanquished the king of Vidarbha and brought about her reunion with the thief released from prison.

Therefore, who can truly known courtesans, who have many hearts, many tongues, many hands, many disguises, who are really devoid of all essence?*

4.40 Varṇana|dayitaḥ kaś cid
dhana|dayito dāsa|karma|dayito 'nyaḥ
rakṣā|dayitaś c' ânyo
veśyānāṃ narma|dayito 'nyaḥ.

iti mahā|kavi|śrī|Kṣemendra|viracite
Kalā|vilāse
veśyā|vṛttam nāma
caturthaḥ sargaḥ.

Courtesans love one man for his praise, another for his wealth, another for his servility, another for his protection, another for diversion. 4.40

The fourth canto,
named the affairs of courtesans,
in the "Grace of Guile" composed by
the great poet Ksheméndra.

THE GRACE OF GUILE
5. FRAUD

Moho nāma janānāṃ
sarva|haro harati buddhim ev' ādau,
gūḍhataraḥ sa ca nivasati
kāyasthānāṃ mukhe ca lekhe ca.

Aindava|kal" êva pūrṇā
niṣpannā sasya/vitta/saṃpattiḥ
grastā kṣaṇena dṛṣṭā
niḥśeṣā divira/rāhu/kalay" êva.

Jñātāḥ saṃsāra|kalā
yogibhir apayāta|rāga|saṃmohaiḥ,
na jñātā divira|kalāḥ
ken' âpi bahu|prayatnena.

Kūṭa|kalā|śata|śibiraiḥ
jana|dhana|vivaraiḥ kṣaya|kṣapā|timiraiḥ
divirair eva samastā
grastā janatā na kālena.

DELUSION INDEED ROBS people of everything.
At its onset it strips away judgement.
Well concealed, it shelters in the mouth
and the writing of the scribe.*

A well-provisioned granary
is like the phase of the moon:
once espied it is, ⁝ *it is observed to be*
completely devoured ⁝ *completely eclipsed*
in an instant ⁝ *for an instant*
by the *scribe's cunning* ⁝ *the power of the sky-going*
at making things vanish ⁝ *eclipse-demon Rahu.**

Yogins,
freed from delusion and craving, can see through
the phantasms of transmigratory existence.
But nobody,
try as he may, can understand
the subterfuges of the scribe.

With a legion of hundreds of fraudulent talents,
with open pockets for the wealth of the people,
inscrutable like a moonless night,—
it is scribes who consume all humanity,
not time.

5.5 Ete hi *kāla/puruṣāḥ*
pṛthutara/daṇḍa/prapāta/hata/lokāḥ
gaṇan'|âgaṇana|piśācāḥ
caranti bhūrja|dhvajā loke.

Kas teṣāṃ viśvāsaṃ
Yama|mahiṣa|viṣāṇa|koṭi|kuṭilānām
vrajati na yasya viṣaktaḥ
kaṇṭhe pāśaḥ Kṛt'|ântena?

Kalam'/âgra/nirgata/maṣī/
bindu/vyājena sāñjan'/âśru/kaṇaiḥ
kāyastha/*khanyamānā*
roditi *khinn"* êva rājya|śrīḥ.

Aṅka|nyāsair viṣamaiḥ
Māyā|vanit"|âlak'|āvalī|kuṭilaiḥ
ko nāma jagati racitaiḥ
kāyasthair mohito na janaḥ?

For, 5.5
these *men of black ink* ⁝ *minions of Death**
wreak havoc among the people ⁝ *kill people*
with *the effluent of their large pens* ⁝ *blows from their huge staffs.*
They are demons of calculation and misreckoning,
who march across the earth
under a banner of birchbark.

Who would place his trust in them,
who are as crooked as the tips
of the horns of Yama's bull,
unless Death, who brings the end
should fasten a noose around his throat?

The patron goddess of the kingdom,
plundered ⁝ *raped*
by *scribes with inky semen*
squirting from the tips of their reed-like penises,
seems to weep in anguish,
shedding *kohl-stained teardrops* ⁝ *the tears of Áñjana,**
*disguised as ink-drops squirting from reed-pens.**

Has anyone in the world not been duped
by the fabrications
of these scribes
who scribble distorted figures,
crooked like the curling locks of lady Maya?

Māyā/prapañca/saṃcaya/
vañcita/viśvair vināśitaḥ satatam
viṣaya/grāma/grāsaiḥ
kāyasthair indriyair lokaḥ.

5.10 Kuṭilā lipi|vinyāsā
dṛśyante kāla|pāśa|saṃkāśāḥ
kāyastha|bhūrja|śikhare
maṇḍala|līnā iva vyālāḥ.

Ete hi Citraguptāḥ
citra|dhiyo *gupta/hāriṇo* divirāḥ
rekhā|mātra|vināśāt
sahitaṃ kurvanti ye rahitam.

Loke kalāḥ prasiddhāḥ
svalpatarāḥ saṃcaranti divirāṇām,
gūḍha|kalāḥ kila teṣāṃ
jānāti Kaliḥ Kṛtānto vā.

The public
is relentlessly devastated by scribal bureaucrats,
who deceive all by false accounting
and officious documentation,
who are parasites on the villages in their influence;
just as the organs of perception,
: which reside in the body,
which grasp the range of sensory objects
and mislead everyone
with illusory manifestation and resorption,
continuously obstruct illumination.

Twisted jottings, 5.10
resembling the nooses of Death,
can be seen coiling like snakes
on the scribe's birch-mountain.

For perverse-minded scribes,
who *steal in secret : stealthily take life,*
are hell's scribal recorders of good and evil deeds.
By deleting a mere line
they can make the "possessor" *(sa-hita),*
the "dispossessed" *(ra-hita).**

Few are the arts of the scribe
which pass as common knowledge.
Perhaps their secret arts are known
to Kali or to the Bringer of the End?

Vakra|lipi|nyāsa|kalā
sakal'|âṅka|nimīlana|kalā
satata|praveśa|saṃgraha|
lopa|kalā vyaya|vivardhana|kalā ca;
Grāhya|pariccheda|kalā
deya|dhan'|ādāna|kāraṇa|kalā ca
utkocair haraṇa|kalā|
paryanta|bhuvaṃ palāyana|kalā ca;

5.15 Śeṣa|stha|viveka|kalā|
cala|rāśi|samagra|bhakṣaṇa|kalā ca
utpanna|gopan|kalā
naṣṭa|viśīrṇa|pradarśana|kalā ca;
Krayamāṇair bharaṇa|kalā
yojana|caryādibhiḥ kṣaya|kalā ca
ekatra pañca|daśyāṃ
luṇṭha|cikitsā|samāsana|kalā ca;
Niḥśeṣa|bhūrja|dāhād
āgama|nāśaś ca paryante
yena vinā vyavahārī
bhūry|āgrahaṇe nirālokaḥ.

Sa/kalaṅkasya kṣayiṇo
nava/nava/rūpasya vṛddhi/bhājaś ca
divirasya kalāḥ kuṭilāḥ
ṣoḍaśa *doṣ"/ākarasy'* âitāḥ.

The art of ambiguous transcription,
the art of obscuring whole figures,
the art of always rifling the collected revenue,
the art of increasing expenditure;
the art of detaching a share of the profit,
the art of legal documentation for appropriating the dues,
the art of larceny through bribery,
the art of making off to a neighbouring region;
the art of removing surplus, 5.15
the art of completely swallowing up moveable property,
the art of withholding any gain,
the art of letting reappear what was wasted or squandered;
the art of gaining wages by purchasing,
the art of causing loss by fiddling travel expenses;
the art of sitting around in one place
for a fortnight for the treatment of lameness,
and finally, the destruction of evidence
by completely burning the birchbark document,
without which the litigant
remains in the dark regarding the retrieval of his gold.

These are the sixteen *crooked arts of the scribe,*
the mine of defects, who is smeared with ink-blots,
who diminishes wealth, who takes on many disguises,
who appropriates a share of one's income.
These are the sixteen *curved digits of the Night-maker,*
who bears a mark, who wanes
and then again assumes a new form,
*waxes, and moves in the sky.**

Kūṭa/sthāḥ kāya|sthāḥ
sarva/na/kāreṇa siddha/mantreṇa
gurava iva *vidita/māyā*
vṛtti/cchedaṃ kṣaṇena kurvanti.

5.20 Hārita|dhana|paṇa|vasanaḥ
caurya|bhayād bandhubhiḥ parityaktaḥ
babhrāma mahīm akhilāṃ
tīvra|vyasanaḥ purā kitavaḥ.

Sa kadā cid etya puṇyaiḥ
Ujjayinīṃ tatra majjanaṃ kṛtvā
vicaran vijane Purahara|
mandiram avalokayām āsa.

Śūny'|āyatane gatvā
varadaṃ devaṃ dṛṣṭvā Mahā|kālam
upalepana|kusuma|phalaiḥ
nirvyāpāraḥ siṣeve saḥ.

Stotra|japa|gīta|dīpaiḥ
vipula|dhyānair niśāsu nirnidraḥ
tasthau tatra sa suciraṃ
duḥsaha|daurgatya|nāśāya.

Tasya kadā cid bhaktyā
śubha|śata|hūtyā prasāditaḥ sahasā
bhava|bhaya|hārī bhagavān
Bhūtapatiḥ saṃbabhāṣe tam:

Scribes *trust in falsehood,*
they have mastered delusion and in an instant
can destroy a livelihood with their magical formula
which is made up entirely of "No's";
Just as gurus,
who have attained the unchanging supreme spirit,
and who have seen through delusion, can terminate
the continuation of rebirth with their perfect mantra
which denies the existence of everything.

Long ago, a severely addicted gambler was relieved of his 5.20
stake of money and home. Cast out by his relatives who feared he would rob them, he roamed the entire earth.

One day, by virtue of his accumulated merit, he reached the sacred city of Ujjáyini. Strolling about there in solitude after his ritual bath, he beheld a temple dedicated to Shiva the Breaker of the Citadel.

He entered the deserted sanctuary and saw the idol of Maha·kala, the God who grants boons. Abstaining from all other activity, he worshipped with offerings of unguents, flowers and fruit.

He remained there for a long time, wakeful at night with hymns of praise, whispered prayers, chants, lighted lamps and deep meditations, seeking deliverance from his unbearable misfortune.

There came a time when, gratified by his devotion and hundredfold-fair invocation, the revered Shiva, Lord of the spirits, the dispeller of the dread of existence, suddenly spoke to him:

5.25 «Putra gṛhāṇ' êty» ukte
devena kapāla|mālikā|śikhare
ekaṃ kapālam asakṛt
cakre saṃjñāṃ Purārāteḥ.
Ardh'|ôkte sthagita|varaḥ
saṃpīḍana|saṃjñayā kapālasya
tūṣṇīṃ cakāra Rudro
dāridryāt kitava|puṇyānām.
Snātuṃ yāte tasmin
vijane devaḥ kapālam avadat tat
dant'|âṃśu|paṭala|pālīṃ
Gaṅgām iva darśayann agre:
«Asya kitavasya sādhoḥ
bhaktasya cira|sthitasya vara|dāne
kasmāt tvayā mam' âiṣā
vihitā saṃpīḍanaiḥ saṃjñā.»
Iti Bhagavatā kapālaṃ
pṛṣṭaṃ provāca sa|smitaṃ śanakaiḥ
viṣama|nayan'|ôṣma|vigalan
maul'|îndu|sudhā|rasair jīvat:
5.30 «Śṛṇu Bhagavan yena mayā
vijñapto 'si sva|bhāva|saral'|ātman
sulabho 'pi bodhyate vā
niṣkāraṇam īśvaraḥ kena?
Eṣa kitavo 'tiduḥkhī|
dāridryād virata|sakala|nija|kṛtyaḥ
prāsāde 'smin racayati
lepana|bali|kusuma|dhūp'|ârgham.

"Son, accept. . . ." No sooner had the God said this much, than a skull at the crest of his chapletof human skulls of human skullhumans repeatedly prodded the Enemy of the Citadel with a signal. 5.25

Rudra, whose boon-granting was stifled in mid-sentence by the tapping signal of the skull, fell silent, since now the meagre merits acquired by the gambler were exhausted.

When that one had departed to bathe, the God spoke in private to that skull, revealing at his front the sharp edge of a skirt of brilliance shooting from his teeth, as though it were the Ganges:

"Why, when I was about to fulfil the wish of this worthy gambler, a long-time devotee, did you prod me with your signal?"

Questioned in this way by the Revered One, the skull smiled and softly replied, simultaneously withering beneath the glare of his third eye and reviving with the nectar-elixir of his crest-moon:

"O Lord whose disposition is forthright, hear why I have apprised you. For who would admonish his master without reason, even if he be easily approachable? 5.30

This miserable cheat, forsaking in his destitution all of his own duties, renders you respectful homage with ablutions, offerings, flowers and incense.

Duḥkhī bhavati tapasvī
    dhana|rahitaḥ sādaro bhavati dharme
bhraṣṭ'|âdhikāra|vibhavaḥ
    sarva|praṇataḥ priyaṃ|vado bhavati.

Arcayati deva|viprān
    namati gurūn vetti nirdhano mitram
kaṭhino 'pi loha|piṇḍas
    taptaḥ karmaṇyatām eti.

Vyasana|paritapta|hṛdayaḥ
    tiṣṭhati sarvaḥ sad|ācāre,
vibhava|mada|mohitānāṃ
    karma|smaraṇe kathā k" âiva?

5.35 Aiśvary'|ârthī Bhagavann
    āśā|pāśena lambamāno 'sau
kurute parāṃ saparyāṃ,
    prāpt'|ârtho dṛśyate na punaḥ.

Sv'|ârth'|ârthinaḥ prayattāḥ
    prāpt'|ârthāḥ sevakāḥ sadā viphalāḥ,
na hi nāma jagati kaś cit
    kṛta|kāryaḥ sevako bhavati.

Deva prāsāde 'smin
    phala|jala|kusum'|ādi|bhoga|sāmagrīm
pūrṇe yāte kitave
    vijane n' ânye kariṣyanti.

Tasmāt puṇy'|ôpanataṃ
    kitavaṃ saṃrakṣa sevakaṃ satatam:
vara|dānam asya bhagavan
    nirvāsanam ātma|pūjāyāḥ.»

A wretch becomes penitent,
a pauper becomes earnest about religion,
divested of rank and prestige he bows to all.

Impoverished, he honors Gods and brahmins,
bows to gurus, and remembers his friends.
Although tough,
  a lump of iron,* once scorched,
  becomes malleable.

Anyone whose heart is burnt by adversity
  adheres to righteous conduct,
but what notion is there of remembering duties
among those stultified by infatuation with their status?

O Revered One, this gambler, striving for power, dangling in the noose of hope, offers fervent adulation. When he has got his reward he won't be seen again. 5.35

Greedy for wealth of their own, servants are diligent, but once they have gained riches they are uselessly idle, for on this earth nobody self-sufficient is a servant.

O God, when this rewarded gambler has gone away, there are no others in this desolate temple to provide fruits, water, flowers and other comforts.

Therefore, hold on to this gambler who is luckily at hand as a servant for good: to grant his wish, O Revered One, is to exile your own worship."

Śrutv" âitad vakrataraṃ
vacanaṃ pṛthu|vismaya|smeraḥ
taṃ papraccha Pinākī:
«kas tvaṃ tattvena? kiṃ karma?»

5.40 Iti pṛṣṭaṃ punar ūce
sapadi kapālaṃ vicintya sad|bhāvam:
«Magadhānām aham abhavaṃ
kāyastha|kule sva|karmaṇo vimukhaḥ.
Snāna/japa/vrata/nirataḥ
tīrtha/rato vidita/sarva/śāstr'/ârthaḥ
tyaktvā Bhāgīrathyāṃ
śarīrakaṃ tvat/padaṃ prāptaḥ.»

Ākarṇy' âitad Bhagavān
ūce: «kāyastha eva satyaṃ tvam
citraṃ kauṭilya|kalāṃ
na tyajasi kapāla|śeṣo 'pi.»

Ity uktvā smita|kiraṇaiḥ
kurvann āśā|latāḥ kusuma|śubhrāḥ
snātv" āgatāya tasmai
kitavāya varaṃ dadau varadaḥ.

Kṛtvā tat|kitava|hitaṃ
paśyata ev' āśu tasya Śaśimauliḥ
niṣkāsitavāṃs tac chira
uttamatama|muṇḍa|mālikā|paṅkteḥ.

Hearing this wily speech, Shiva, the bearer of the bow, smiling wide in wonder, demanded: "Who are you really? What was your profession?"

Thus questioned, the skull recalled his origins and quickly 5.40
replied: "I was born into a scribes' family in Mágadha, averse to the legacy of my birth.

I delighted in ritual bathing, prayers and vows, was attracted to places of pilgrimage and conversant with the import of all the sacred texts. I abandoned my wretched body in the Ganges and reached your abode.

*⁝ Actually, I embraced the legacy of my birth. I desisted from ritual bathing, prayers and vows, was fond of stratagems and had no idea of the meaning of any of the scriptures. After giving up my soul, I reached your abode by way of partaking of someone else's share."**

On hearing this, the Adored One exclaimed: "So you are a scribe! It is true! Strange that you cannot relinquish your art of perfidy even though only your skull remains."

This said, he illuminated the vine of the celestial quarters with the radiance of his bright smile, so that it appeared white with flowers. Then, the granter of boons fulfilled the wish of the gambler who had returned from his bath.

After he had ensured the gambler's welfare before the scribe's very eyes, moon-crested Shiva at once banished that head from his most excellent chaplet of skulls.

5.45 Ity evaṃ kuṭila|kalāṃ
sahajāṃ malināṃ jana|kṣaye niratām
Yama|daṃṣṭrām iva muñcati
kāyastho n' âsthi|śeṣo 'pi.

Susthaḥ ko nāma janaḥ
satat'|âśuci|bhāva|dūṣita|kalānām
doṣa|kṛtāṃ śakṛtām iva
kāyasthānām avaṣṭambhaiḥ?

Asura|racita|prayatnād
vijñātā divira|vañcanā yena
saṃrakṣitā mati|matā
ratna|vatī vasumatī tena.

iti mahā|kavi|śrī|Kṣemendra|viracite
Kalā|vilāse
kāyastha|caritaṃ nāma
pañcamaḥ sargaḥ.

Thus a scribe, even if he is mere bones, 5.45
cannot renounce his innate unclean art of crookedness, which,
like the fang of death,
is bent on destroying people.

Who could possibly remain healthy with a blockage
of the seven bodily substrata
which are perpetually defiled by impure substances,
and which produce harmful matter such as excrement?
⁝ Who could remain prosperous with the meddling
of scribes,
whose craft is always tainted by unscrupulous motives,
who defile like excrement?

The wise man,
who has scrutinised the scribe's duplicity
with the care appropriate to the writings of a demon,
protects the earth rich in treasures.

The fifth canto,
named the exploits of the scribe,
in the "Grace of Guile"
composed by the great poet Ksheméndra.

THE GRACE OF GUILE
6. INTOXICATION

Ekah sakala|janānāṃ
hṛdayeṣu kṛt'|āspado madaḥ śatruḥ
yen' āviṣṭa|śarīro
na śṛṇoti na paśyati stabdhaḥ.

Vijit'|ātmanāṃ janānām
abhavad yaḥ kṛta|yuge damo nāma
so 'yaṃ viparītatayā
madaḥ sthitaḥ kali|yuge puṃsām.

Maunaṃ vadana/nikūṇanam
ūrdhv'/ēkṣaṇam anya/lakṣyatā c' âkṣṇoḥ
gātra/vilepana/veṣṭanam
agryaṃ rūpaṃ madasy' âitat.

Śaurya|mado rūpa|madaḥ
śṛṅgāra|madaḥ kul'|ônnati|madaś ca
vibhava|mada|mūla|jātā
mada|vṛkṣā dehinām ete.

6.5 *Śūl'/ārūḍha/samāno*
vāta|stabdh'|ôpamo 'tha bhūta|samaḥ,
bahu/bhoge vibhava|madaḥ
prathama|jvara|saṃnipāta|samaḥ.

A FOE IS LODGED IN THE HEARTS of all people:
Intoxication. Possessed by it,
one sees nothing, hears nothing,
is transfixed.

The pursuit of "self-restraint" *(da-ma)*,
common among the enlightened people of the golden age,
has in this decadent age
inverted to "self-indulgence" *(ma-da)*.

The first signs of intoxication are
taciturnity ⁝ *vows of silence,*
sneering ⁝ *pursing the lips for breath-control,*
ambition ⁝ *gazing upwards between the eyebrows,*
looking at something else ⁝ *focussing the eyes on the beyond,*
and *daubing the limbs with lotions* ⁝ *dusting the limbs and clasping them together.**

The mania of valor,
the giddiness of vanity,
the dizziness of infatuation
and the delirium of nobility,
—these are mankind's trees of intoxication*
sprung from one root: pomposity.

A pompous man* 6.5
in the midst of affluence ⁝ *over-indulging,*
seems wracked by the onset of a morbid fever.*
He seems to be *impaled on a stake* ⁝ *suffering from a colic,*
appears to be bloated with blocked wind,
resembles a wraith.

Śaurya|mado bhuja|darśī
    rūpa|mado darpaṇ'|ādi|darśī ca
kāma|madaḥ strī|darśī
    vibhava|madas tv eṣa jāty|andhaḥ.

Antaḥ|sukha|rasa|mūrcchā|
    mīlita|nayanaḥ *samāhita|dhyānaḥ*
dhana|mada eṣa narāṇām
    ātm'|ārām'|ôpamaḥ ko 'pi.

Unmādayaty aviṣaye
    vividha|vikāraḥ samasta|guṇa|hīnaḥ
mūḍha|madas tv anyo 'yaṃ
    jayati vicitro nirālambaḥ.

Stambhān na paśyati bhuvaṃ
    khecara|darśī sadā tapasvi|madaḥ,
bhakti|mado 'dbhuta|kārī
    vismṛta|dehaś calaḥ prakṛty" âiva.

The valor-maniac admires the arm,
the vain man gazes at mirrors and such like,
the infatuated man leers at women,
but the pompous man is born blind.

The "daze of riches"
manifests itself in people somehow
  like the bliss of self-realisation:
brooding on hoarded wealth, ⁝ *absorbed in meditation,*
the eyes are shut
  in a *swoon* ⁝ *repose*
  at the *sweet taste of a hidden elation* ⁝ *delight of inner rapture.**

Yet another is the unstoppable "imbecile fixation."
It *deranges* ⁝ *causes euphoria*
without incitement ⁝ *when sensory objects are shunned,*
is degenerative in many ways ⁝ *has many stages,*
has no virtues at all ⁝ *is free from all attributes.*
It is *eccentric and baseless* ⁝ *wondrous and supportless.*

Due to its paralysing nature,
the "stupor of the ascetic" does not see the ground
  but instead looks always toward the sky-going celestials.
The "befuddlement of devotion,"
  unsteady by nature,
performs miracles but neglects its own body.

6.10 Ākopa|rakta|nayanaḥ
para|vāṅ|mātr'|âsahaḥ pralāpī ca
viṣamaḥ śruta|mada|nāmā
dhātu|kṣobho nṛṇāṃ mūrtaḥ.

Satata|bhru|kuṭi|karālaḥ
paruṣ'|ākrośī haṭh'|ābhighāta|paraḥ
adhikāra|madaḥ puṃsāṃ
sarv'|āśī rākṣasaḥ krūraḥ.

Pūrva|puruṣa|pratāpa|
prathita|kathā|vismṛt'|ânya|nija|kṛtyaḥ
kula|mada ekaḥ puṃsāṃ
su/dīrgha/darśī mah"/âjñānaḥ.

Varjita/sakala/sparśaḥ
sarv'/âśuci/bhāvanān nirālambaḥ
ākāśe 'pi sa/lepaḥ
śauca|mado *nitya/saṃkocaḥ.*

S'|âvadhayaḥ sarva|madā
nija|nija|mūla|kṣaye vinaśyanti,
vara|mada ekaḥ kuṭilo
vijṛmbhate niravadhir bhogī.

The harrowing "delirium of erudition" 6.10
is an embodied upheaval of the bodily elements:
The eyes are reddened by rising anger,
one is unable to bear the mere voice of others,
but is oneself a prattle.*

The "hysteria of authority" is an all-devouring,
brutal demon afflicting mankind.
It is loathsome with incessantly knitted eyebrows,
crudely abuses people,
and is prone to violent assault.

The "delirium of noble lineage"
is preoccupied with tedious tales of ancestral glory
but forgets its own duty towards others.
Unique among men,
it is *a farsighted, great folly* ⁝ *an acute vulture*.*

The "lunacy of purity"
cowers perpetually ⁝ *is an uninterrupted yogic withdrawal*.
recoils from the slightest contact ⁝ *shuns any sensory contact*,
is *friendless* ⁝ *a supportless trance*
because it imagines everyone to be impure ⁝ *by realising that all sensory objects are unreal*,
and *fears contamination even from the sky* ⁝ *perceiving even emptiness as an obstacle*.

All these forms of insobriety are limited,
they pass away when their respective root is cut.
The "conceit of self-importance" stands alone:
an endless coiling serpent with gaping jaws.*

6.15 Pāna|madas tu jaghanyaḥ
sarva|jugups"|āspadaṃ mahā|mohaḥ
kṣaṇiko 'pi harati sahasā
varṣa|sahasr'|ârjitaṃ śīlam.

Vidyāvati vipra|vare
gavi hastini kukkure śva|pāke ca
madya|madaḥ sama|darśī
sva|para|vibhāgaṃ na jānāti.

Vigalita|sad|asad|bhedaḥ
sama|kāñcana|loṣṭa|pāṣāṇaḥ
prāpto yogi|daśām api
narakaṃ kṣībaḥ svayaṃ patati.

Roditi gāyati vihasati
dhāvati vilapaty upaiti saṃmoham
bhajate vividha|vikārān
saṃsār'|ādarśa|maṇḍalaḥ kṣībaḥ.

Para|pati|cumbana|saktāṃ
paśyati dayitāṃ na yāti saṃtāpam;
kṣībo 'pi gāḍha|*rāgī*
pītvā madhu vīta|rāgaḥ kim?

But liquor-induced drunkenness is vilest, 6.15
a condition entirely repulsive, a sheer stupidity.
Though lasting but a fleeting moment,
it abruptly strips away merit
amassed in thousands of years.

Drunkenness regards as equal
a learned and saintly brahmin, a cow,
an elephant, a dog and a dog-cooker,
and does not understand the distinction
between "mine" and "another's."*

Unhampered by the distinction between real and unreal,
considering gold, mud and stones to be the same,
the drunkard,
even though he has thus attained the state of the Yogin,
propels himself into hell.*

The drunkard is a mirror image of transmigration:
He weeps, he sings, he laughs,
he runs and bawls, falls prey to bewilderment,
swings from mood to mood.*

He can see his wife
engrossed in kissing the husband of another woman
and yet feel no outrage.
Has the drunkard,
even though he is extremely *flushed* ⁝ *passionate*,
been freed from desire by guzzling liquor?

6.20 Visṛjati vasanaṃ dūre
vyasanaṃ gṛhṇāti duḥsahaṃ kṣībaḥ
añjali|pātraiḥ pibati ca
nija|mūtra|vijṛmbhitaṃ candram.

Cyavanaḥ purā maharṣiḥ
yauvanam Aśvi|prayogato labdhvā
yajñe svayaṃ kṛta|jñaḥ
tau cakre Soma|bhāg'|ârhau.
Kruddhas tam etya Śakraḥ
provāca: «mune! na vetsi kim api tvam?
bhiṣajāv apaṅkti|yogyau!
Som'|ârhāv Aśvinau kasya?»
Iti bahuśaḥ Sura|patinā
pratiṣiddho 'pi sva|tejasā Cyavanaḥ
na cacāla niścit'|ātmā
nija|kṛtyād Aśvinoḥ prītyā.
Tat|kop'|ôdyata|vajraṃ
Jambhārer āyataṃ bhuja|stambham
astambhayan mun'|îndraḥ
prabhāva|saṃbhāvanā|pātram.
6.25 Asṛjac ca tad|vadhāya
Pralamba|kāy'|ôpamaṃ catur|daṃṣṭraṃ
yojana|sahasra|vipulaṃ
kṛtyā|rūpaṃ mah"|Āsuraṃ ghoram.
Ten' āviṣṭaḥ sahasā
bhīto Vajrī tam āyayau śaraṇam
«Somo 'stu Deva|bhiṣajoḥ»
iti c' ôvāca praṇaṣṭa|dhṛtiḥ.

The drunkard casts off his garments *(vasana)* far away 6.20
and takes up unbearable depravity *(vyasana)*.
With his cupped hands he sips the moon
waxing in his own urine.

Long ago, the great seer Chyávana had regained his youth by the ministration of the twin Ashvins. Grateful, he honored them by entitling them to draughts of Soma at his sacrifice.*

The enraged Indra appeared to him and reprimanded: "Sage! Don't you know anything? Physicians are unacceptable as company at meals! Who would honor them with Soma libations?"

Though the Lord of the Gods thus repeatedly forbade him, the determined Chyávana, secure in his own might, out of love for the Ashvins, did not waver from his resolve.

The best of seers paralysed Indra's huge, pillar-like arm, an object of awe due to its power, with thunderbolt raised up in rage at him.

Then, to slay Indra, he fashioned a hideous, colossal 6.25
Ásura whose body resembled that of Pralámba,* with four fangs, whose bulk measured a thousand leagues in extent, an incarnation of evil sorcery.

Indra the thunderbolt-bearer was violently possessed by him. Dismayed, he came running to Chyávana seeking shelter, and failing in courage, he conceded: "The Gods' twin physicians may have their share of Soma!"

Munir api karuṇā|sindhuḥ
bhītaṃ praṇataṃ mah"|Ēndram āśvāsya
Madam utsasarja ghoraṃ
dyūta|strī|pāna|mṛgayāsu.

So 'yam asuraḥ pramāthī
muninā kruddhena nirmito hṛdaye
nivasati śarīra|bhājāṃ
stambh'|ākāro guṇair baddhaḥ,

Maune śrī|mattānāṃ
niḥspanda|dṛśi pravṛddha|vibhavānām
bhrū|bhaṅga|mukha|vikāre
dhanikānāṃ bhrū|puṭe viṭ'|ādīnām,

6.30 Jihvāsu dūta|viduṣāṃ
rūpavatāṃ daśana|keśa|veśeṣu
vaidyānām oṣṭha|puṭe
grīvāyāṃ guru|niyogi|gaṇakānām;
Skandha|taṭe subhaṭānāṃ
hṛdaye vaṇijāṃ kareṣu śilpavatām
gala|patr'|âṅguli/*bhaṅge*
chātrāṇāṃ stana|taṭeṣu taruṇīnām;
Udare śrāddh'|ârhāṇāṃ
jaṅghāsu ca lekha|hāra|puruṣāṇām
gaṇḍeṣu kuñjarāṇāṃ
barhe śikhināṃ gatau ca haṃsānām.

The seer for his part, a river of compassion, consoled great Indra as he was frightened and humbled, and sent forth the terrible demon "Intoxication" into gambling, women, drink and hunting.

That rending demon, fashioned by the angry seer, now dwells in the hearts of living beings in the guise of paralysis, held in check by virtues.*

In the silence of those drunk with wealth,
in the immobile stare of those grown in stature,
in the faces of the wealthy, disfigured by frowning,
in the knitted eyebrows of rakes etc.;
In the tongues of envoys and scholars, 6.30
in the teeth, hair and garments of the beautiful,
in the puckered lips of physicians,
in the necks of gurus, of petty officials, and astrologers;
In the bulging shoulders of champions,
in the hearts of merchants,
in the hands of craftsmen,
in the *stretched out* throats,
    torn birchbark-manuscripts
    and *bent* fingers of students,
in the upright breasts of slender ladies;
In the bellies of those entitled to funerary offerings,
and in the calves of couriers,
in the cheeks of elephants,
in the tailfeathers of peacocks,
and in the gait of swans.

Ity evaṃ madanāmā
    mahā|graho bahu|vikāra|dṛḍha|mohaḥ
aṅge kāṣṭhī|bhūto
    vasati sadā sarva|bhūtānām.

iti mahā|kavi|śrī|Kṣemendra|viracite
Kalā|vilāse
mada|varṇana|nāma
ṣaṣṭhaḥ sargaḥ.

In this way the mighty demon called Intoxication,
having become insensible like a log,
a profound delusion assuming many forms,
for ever inhabits the bodies of all living beings.

The sixth canto, named the description of intoxication,
in the "Grace of Guile" composed by
the great poet Kshemendra.

THE GRACE OF GUILE
7. DEPRAVITY

ARTHO NĀMA janānāṃ
jīvitam akhila|kriyā|kalāpasya.
tam api haranty ati|dhūrtāś
chagala|galā gāyanā loke.

Niḥśeṣaṃ kamal'|ākara|koṣaṃ
jagdhv" âpi kumudam āsvādya
kṣīṇā gāyana|bhṛṅgā
mātaṅga|praṇayitāṃ yānti.

Ghaṭa|paṭa|śakaṭa|skandhā
bahu|ḍimbhā mukta|keśaka|kalāpāḥ
ete yoni|piśācā
bhūpa|bhujo gāyanā ghorāḥ.

THE INCENTIVE for the vast profusion of human striving is prosperity.
It is this
that utterly unscrupulous, goat-throated singers
plunder in this world.

Even though they have completely exhausted
the buds of the red day-lotus pond
and finished off the white lilies,
the singer-bees, still emaciated,
yearn for the fragrant rut-fluid of elephants.
⁝ After completely depleting their patron's treasury
abounding in riches
and then tasting his anger,
the singer-rakes, impoverished,
*solicit the meanest outcastes.**

Followed by caravans of carts crammed with
pots and blankets, a train of brats in tow,
with their dishevelled hair unkempt,
awful are these singers, royal parasites,
reared on meat.
⁝ Followed by troops in wedge-formation,**
striking kettle-drums of war, in great affray,*
equipped with quivers of powerful missiles* and*
*arrows,**
terrible are these goblin-spawned,
regicidal warriors of the God of war.**

Tamasi varākaś cauro
hāhā|kāreṇa yāti saṃtrastaḥ,
gāyana|cauraḥ prakaṭaṃ
hāhā kṛtv" âpi nayati lakṣaṃ ca.

7.5 Pāpādhadhaninigamasā|
dhādhāmāmāsamāsagādhāmā
kṛtvā svara|pada|pālīṃ
gāyana|dhūrtāś caranty ete.

Kuṭil'|āvarta|bhrāntaiḥ
vaṃśa|vikāraiś ca mukha|vikāraiś ca
gāyati gāyana|saṃgho
mardala|hastaś ciraṃ maunī.

Āmantraṇa|jaya|śabdaiḥ
pratipada|jhaṃkāra|gharghar'|ārāvaiḥ
svayam|ukta|sādhu|vādair
antarayati gāyano gītam.

The wretched thief moans: 'Ah! Ah!'
  and shudders as he skulks in the darkness.
The singer-thief also intones 'Ah! Ah!'
  in broad daylight and carries off a fortune.

"Pā pā dha dha ni ni ga ma sā 7.5
  dhā dhā mā mā sa mā sa gā dhā ma"
  rehearsing phrases* of the notes
  of the musical scale in this way,
  these singers are on the prowl.

The troupe of singers performs their song,
  drum in hand,
  it is faulty with convoluted "revolving ornamentations,"
  with mutilated "flute ornamentations,"
  with a disfigured opening theme,
  : reeling with crooked gyrations,
  and with twisted spines, with contorted faces,*
  their hands trembling like rattle-drums,
followed by lengthy silence.

The bard encumbers the song
  with salutes and hails of: "Victory!,"
  with gurgling noises, cymbal crashes,
  with buzzing twangs after every musical phrase,
  and applauds himself with cries of "Bravo!."

Jala|patite saktu|kaṇe
matsyair bhukte 'sti k" âpi dharm'|āptiḥ,
gāyana|dattāsu paraṃ
koṭiṣv api bhavati prajā|pīḍā.

Mugdha|dhanānāṃ Vidhinā
ruddhānām andha|koṣa|kūpeṣu
vihito vivṛta|mah"|āsyo
gāyana|nāmā praṇāl'|âughaḥ.

7.10 N' âitat prakaṭita|daśanā
gāyana|dhūrtāḥ sad" âiva gāyanti;
ete gat'|ânugatikān
hasanti mugdhān gṛhīt'|ârthāḥ.

Prātar gāyana|dhūrtā
bhavanti dhīrāḥ sahāra|keyūrāḥ
madhy'|âhne dyūta|jitā
nagnā bhagnā nirādhārāḥ.

Should a morsel of gruel be dropped into the water
and be swallowed by fish,
there may accrue some gain of merit.
But when donations are made to singers,
even if they be tens of millions,
public misery ensues.*

The Creator has made provision
for a large-mouthed, gaping overflow
called "singer"
on stagnant treasury-wells
for the clogged-up wealth of idiots.

It is not even the case 7.10
that this protruding-toothed rabble of minstrels
is always busy singing;
they are also busy laughing
at simpletons who follow the crowd
after they have grabbed their money.

Early in the morning,
the singer-libertines are undaunted,
adorned with pearl necklaces and gold armbands.
At midday,
beaten at dice, they stand disrobed,
humiliated and bereft of patronage.
: At dusk,
the singer-rakes are virile in thrilling love-sport,**
at midday,
exhausted by love-play, they are still undressed,
*aching and sapped of essence.**

Stuti|vāgurā|nibaddhaiḥ
vacana|śaraiḥ kapaṭa|kūṭa|racanābhiḥ
gītair gāyana|lubdhā
mugdha|mṛgāṇāṃ haranti *sarvasvam.*

Naṣṭa|svara|pada|gītaiḥ
kṣaṇena lakṣāni gāyano labdhvā
«dāsī|sutena dattaṃ
kim?» iti vadan duḥkhito yāti.

Varjita|sādhu|dvija|vara|
vṛddhāyāḥ sakala|śoka|kalitāyāḥ
śāpo 'yam eva Lakṣmyā
gāyana|bhojy" âiva yat satatam.

7.15 Devaḥ purā surāṇām
adhinātho Nāradaṃ cir'|āyātam
papraccha loka|vṛttaṃ
caritaṃ c' âitan mahīpānām.
So 'vadad «avani|patīnāṃ
jayināṃ bahu|dāna|dharma|yajñānām
caratā mayā nṛ|loke
sura|pati|yogyāḥ śriyo dṛṣṭāḥ.

Minstrel-hunters
take the *wealth* ⁝ *life*
of their *foolish victims* ⁝ *innocent deer*
by means of songs, composed with praise-snares,
with lyric-arrows, with arrangements
in the form of concealed traps.

Presented immediately with great largesse
for songs whose note-phrases have already faded away
the musician grumbles:
"What has he coughed up, that son of a slave,"
and walks out disgruntled.

Such is the curse of Lakshmi,
the Goddess of fortune,
that though haunted by everybody's grief,
she must shun saintly Brahmins
and eminent, distinguished elders,
ever to be enjoyed by singers.

Long ago the god Indra, overlord of the celestials, en- 7.15
quired from the sage Nárada, who had arrived after a long
time, for news of the world, and how fared the earth-
protecting kings.

He replied: "As I wandered in the world of men I saw among the victorious rulers of the earth, abounding in charity, Dharma and sacrifices, splendors befitting the king of gods.

Anu ca tvāṃ spardhante
vibhavair Varuṇaṃ Dhan'|âdhināthaṃ ca.
śata|makha|saṃjñām asakṛd
bahutara|yajñā hasanty eva.»

Śrutvā tan muni|vacanaṃ
jāta|dveṣaḥ Śatakratuḥ kopāt
hartuṃ dhanaṃ piśācān
visasarja bhuvaṃ nar'|êndrāṇām.

Te gīta|nāma|mantrāḥ
sura|pati|diṣṭāḥ piśāca|saṃghātāḥ
hartuṃ sakala|nṛpāṇāṃ
dhanam akhilaṃ bhū|talaṃ prayayuḥ.

7.20 Māyādāsaḥ prathamaṃ
Ḍambaradāsaśca Prasiddhidāsaś ca
Kṣayadāsa|Luṇṭhadāsau
Kharadāso Vajradāsaś ca,

Vāḍavadāsaś c' âṣṭau
te gatvā martya|lokam ati|bhaya|dāḥ
vivṛt'|āsya|ghora|kuharā
gāyana|sṛṣṭiṃ sasarjur ati|vikaṭām.

Tair ete hata|vibhavā
diśi diśi hṛta|sakala|loka|sarvasvāḥ
yajñ'|ādiṣu bhū|patayo
jātāḥ śithil'|ôdyamāḥ sarve.

And they rival you, Váruna, and the God of wealth taken together with riches. They mock your title "having-a-hundred-sacrifices" as they perform such worship not once, but many times over."

When he had heard the sage's words, Indra, the hundredfold powerful one, his hostility flaring up, sent forth demons to the earth, to plunder the wealth of the kings of men.

This company of demons, Mantra-regents* called "songs" commanded by Indra, the Lord of the Gods, advanced against the earth, to seize the entire wealth of all kings.

Foremost among them was 7.20
the "Servant of ilusion,"
next the "Servant of verbosity,"
the "Servant of notoriety,"
the "Servant of ruin,"
the "Servant of pillage,"
the "Servant of harshness,"
the "Servant of the thunderbolt,"
and the "Servant of the submarine inferno."

These eight extremely fearsome beings came into the world of mortals, a hideous guttural roar in their gaping jaws, and summoned forth the utterly horrible creation of musicians.

All around, they impoverished these kings who seized the wealth of the whole population. All of the earthly king's zeal for sacrifices and such like diminished.

Ete hi karṇa|vivaraiḥ
pravíśya gīta|cchalena bhū|pānām
sahasā haranti hṛdayaṃ
karṇa|piśācā mahā|ghorāḥ.

Tasmād eṣāṃ rāṣṭre
na dadāti vikāriṇāṃ praveśaṃ yaḥ
tasya sakal'|ârtha|saṃpad|
yajñavatī Bhūmir ādhīnā.

7.25 Naṭa|nartaka|cakra|carāḥ
kuśīlavāś cāraṇā viṭāś c' âiva
aiśvarya|śāli|śalabhāś
caranti; tebhyaḥ śriyaṃ rakṣet.

Gāyana|saṃghasy'| āikyād
uttiṣṭhati gīta|niḥsvanaḥ sumahān
asthāne dattāyā
Lakṣmyā iva saṃbhram'|ākrandaḥ.

iti mahā|kavi|śrī|Kṣemendra|viracite
Kalā|vilāse
gāyana|varṇana|nāma
saptamaḥ sargaḥ.

For, these terrifying ear-demons enter, in the guise of songs, through the auditory passages of earth ruling lords, and violently take hold of the heart.

Therefore, to him who refuses these corruptors entry into his kingdom, the lady Earth, abounding with all fortune, success and sacrifices, remains subservient.

Actors, dancers, jugglers, mimes, minstrels and procurers 7.25
swarm around as locusts on the rice of dominion; fortune must be defended from them.

A mighty din of singing resounds
from the united horde of minstrels,
the distressed cry, as it were, of Lakshmi
offered in unbefitting matrimony,
: the confused disharmony of a Lakshmi-verse recited
in the wrong musical register.

The seventh canto, named the description of singers,
in the "Grace of Guile" composed by
the great poet Ksheméndra.

THE GRACE OF GUILE
8. DECEPTION

Tatr' âpi *hema/kārā*

haraṇa/kalā/yoginaḥ pṛthu/dhyānāḥ

ye dhāmni bahala/lakṣmyāḥ

śūnyatvaṃ darśayanty eva.

Sāraṃ sakala|dhanānāṃ

sampatsu vibhūṣaṇaṃ vipadi rakṣā

ete haranti pāpāḥ

satataṃ tejaḥ paraṃ hemnaḥ.

Sahas' âiva dūṣayanti

sparśena suvarṇam upahata|cchāyam

nity'|âśucayaḥ pāpāḥ

caṇḍālā hema|kārāś ca.

Masṛṇa|kaṣ'|âśmani nikaṣo

manda|ruciḥ kraya|gatā kalā teṣām

paruṣa|kaṣ'|âśmani nikaṣo

vikraya|kāle 'pi lābha|kalā.

O F SIMILAR TEMPER, *also, are goldsmiths,*
adepts in the art of gold : making things
disappear,
*who, thanks to a far-fetched, visionary imagination,**
can make a show of insolvency in the midst
of their fabulously prosperous residences.
: There are also Yogins
with the ability to endure the hardship* of snow,**
who, absorbed in profound meditation,
manifest the attainment of emptiness
in a state replete with beatitude.**

These wicked goldsmiths incessantly seize
the essence of all possessions,
an ornament in prosperity
and a security in misfortune,–
the supreme splendor of gold.

A brief contact, and wicked outcastes, ever unclean,
pollute the higher castes,
corrupting their purity,
and just so, evil, unsavory goldsmiths
tarnish gold with their impetuous fumbling,
dimming its lustre.

Their ploy when buying
is a streak of dim lustre
on a soft touchstone.
At the time of selling,
the ploy of making profit is a streak
on a coarse stone as assay.*

8.5 S'|ôpasnehaḥ svedyaḥ
sikthaka|mudro 'pi vālukā|prāyaḥ
s'|ôṣmā ca yukti|bhedāt
tul'|ôpalānāṃ kalāḥ pañca.

Dvi/puṭā sphoṭa|vipākā
suvarṇa|rasa|pāyinī sa|tāmra|kalā
sīsa|mala|kāca|cūrṇa|
grahaṇa|parā ṣaṭ|kalā mūṣā.

8.7-8 *Vakra/mukhī viṣama/puṭā*
suṣira/talā nyasta/pāradā mṛdvī
kaṭu/kakṣyā granthimatī
kuśikyitā bahu/guṇā puro/namrā
vāta/bhrāntā tanvī
gurvī vā paruṣa/pātra/dhṛta/cūrṇā
nirjīvanā sajīvā
ṣoḍaśa hemnas tulāsu kalāḥ.

The swindles with balance-stones are five: 8.5
Though stamped with an official-looking seal* of beeswax
they are made mostly of sand, and depending on the ploy,
they are soaked in water, dried, or heated.

Six are the foibles of the crucible:
It *is a double vessel* ⁝ *has a double bottom**,
easily undergoes the calamity of bursting asunder,
it drinks up liquid gold,
it has a copper inlay, and is designed
to retain led and alkaline salt powder.

The scales for weighing gold have sixteen failings:
a bent indicator, unevenly matched bowls,
a perforated layer, they are loaded with mercury,
they are bendable, have an inert scale,
their cords are knotty, badly strung, and many-stranded,
they are out of balance before used,
can be disturbed by the wind, are too light, or too heavy,
they retain gold-dust in their coarse bowls,
and are magnetically static, or volatile.
⁝ *these are the sixteen traits of winter:*
the points of the compass become hostile,
the hollows become impassable, the ground cracks open,
it becomes soft as if with quicksilver scattered about.
With severe wraps, knotted together,
indecorously looped around the body many times,
one leans forward, shaken by stormy winds,
whether one is thin or stout,
snowy powder clings to coarse garments,
*and inanimate objects are blown about as though alive.**

Mandaḥ s'|āvego vā
    madhya|cchinnaḥ sa|śabda|phūt|kāraḥ
pātī śīkara|kārī
    phūt|kāraḥ ṣaṭ|kalas teṣām.

8.10 Jvāl'|āvalayī dhūmī
    visphoṭī mandakaḥ sphuliṅgī ca
pūrva|dhṛta|tāmra|cūrṇaḥ
    teṣām api ṣaṭ|kalo vahniḥ.

8.11-12 Praśnāḥ kathā vicitrāḥ
    kaṇḍūyanam aṃśuk'|ântarā|drstih
dina|vel"|ârka|nirīksaṇam
    ati|hāso makṣik'|ākṣepaḥ
kautuka|darśanam asakṛt
    sva|jana|kaliḥ salila|pātra|bhaṅgaś ca
bahir api gamanaṃ bahuśo
    dvā|daśa ceṣṭā|kalās teṣām.

Ghaṭitasy' ôpari pākaḥ
    kṛtrima|varṇa|prakāśan'|ôtkarṣī
tanu|gomay'|âgni|madhye
    lavaṇa|kṣār'|ânulepena.

Sāmānya|loha|pātrā
    bhūmi|nyaste 'pi kānta|loha|tale
dhāvati vadanena tulā
    rikt" âpi muhuḥ supūrṇ" êva.

Their blowing is sixfold:
puffing feebly or restlessly,
breaking off in the middle,
wheezing noisily, spluttering and hissing.

Their fire also has six aspects: 8.10
it can be ringed in flames,
smoky, roaring, smouldering, shedding sparks,
and is supplied with copper dust* placed in front of it.

Twelve are the traits of their behavior:
Questions, weird tales, scratching,
looking inside their garments,
checking the sun for time of day,
excessive laughter, swatting flies,
showing impatience,
much quarrel with their own people,
smashing the water-pot, and frequently going out.*

By smearing it with saline acid
in a gentle fire of cow-dung,
the finish of the worked article
becomes dazzlingly radiant with artificial color.

And because there is a magnetic layer
concealed in the ground,
the indicator of the scales,
with its bowls made of common iron,
suddenly jumps as if they were full,
though they are empty.

8.15 Pratibaddhe jatu|yogye
    prakṣipt'|ântar|nigūḍha|kanaka|kaṇam
tulite pūraṇa|kāle
    mukhena hartuṃ samāyāti.

Ujjvalane 'pi ca teṣāṃ
    pātanam ati|sukaram aśma|kāle ca
sadṛśa|vicitr'|ābharaṇe
    parivartana|lāghav'|âpasāraś ca.

Pūrṇ'|ādānaṃ ghaṭane
    dāne kṣāmārpaṇaṃ prabhā|yogaḥ
kāl'|āharaṇa|vināśaḥ
    pratipūraṇa|yācanaṃ bahu|śleṣaḥ.

Ekā|daśa yukti|kalāḥ
    teṣām etāḥ samāsena
ek" âiva kalā mahatī:
    niśi gamanaṃ sarvam ādāya.

Etā hema|karāṇāṃ
    vicāra|labhyāḥ kalāś catuḥ|ṣaṣṭiḥ
anyās tu nigūḍhā|kalāḥ
    Sahasra|netro 'pi no vetti.

At the time of completion, 8.15
when the ornament is being weighed,
he proceeds to extract a concealed lump of gold,
which he had secreted within while the ornament
was being inlaid with the use of lac,
through a hole.

†When the fire flares up,
or when they are working with a touch-stone
it is exceedingly easy for them to strike off a piece,
or an exchange with a similar shining ornament
might occur.†*

†They receive the full weight of gold for their work,
deliver...
they apply a glossy shine,
make timely collection impossible,
demand more material,
and use much double-talk.†

In brief these are their eleven practical arts.
Their ultimate art is to sneak away in the night,
taking everything with them.

Such are the sixty-four arts of goldsmiths
which can be inferred by reason,
but even thousand-eyed Indra does not know their other,
secret arts.

8.20 Meruḥ sthito vidūre
manuṣya|bhūmiṃ bhiyā parityajya
bhīto 'vaśyaṃ cauryād
caurāṇāṃ hema|kārāṇām.
Kanaka|śilā|śata|saṃdhi|
prasṛta|mahā|vivara|koṭi|saṃghātaiḥ
utkīrṇa|śithila|śikharaḥ
purā kṛto mūṣakair Meruḥ.
Tatr' âkhil'|ākhu|senā|
nikhāta|nakhar'|âvalekhan'|ôtkhātaiḥ
śithilita|mūlaḥ sahasā
babhūva Meruḥ purā niyatam.
Mūṣaka|nakhar'|ôtkhātaḥ
SuMerur uccaistarāṃ śuśubhe,
uddhūta|kanaka|dhūlī|
paṭalaiḥ kapilā babhuḥ kakubhaḥ.
Tasmiñ jarjara|śikhare
vivar'|ôdara|dalita|kaṭaka|kūṭa|taṭe
kalp'|ânt'|āgamane
bhayam āvir abhūd akhila|Devānām.
8.25 Tān ūce divya|dṛśā
vilokya sarvān mun'|īśvaro 'gastyaḥ:
«ete hi Brahma|ghnā
niśācārās tridaśa|saṃgare nihatāḥ.
Jātā mūṣaka|rūpā
Meru|nipāte kṛt'|ārambhāḥ
vadhyāḥ punar api bhavatām
āśrama|bhaṅgān munīnāṃ ca.»

Forsaking the world of men in fear, Mt. Meru towers far 8.20
away. Without a doubt he was afraid of the plundering of the thieves called goldsmiths.

Long ago, rats, by the sheer number of huge tunnels driven into the veins* of hundreds of gold-ore deposits, made the peak of Mt. Meru teeter on the brink of collapse by erosion.

Inevitably, the foundations of Mt. Meru were vehemently shaken by the excavations burrowed by the claws of this whole army of rats.

Mt. Meru, laid waste by the rat's claws, became exceedingly beautiful, its peaks shone with a reddish hue, covered by a veil of thrown up gold-dust.

Because its summit was shattered, because its ridges, peaks and slopes were rent asunder by chasms and clefts, all of the Gods became alarmed that the end of the eon was upon them.

Ágastya, lord of sages, scrutinised the calamity with his 8.25
divine eye and said to them all: "Forsooth, it is the night-stalkers, slayers of brahmins, who were annihilated in the war with the Gods!*

Reborn as rats, they are making efforts to topple Mt. Meru. You must destroy them again, for they have also destroyed the sanctuaries of the sages."

Śrutv" âitan muni|vacanaṃ
dhūmena bil'|āvalīṃ samāpūrya
śāpena pūrva|dagdhāñ
jagdhus tridaśā mahā|mūṣān.

Te hema|harāḥ
suvarṇa|kārāḥ kṣitau jātāḥ
janm'|âbhyāsād aniśaṃ
kāñcana|cūrṇaṃ nikarṣanti.

Tasmān mahī|patīnām
asaṃbhave garada|cora|dasyūnām
ekaḥ suvarṇa|kāro
nigrāhyaḥ sarvathā nityam.

iti mahā|kavi|śrī|Kṣemendra|viracite
Kalā|vilāse
suvarṇa|kār'|ôtpattir nāma
aṣṭamaḥ sargaḥ.

When they heard these words of the sage, the Gods filled the row of holes with smoke and burnt the great rats, who, in their previous existence, had been burnt by a curse.

These gold-robbers were then resurrected on earth as goldsmiths.* In each rebirth they ceaselessly scratch together gold-dust.

Therefore, in the absence of poisoners, thieves, or bandits, kings must ruthlessly persecute goldsmiths without reprieve.*

The eighth canto,
named the origin of goldsmiths,
in the "Grace of Guile" composed by
the great poet Ksheméndra.

THE GRACE OF GUILE
9. QUACKERY

V ĀÑCAKA|MĀYĀ mahatī
    mahī|tale jaladhi|mekhale nikhile
naṣṭa|dhiyāṃ matsyānāṃ
    jāl'|ālī *dhīvarair* vihitā.

Sarvasvam eva paramaṃ
    prāṇā yeṣāṃ kṛte prayatno 'yam,
Vaidyā vedyāḥ satataṃ
    yeṣāṃ haste sthitās te 'pi.

Ete hi dehi|dāhā
    virahā iva duḥsahā bhiṣajaḥ;
grīṣma|divasā iv' ôgrā
    bahu|tṛṣṇāḥ śoṣayanty eva.

Vividh'|âuṣadhi|parivartair yogaiḥ
    jijñāsayā sva|vidyāyāḥ
hatvā nṛṇāṃ sahasraṃ
    paścād vaidyo bhavet siddhaḥ.

9.5 Vinyasya rāśi|cakraṃ
    graha|cintāṃ nāṭayan mukha|vikāraiḥ
anuvadati cirād gaṇako
    yat kiṃ cit prāśniken' ôktam.

Gaṇayati gagane gaṇakaḥ
    candreṇa samāgamaṃ Viśākhāyāḥ
vividha|bhujaṃga|krīḍ"|āsaktāṃ
    gṛhiṇīṃ na jānāti.

THERE IS A GREAT VEIL of deception
covering the surface of
the whole, sea-girdled earth,
a train of nets set up by *fishermen : cunning men*
for fish whose wits have perished.*

The vital breaths are the ultimate possession,
all this striving is for their sake.
Know those, in whose hands they are at all times,
to be the *Gods of the Vedas : physicians.**

For, these dire physicians
burn the body like separation from a lover;
like ferocious summer days,
they bring much thirst, and dehydrate.

The physician becomes a renowned success
after he has killed a thousand patients with his concoctions,
swapping around their various constituent drugs
in an attempt to figure out his own science.

After sketching the zodiac, 9.5
and affecting concern about the planets by pursing his lips,
after a long pause,
the astrologer finally paraphrases
whatever the questioner had asked.

The astrologer calculates
the *rendez-vous* of the constellation Vishákha*
with the moon in the sky,
unaware that his wife at home
is addicted to love-play with numerous paramours.

Prathamaṃ sva|vittam akhilaṃ
kanak'|ârthī bhasmasāt svayaṃ kṛtvā
paścāt sadhanān rasikān
vināśayaty eṣa varṇikā|nipunaḥ.

«Śata|vedhī siddho me
sahasra|vedhī raso 'pi niryātaḥ»
iti vadati dhātu|vādī
nagno rūkṣaḥ kṛśo malinaḥ.

Tāmra|ghaṭ'|ôpama|śīrṣo
dhūrto 'pi rasāyanī jarā|jīrṇaḥ
keś'|ôtpādana|kathayā
khalvāṭān eva muṣṇāti.

9.10 Prahlādana|śuci|tāraka|
śambara|ramaṇīj|ane 'pi baddh'|āśaḥ
bilv'|ādibhir ati|kāmī
hutvā dhūm'|ândhatām eti.

«Khecarat" āpta|prāyā
yatnād yadi labhyate nabhaḥ|kusumam;
uktāḥ prayoga|vidbhir
maśak'|âsthiṣu siddhayo vividhāḥ.

First, the gold-maker*
reduces his own fortune to ashes in failed experiments.
Then, having become skilled in gold-plating,
he goes on to ruin wealthy alchemists.

The alchemist boasts:
"I have mastered the art of hundredfold-piercing mercury
and perfected even the thousandfold-piercing mercury."
—He is naked,
shrivelled,
emaciated,
filthy.

The quack rejuvenator,
with a head bald like a copper pot,
withered with old age,
pilfers bald men with tales of sprouting hair.*

The lecher, 9.10
yearning for gorgeous mistresses
with exhilarating bright eyes,
makes burnt offerings of *bilva*s etc.
and is blinded by the smoke.*

"The state of being a sky-goer is readily attained
if one strives to get a sky-flower;*
sorcerers have revealed
that there are many powers in mosquito-bones.*

Kṛṣṇ'|âśva|śakṛd|vṛtyā
paśyati gagane sur'|Ēndra|caritāni;
maṇḍūka|vasā|lipto
bhavati pumān vallabho 'psarasām.»

Ity uktvā punar āśāṃ
diśi diśi vilasanti dhūrta|saṃghātāḥ
yair vividha|siddhi|lubdhāḥ
kṣiptāḥ śataśo narāḥ śvabhre.

Vaśy'|ākarṣaṇa|yogī
pathi pathi rakṣāṃ dadāti nārīṇām,
rati|kāma|tantra|mūlaṃ
mūlaṃ mantraṃ na jānāti.

9.15 Bahavo rathyā|guravo
laghu|dīkṣāḥ svalpa|yogam utpādya
vyādhaya iva vardhante
mugdhānāṃ draviṇa|dāra|harāḥ.

«Hasta|sthā dhana|rekhā
vipulatar" âsyāḥ patis tu cala|cittaḥ»
mṛdnāti kula|vadhūnām
ity uktvā kamala|komalaṃ pāṇim.

With an eye-salve made of the dung
of a black horse
one sees the doings of Indra in the sky;
smeared with frog-fat,
a man can become the lover of celestial nymphs."

With such assertions,
hordes of swindlers perpetually fan hopes the world over,
casting down hundreds of men,
lusting for all kinds of powers,
into the chasms of hell.

On every street,
an adept at love-enchantment offers amulets to women,
without knowing
the magical roots* used in the science
nor the root-mantra.

Numerous street-gurus, 9.15
who have received only minor initiations
and mastered but little yoga,
rob the wealth and wives of the innocent,
proliferating like diseases.

Alleging that:
"The wealth-line in her hand is extensive,
but her husband is a half-wit,"
the palmist squeezes the tender hands of noble ladies.

Khaḍge 'ṅguṣṭhe salile
paśyati vividhaṃ jana|bhramaṃ kanyā
na prāpyate tu cauro
moho 'sāv indra|jālasya.

Khādati pibati ca dhūrtaḥ
pralāpa|kārī nṛṇāṃ tal'|āghātaiḥ
ceṭ'|āveśaṃ kṛtvā
nirmantra|kṣudra|dhūpena.

«Kakṣa|puṭe Nāgārjuna|
likhitā vartir vidhīyatāṃ dhūpe
sā dagdhā mohād! iti»
dhūrto 'gnau kṣipati para|vittam.

9.20 Yakṣī|putrāś corā
vijñeyāḥ kūṭa|dhūpa|kartāraḥ
yeṣāṃ pratyakṣa|phalaṃ
dāridryaṃ rāja|daṇḍaś ca.

«Bahutara|dhanena vaṇijā
putrī sā putravad|gṛhīt" êva
mad|adhīn" êti» kathābhiḥ
kany"|ârthaṃ bhujyate dhūrtaiḥ.

Cintyaś c' êṅgita|vādī
marma|jño hṛdaya|caura ev' âsau
tiṣṭhati para|prayukto
mithyā|badhiro 'thavā mūkaḥ.

The virgin sees a diverse crowd of people
in a sword-blade, in her thumb-nail, or in water,
but the thief is not caught,
such is the futility of divinatory magic.*

The fraud gorges himself and drinks,
he prattles on, applauded by the public,
after he has made his low-born side-kick become possessed
using just a little incense and no mantras.*

"The collyrium described by Nagárjuna in the *Kaksha·puta**
must be prepared in the smoke of incense.
By accident it has burnt!" With this excuse the villain
throws the wealth of other people
into the fire.

Sons of *yakshis* must be known as 9.20
thieves who produce narcotic fumigants;
for them the visible reward
is poverty and punishment by the king.*

"An extremely wealthy merchant
has appointed his daughter,
who is dependent on me,
as legal heir in place of a son,"*
with such tales
villains gorge themselves at the expense of a girl.

Suspect is also the specialist of physiognomy.*
A knower of vulnerabilities, he is a heart-thief.
He makes his appearance feigning to be deaf or mute,
masterminded by an adversary.

Bhasma|smerā veśyā
vṛddhā śramaṇā sa|daivatā gaṇikā
etāḥ kula|nārīṇāṃ
caranti dhana|śīla|hāriṇyaḥ.

«Vidhavā taruṇī sa|dhanā
vāñchati divyaṃ bhavad|vidhaṃ ramaṇam»
dhūrto jaḍam ity uktvā
sarvasvaṃ tasya bhakṣayati.

9.25 Pratyaha|vetana|yuktāḥ
karmasu ye kāru|śilpino dhūrtāḥ
vilasanti karma|vighnaiḥ
vijñeyāḥ kāla|caurās te.

Akṣa|vyājair vividhaiḥ
gaṇanā|hast'|ādi|lāghavair nipuṇāḥ
dhūrtāś caranti gūḍhaṃ
prasiddha|kitavā videśeṣu.

Bhojana|mātr"|ôtpattiḥ
bahu|vyayo dyūta|madya|veśyābhiḥ
vijñeyo gṛha|cauro
bandhu|jano veśma|dāso vā.

«Kṛtakaṃ śāstram asatyaṃ,
sākṣād|dṛṣṭaś ca kena para|lokaḥ?»
iti vadati yaḥ sa śaṅkyo
niraṅkuśo matta|mātaṅgaḥ.

A prostitute pallid with sacred ash,
an old nun, or a courtesan carrying an idol;
these destroyers
 of the wealth and virtue of noble ladies
are on the prowl.

"A young, rich widow
lusts after a divine lover like you,"
saying this to a dim-wit
the villain eats into his money.

Corrupt artisans and craftsmen, 9.25
day-labourers who divert themselves
with disruptions to their job,
should be known as time-thieves.

Expert gamblers,
villains adept in dice-tricks, miscalculation,
 and sleight of hand etc.,
pass unmarked in foreign lands.*

A relative,
who shows himself only at mealtimes,
who squanders a lot
 on gambling, wine and loose women,
should be known as a house-thief
 or house-fiend.

"Sacred scripture is fabrication and false.
Who has actually seen the hereafter?"
He who speaks thus should be feared
like a rutting elephant running out of control.

Bahu|lābha|lubdha|manasāṃ
haranti ye duḥsahena lobhena
ṛṇa|dhanam adhika|vidagdhā
vijñeyā lābha|caurās te.

9.30 Deś'|ântara|saṃbhavibhiḥ
bhoga|varair varṇanā|ramyaiḥ
ye 'pi nayanti videśaṃ
paśu|sadṛśān deśa|caurās te.

Adhika|raṇ'|âmbudhi|madhye
jvalanti vaḍav"|âgnayaḥ sakala|bhakṣāḥ
jita|jana|vinimayino ye
bhaṭṭ'|ākhyā jñāna|corās te.

Vibhav'|âmbho|ruha|madhupā
duḥsaha|vipad|anila|vega|vimukhā ye
suhṛdas te sukha|caurāḥ
caranti lakṣmī|lat"|āhūtāḥ.

Those who, skilled at excess,
with unbearable greed,
rake in the debts
of those hoping to make much profit,
should be known as profit-thieves.

Those who entice people abroad like cattle, 9.30
with the choice enjoyments
available in other lands,
enchanting with the praises heaped upon them,
are land-thieves.*

Those, who bear the title "honorable,"
who are all-devouring submarine fires
smoldering in the midst of
the oceans of law-courts,
who collude with the defeated party
to arrange the outcome,
are knowledge-thieves.

Friends, who are
honey-drinking bees on the lotus of prosperity,
who are blown away by the force
of the wind of unpalatable hardship,
are comfort-thieves, who rove about
attracted by the vine of fortune.

Yad yat kiṃ cid apūrvaṃ
para|carit'|ākalpanād asaṃbaddham
varṇayati harṣa|kārī
bahu|vacanaḥ karṇa|cauro 'sau.

Doṣeṣu guṇa|stutibhiḥ
śraddhām utpādya *catura|vacanā* ye
kurvanty abhinava|sṛṣṭiṃ*
sthiti|caurās te nirācārāḥ.

9.35 Ātma|guṇa|khyāti|parāḥ
para|guṇam ācchādya vipula|yatnena
prabhavanti parama|dhūrtā
guṇa|caurās te vimūḍha|hṛdayeṣu.

Vallabhatām upayātāḥ
para|vāllabhyaṃ vicitra|paiśunyaiḥ
ye vārayanti dhūrtā
mātsaryād vṛtti|caurās te.

Śama|dama|bhakti|vihīnas
tīvra|vrata|durgraha|grastaḥ
abhibhavati pratipattyā
sādhuj|anaṃ kīrti|cauro 'sau.

The entertainer who recounts all kinds of things
which are unheard of,
which are incoherent,
because he does not formulate
what was done by others,
is a talkative ear-thief.

Those, who, with *pleasing voices ⁝ clever words*
generate faith
by praising virtues where there are only defects,
create a rival world-order,
are lawless thieves of the bounds of morality.

Those utter villains, who, 9.35
intent on proclaiming their own virtues,
exert themselves mightily to obscure the virtues of others,
are virtue-thieves,
they wield influence among the simple-minded.

Those villains, who have won royal favor,
who out of jealousy obstruct others from royal favor
by all manner of backbiting,
are livelihood-thieves.

A man lacking in tranquility, restraint and devotion,
but seized by a mania to observe severe religious vows
overwhelms good people with his determination.
He is a renown-thief.

Nānā|hāsa|vikāraiḥ
bahu|vaidagdhyaiḥ sa|narma|parihāsaiḥ
ramayati divasam aśeṣaṃ
prakṛti|vyāpāra|cauro 'sau.

Bhakṣita|nija|vibhavā ye
para|vibhava|kṣapaṇa|dīkṣitāḥ paścāt
aniśaṃ veśy"|āveśa|
stuti|mukharās te viṭāś cintyāḥ.

9.40 Ati|śucitayā na vṛttiṃ
gṛhṇāti karoti c' âgryam adhikāram
yo niyama|salila|matsyaḥ
parihāryo 'sau tu niḥspṛha|niyogī.

Rathyā|vaṇijaḥ pāpāḥ
svayam etya gṛheṣu yat prayacchanti
tat kṣaṇa|ratnam udāraṃ
bhavati paraṃ kāca|śakalam api.

Chand'|ânuvartino ye
śvabhr'|āpāte 'pi sādhu|vāda|parāḥ
sarvasva|hāriṇas te
madhurā viṣavad viśanty antaḥ.

The thief of habitual occupation fritters away
 the whole day
shifting into diverse types of laughter,
with many clever quips
abounding in jokes and farces.

Those who have squandered
 all of their own money
and then devote themselves to wasting the wealth of others,
who incessantly prattle on
 acclaiming brothels,
are suspect as pimps.*

The abstemious commissioner,* 9.40
who discharges the highest office
but does not accept any wages
 out of inordinate purity,
must be shunned
as a shark in the water of moderation.

Wicked street-peddlers call at houses uninvited.
Whatever they proffer,
becomes in a flash a jewel of distinction,
be it nothing but a bit of glass.

Sycophants, who are ready to cry "Bravo!"
even when one plummets into a chasm,
rob everything with a pleasing voice,
they spread within like poison.

«Tava nara|patiḥ prasādī
guṇa|gaṇana|paraḥ param» vijane
uktv" êti rāja|dāsaiḥ
sevaka|lokaḥ sadā muṣitaḥ.

«Svapne may" âbja|hastā
dṛṣṭā Śrīs tvad|gṛhaṃ praviṣṭā ca
mās'|ôpavāsa|tuṣṭā
Devī Śrīḥ sādarā prāha:

9.45 ‹Mad|bhaktas te dāsyati
sarvaṃ.› labdho mayā tat tvaṃ»
ity uktvā saralānāṃ
vilasanti gṛhe gṛhe dhūrtāḥ.

Pura|viplava|nagar'|ôdaya|
yajña|vivāh'|ôtsav'|ādi|jana|saṃghe
praviśanti bandhu|veṣāḥ
pare 'pi sarv'|âpahārāya.

Parijana|pān'|âvasare
pibati na madyaṃ, niśāsu jāgarti
dhyāna|paraḥ, svair'|ârthī,
kim api ca kartuṃ kṛt'|ôdyogaḥ,

"The King is favorably inclined towards you,
he knows well to appreciate your many virtues."
With such private avowals, the royal menials
ever rifle the servants.

"In a dream*
I saw the Goddess of fortune,
and she entered your house
  with a lotus in her hand.
Gratified by my month-long fast,
the Goddess Lakshmi, though usually diffident,
spoke to me:

'My devotee will give you everything'. 9.45
So I have come to you."
With such pretenses, villains take advantage
of the simple-minded faithful,
  house by house.

When crowds congregate
because the city is in affray,
because of sacrifices,
wedding-festivals or the like,
strangers dressed as kinsmen
intrude to carry off valuables.

When the company drinks
  he does not touch wine.
He stays awake at night
  absorbed in brooding.
He is inclined to be self-willed,
and has hatched plans for some venture.

Na dadāti prativacanaṃ,
 prativakti ca gadgad'|âkṣarair viṣamam
naṣṭa|mukhaḥ s'|ôcchvāsaḥ
 pravepate tat|kṣaṇaṃ coraḥ.

Yaś c' âdhika|pariśuddhiṃ
 prārthayate raṭati yaś ca s'|āṭopaṃ
ghor'|âpahnava|kārī
 śaṅk'|āyatanaṃ sa pāpaḥ syāt.

9.50 Pratyakṣe 'pi parokṣe
 kṛtam akṛtaṃ kathitam apy anuktaṃ ca
yaḥ kurute nirvikṛtiḥ
 sa paraṃ puṃsāṃ bhaya|sthānam.

Kṛta|kṛtaka|mugdha|bhāvaḥ
 ṣaṇḍha iva strī|svabhāva|saṃlāpaḥ
vicarati yaḥ strī|madhye
 sa Kāma|devo gṛhe dhūrtaḥ.

He gives no answer.
Or he gives a reply
muffled with stammering.
He hides his face, he sighs,
he trembles in an instant:
the thief.

He, who demands inordinate purity
  and clamors arrogantly,
that miscreant is a source of suspicion,
a source of terrifying dissimulation.

He who, 9.50
  whether it was witnessed or not,
turns what has happened
  into what has not happened,
and what was said
  into what was not said,
without batting an eyelid,
he is the ultimate source of danger
  for men.

The villain
who affects an artificial innocence,
who, like a eunuch,
talks in the manner of a woman,
who loiters around the women
is the God of love
  in the house.

Satatam adho|mukha|dṛṣṭiḥ
  sati vibhave malina|gātra|vasanaś ca
vilasan koṣa|niyuktaḥ
  koṣa|gṛhe *mūṣakaś* cintyaḥ.

Tiṣṭhati yaḥ sakala|dinaṃ
  gṛha|dāsaḥ prīti|veśma|bhavaneṣu
gṛha|dīrgha|kathāḥ kathayan
  sa caraḥ sarv'|ātmanā tyājyaḥ.

Nindye bahu|daṇḍ'|ârhe
  karmaṇi yaḥ sarvathā pratārayati
ā|jīva|bhīti|bhojyas
  tena nibaddhaḥ payo|rāśih.

9.55 Dṛṣṭvā guhyam aśeṣaṃ
  tasya rahasyaṃ ca līlayā labdhvā
dhūrtena mugdha|lokas
  tena śilā|paṭṭake likhitaḥ.

The treasurer
whose eyes are always cast down,
whose body and clothes are filthy
even though he has money,
who frolics in the treasury,
should be feared as a *thief* : *rat*.*

The servant attached to a house
who stays all day
  in the inner apartments
  as a favor,
telling long-winded tales about the house,
must be scrupulously avoided as a spy.

He who persistently instigates others to commit
sinful undertakings meriting severe punishment,
has dammed the ocean
which he must enjoy with apprehension
for the remainder of his life.

The villain, 9.55
once he has seen all
  of the private affairs
  of unsophisticated people,
and has without difficulty uncovered their secrets,
proceeds to inscribe them
  on a stone slab.

Rāja|viruddhaṃ dravyaṃ
rūpyaṃ vā kūṭa|lekhyam anyad vā
nikṣipya yāty alakṣyaṃ
dhūrtas teṣāṃ vināśāya.

Kṣudraḥ kṣīṇo 'pi gṛhe
labdh'|āsvādaḥ kṛto dhanair yena
viṣa|śastra|pāśa|hastaḥ
sa Pāśa|hasto dhṛtas tena.

Lajjā|dhanaḥ kulīnaḥ
saṃbhāvita|śuddha|śīla|maryādaḥ
nārīkriyate dhūrtaiḥ
prāyeṇa sa|garbha|nārībhiḥ.

Dṛṣṭābhir abhijñābhiḥ
krūrābhiḥ kṛtaka|vacana|mudrābhiḥ
dhūrto muṣṇāti vadhūṃ
mugdhāṃ viproṣite patyau.

9.60 Sa|jane 'pi sādhu|veṣā
vidhṛt'|ābharaṇāś ca helayā dhūrtāḥ
dhīrā haranti satataṃ
dṛṣṭe hāso 'nyathā lābhaḥ.

To ruin them,
the villain plants illegal goods,
money banned by the king,
a forged document or something similar,
and then absconds unnoticed.

Someone who affords succor in his own house
to an emaciated wretch at his own expense,
is then held to ransom
by that veritable God of death
holding a poisoned knife and a noose.

By means of pregnant women,
villains commonly make a woman
of an easily embarrassed, highborn man
who respects the boundaries of pure conduct.*

When her husband is abroad,
a villain robs his innocent wife,
with cruel, made-up messages and seals,
with tokens of recognition which he has observed.

Even in the midst of people, 9.60
bold gentlemen-thieves dressed in respectable finery,*
  bedecked with ornaments,
are ceaselessly stealing without effort.
If it is noticed, it is a joke,
if not, it is a gain.

Deśe kṛtvā sphīte
kumbha|dhan'|āḍambarair gṛhaṃ pūrṇam
nikṣepa|lakṣa|hārī
varṣeṇa palāyate dhūrtaḥ.

Suṣira|maya|kanaka|bhūṣaṇa|
tanu|vasanaiḥ saṃvṛtāś ca pūjyante
ripu|bhagna|rāja|putra|
vyājena gṛhe gṛhe dhūrtāḥ.

Ādāya deśa|vṛṣabhaṃ
puṇya|cchāgaṃ ca dhūrta|vikrītaṃ
mugdhasya duḥkha|pākaḥ
samargha|lābh'|ôdito harṣaḥ.

S'|âdhi|kṣepas tyāge
mahatāṃ saṃpatsu yaḥ kṛt'|āsūyaḥ
tasmai bhayena vittaṃ
rikto 'pi dadāti yatnena.

9.65 Niḥsāra|bhūrja|sāraiḥ
kṛtvā gantrī|yutaṃ mahā|sārtham
dhūrto diśi diśi vicaran
dhanika|sahasrāṇi muṣṇāti.

Dhūrtaḥ prasanna|veṣo
nirdiśya Surāpagā|gayā|yātrām
bandhu|nidhāya sārthe
draviṇaṃ gṛhṇāti mugdhebhyaḥ.

Once the con-man,
who steals hundreds of thousands worth of deposits,
has crammed his house in a prosperous foreign land
  with piles of treasure-vats,
he disappears within a year.

Bedecked with hollow golden ornaments and fine garments,
impostors are honored in house after house
in the guise of princes usurped by a common enemy.

After a fool has bought a lucky goat
from a swindler with a country bull,
his glee at a valuable bargain
ripens into grief.

Even an impoverished man, out of fear,
is intimidated into giving money to an extortionist
who is abusive when ignored,
who is envious of the prosperity of eminent people.*

With wares which are really worthless bundles of birchbark, 9.65
a villain sets up a vast caravan furnished with carts,
crisscrosses the world,
and robs thousands of wealthy people.

A fraud, dressed in discreet robes,
announces a pilgrimage to the river Ganges
and then takes money from simple people
in order to deposit
the cremated remains of relatives.

Muṣṇāti sārtha|ramaṇī
    śāṭīm ādāya nidrayā mugdham.
dhūrtena kūṭa|rūpaṃ
    dattvā niśi vañcyate s" âpi.

Badhiraṃ vā mūkaṃ vā
    vaṇijaṃ nikṣipya bhāṇḍa|śālāyām
dhūrto nayati tvarayā bahu|mūlyaṃ varṇaka|dravyam.

Kiṃ cit paricaya|mātraiḥ
    kiṃ cid dhārṣṭyena katthanaiḥ
kiṃ cid vivāda|kalahaiḥ sarva|jño vañcakaś carati.

9.70 *Mithyā|ḍambara|dhaniko*
    mala|patraka|paṇḍitaḥ kathā|jñānī
varṇana|śūraś ca paraḥ
    Catur|mukho jṛmbhate dhūrtaḥ.

Sarv'|âvayava|vidhūnana|
    kṛta|saṃketān vibhajya geheṣu
bhoktuṃ vrajati digantān
    vedh'|ācāryo mahā|dhūrtaḥ.

The caravan-harlot
steals the gown of a dozing simpleton.
Given a counterfeit coin by a villain,
she is cheated the same night.

A villain locks a deaf or dumb merchant
in his store-house
and quickly makes off
with heaps of stock and gold.

The cheat* sets out, omniscient,
  in part through mere acquaintance,
  in part through audacity,
  in part through boasting,
  in part through quarrel and disagreement.

Loudly asserting falsehoods, learned by reading title-pages, 9.70
expert in disputation, heroic in embellishment,
the villain is prominent as another four-faced Brahma
: who powerfully confounds falsehood,
who is the scholar seated on stainless lotus-petals,
who knows sacred lore,
*who is heroic in creating the universe.**

After investing houses with stooges ready to fake
violent tremors in their whole bodies,
the great deceiver roams hither and thither
to enjoy himself as a master of piercing-initiation.*

«Śata|vārṣikam āmalakaṃ
bhuktvā śrī|parvatād ahaṃ prāptaḥ»
dhūrto vadati gurūṇāṃ
purataḥ «Śakuniṃ smarām' îti.»

Ete leśena mayā
kathitā māyā|kalāś catuḥ|ṣaṣṭiḥ;
ko vetti vañcakānāṃ
māyānāṃ śata|sahasrāṇi?

iti mahā|kavi|śrī|Kṣemendra|viracite
Kalā|vilāse
nānā|dhūrta|varṇanaṃ nāma
navamaḥ sargaḥ.

The villain proclaims in front of the gurus:
"I have come from Mt. Shri·párvata
where I have eaten
a hundred year old Myrobalan fruit.
I remember Shákuni."*

These, succinctly told,
are the sixty-four arts of deceit.
Who knows
the hundreds of thousands of tricks of swindlers?

The ninth canto,
named the description of assorted villains,
in the "Grace of Guile" composed by
the great poet Ksheméndra.

THE GRACE OF GUILE
10. VIRTUE

ETĀ VAÑCAKA|MĀYĀ
vijñeyā na tu punaḥ svayaṃ sevyāḥ
dharmyaḥ kalā|kalāpo
viduṣā|mayam īpsito bhūtyaiḥ.

Dharmasya kalā jyeṣṭhā
bhūta|day"|ākhyā par'|ôpakāraś ca
dānaṃ kṣam" ânasūyā
satyam alobhaḥ prasādaś ca.

Arthasya sad"|ôtthānaṃ
niyamaḥ paripālanaṃ krama|jñānam
sthāne tyāgaḥ paṭutā|
anudvegaḥ strīṣv aviśvāsaḥ.

Kāmasya veṣa|śobhā
peśalatā cārutā guṇ'|ôtkarṣaḥ
prītiḥ praṇayo līlā| citta|jñānaṃ ca kāntānām.

10.5 Mokṣasya viveka|ratiḥ
praśamas tṛṣṇā|kṣayaḥ sva|saṃtoṣaḥ
saṅga|tyāgaḥ sva|layaḥ
sāmyaṃ parama|prakāśaś ca.

Etāś catuṣṭaya|kalā
dvā|triṃśat|krama|dhṛtāḥ samastā vā
saṃsāra|vañcakānāṃ
bhavanti vidyāvatām.

One must know these tricks of charlatans,
but one should not pursue them oneself.
The wise seek their welfare
in the profusion of virtuous arts.

The most excellent arts of righteousness are known as
compassion for living beings, assistance to others,
charity, forbearance, goodwill, truthfulness,
contentment, and serenity.*

Of gain they are
unflagging exertion, regularity, saving,
knowledge of business, selling in due time,
proficiency, calm, and distrust in women.

Of pleasure they are
beautiful clothes, gentleness, elegance, excellent virtues,
affection, trust, playfulness,
and knowing the mind of the beloved.

Of liberation they are 10.5
a love of discernment, tranquility, eradication of craving,
self-contentment, giving up clinging, merging into the self,
equanimity, supreme illumination.

For wise deceivers of transmigration
these are the thirty-two arts
of the quartet of worldly aims
practised in order or all at once.*

Mātsarya|parityāgaḥ
priya|vāditvaṃ sadhairyam akrodhaḥ
vairāgyaṃ ca par'|ârthe
sukhasya siddhāḥ kalāḥ pañca.

Sat|saṅgaḥ kāma|jayaḥ
śaucaṃ guru|sevanaṃ sad|ācāraḥ
śrutam amalaṃ yaśasi ratiḥ
mūla|kalāḥ sapta śīlasya.

Tejaḥ sattvaṃ buddhiḥ
vyavasāyo nītir iṅgita|jñānam
prāgalbhyaṃ susahāyaḥ
kṛta|jñatā mantra|rakṣaṇaṃ tyāgaḥ;

10.10 Anurāgaḥ pratipattiḥ
mitr'|ârjanam ānṛśaṃsyam astambhaḥ
āśrita|jana|vātsalyaṃ
daśa|sapta kalāḥ prabhāvasya.

Maunam alaulyam ayācñā
mānasya ca jīvitaṃ kalā|tritayam
etāḥ kalā vidagdhaiḥ
sva|gatāḥ kāryāś catuḥ|ṣaṣṭiḥ.

śakta|virodhe gamanaṃ
tat|praṇatir vā bal'|ôdaye vairam
ārtasya dharma|caryā
duḥkhe dhairyaṃ sukheṣv anutsekaḥ;

Vibhaveṣu saṃvibhāgaḥ
satsu ratir mantra|saṃśaye prajñā
nindyeṣu parāṅ|mukhatā
bheṣajam etat kalā|daśakam.

Giving up envy, kindly speech, fortitude,
freedom from anger,
and dispassion towards the wealth of others,
are the five magical arts of happiness.*

The seven fundamental arts of integrity are:
association with the good,
vanquishing sensual desires, purity,
service to the preceptor, good conduct, stainless learning,
and striving for a good reputation.

Dignity, character, intelligence, determination, statecraft,
knowledge of gestures betraying secret intentions, boldness,
loyal friends, gratitude, confidentiality, generosity;
Devotion, sanctioned authority, acquisition of friends, 10.10
mercy, modesty, and kindness towards dependents
are the seventeen arts of power.

Reserve, firmness and not begging,
this triad of arts is the life of honor.
The wise should make
these sixty-four arts their own.

When opposed by a greater power
one should leave or bow to it,
one should show hostility when force is brought to bear,
righteous conduct towards the oppressed,
fortitude in suffering, courtesy in happiness;
Sharing in wealth, fondness for good people,
clear insight when counsels are doubtful,
and aversion to reprehensible people;
these ten arts are remedial.

Guru|vacanaṃ satyānāṃ
  kāryāṇāṃ go|dvi|jāti|sura|pūjā
lobhaḥ pāpatamānāṃ
  krodhaḥ sarv'|ôpatāpa|janakānām;

10.15 Prajñā sarva|guṇānāṃ
  yaśasvitā vipula|vitta|vibhāvānām
sevā duḥkhatarāṇām
  āśā pṛthu|kāla|bhujaga|pāśānām;

Dānaṃ ratna|nidhīnāṃ
  nirvairatvaṃ sukha|pradeśānām
yācñā māna|harāṇāṃ
  dārirdyaṃ śāpa|tāpas'|ârthānām;

Dharmaḥ pātheyānāṃ
  satyaṃ mukha|padma|pāvanatarāṇām
vyasanaṃ roga|gaṇānām
  ālasyaṃ gṛha|samṛddhi|nāśānām;

Niḥspṛhatā ślāghyānāṃ
  priya|vacanaṃ sarva|madhurāṇām
darpas timira|bharāṇāṃ
  dambhaḥ sarv'|ôpahāsa|pātrāṇām;

Adrohaḥ śaucānām
  acāpalaṃ vrata|viśeṣa|niyamānām
paiśunyam apriyāṇāṃ
  vṛtti|cchedo nṛśamsa|caritānām;

10.20 Kāruṇyaṃ puṇyānāṃ
  kṛta|jñatā puruṣa|ratna|cihnānām
māyā moha|matīnāṃ
  kṛta|ghnatā naraka|pāta|hetūnām;

In this world,* it is renown,
which is the guru's word among truths,
the worship of cows, brahmins and Gods among deeds,
greed among heinous sins,
wrath among all that leads to sorrow;
Wisdom among all virtues, 10.15
prestige among all the dignities of vast affluence,
servitude among miseries,
hope among thick snares and black cobras;*
Charity among jewel treasures,
freedom from enmity among the happy realms,
begging among erasers of honor,
poverty among all penitences caused by curses;
Righteousness among waybreads,
truth among the purifiers of one's mouth-lotus,
vice among epidemics of diseases,
sloth among the destroyers of the prosperity of a house;
Desirelessness among things worthy of praise,
kind words among all that is sweet,
arrogance among all that is impenetrably dark,
false piety among all that is laughable;
Absence of malice among purities,
steadfastness among the observances imposed
  by difficult vows,
slander among unpleasant deeds,
severing a livelihood among mean acts;
Compassion among meritorious feats, 10.20
gratitude among the marks of the superior man,
deceit among foolish ideas,
ungratefulness among the causes for a downfall to hell;

Madanaś chala|caurāṇāṃ
strī|vacanaṃ jñāti|bhedānām
krūraś caṇḍālānāṃ
†māyāvī kali|yug'|âvatārāṇām†;
śāstraṃ maṇi|dīpānām
upadeśaś cābhiṣekāṇāmab:
sneho viṣama|viṣāṇāṃ
veśyā|rāgo visarpa|kuṣṭhānām;
Bhāryā gṛha|sārāṇāṃ
putraḥ para|loka|bandhūnām
śatruḥ śalya|śatānāṃ
duṣputraḥ kula|vināśānām;
Tāruṇyaṃ ramyāṇāṃ
rūpaṃ rucir'|ôpacāra|veṣāṇām
vṛddhatvaṃ kleśānāṃ
rogitvaṃ nidhana|tulya|duḥkhānām;
10.25 Prabhu|śaktir bhāgyānāṃ
putra|janiḥ sarva|saukhyānāṃ
mānaḥ puṣṭi|karāṇām
ācāraḥ karma|dharma|niratānām;
Saṃtoṣo rājyānāṃ
sat|saṅgaś cakra|varti|vibhāvānāmab:
cintā śoṣa|karāṇāṃ
vidveṣaḥ koṭar'|âgni|dāhānām;

The God of love among sneaky thieves,
women's words among dividers of kinsmen,
a cruel one among *chandálas*,*
a necromancer among those incarnated
in the age of darkness;
Scripture among jewel-lamps,
instruction among consecrations,
love among cruel poisons,
attraction to prostitutes among spreading rashes
and leprosies;*
A wife among domestic properties,
a son among relatives helpful for the next life,*
an enemy among hundreds of barbs,
a bad son among the destroyers of families;
Youth among lovely things,
beauty among splendid pomp and garments,
old age among afflictions,
sickness among agonies equal to death;
Sovereignty among good fortunes, 10.25
the birth of a son among all joys,
self-respect among invigoraters,
customary observance among those devoted
to ritual and religion;
Satisfaction among kingdoms,
good company among the glories of emperors,
worry among things which parch,
hatred among fires smoldering in hollow trees;

Maitrī viśrambhānāṃ
niryantraṇatā mah"|ârha|bhogānām
saṃkoco vyādhīnāṃ
kauṭilyaṃ nirjal'|ândha|kūpānām;
Ārjavam amalatarāṇāṃ
vinayo vara|ratna|mukuṭānām
dyūtaṃ durvyasanānāṃ
strī|jitatā madhumatāṃ piśācānām;
Tyāgo maṇi|valayānāṃ
śrutam ujjvala|karṇa|ratnānām
khala|maitrī capalānāṃ
durjana|sevā vṛthā|prayāsānām;
10.30 Nirvṛtir udyānānāṃ
priya|darśanam amṛta|varṣāṇām
tattva|ratir labhyānāṃ
mūrkha|sabhā guṇa|viveka|nāśānām;
Kuṭajaḥ sa|phala|tarūṇāṃ
saubhāgyaṃ kṛta|purāvatārāṇām
rāja|kulaṃ śakyānāṃ
strī|hṛdayaṃ prakṛti|kuṭilānām;
Aucityaṃ stutyānāṃ
guṇa|rāgaś candan'|ādi|lepānām
kanyā śoka|karāṇāṃ
buddhi|vihīno 'nukampyānām;
Vibhavaḥ saubhāgyānāṃ
jana|rāgaḥ kīrti|kandānām
madyaṃ vetālānāṃ
mṛgayā gaja|gahana|yakṣāṇām;

Amiability among intimate confidences,
independence among priceless enjoyments,
self-abasement among diseases,
duplicity among waterless concealed wells;
Sincerity among unsullied things,
modesty among diadems of choice gems
gambling among depravities
defeat by women among appealing goblins;
Renunciation among jewelled bracelets,
learning among dazzling earrings set with gems,
friendship with villains among uncertainties,
service to the wicked among futile endeavours;
Beatitude among gardens, 10.30
the glance of a friend among nectar-showers,
rejoicing in truth among things within reach,
an assembly of fools
among destroyers of the discernment of virtues;
The *kútaja** among fruit-bearing trees,
good fortune among the consequences of former deeds,
the royal family among wherewithals,
a woman's heart among the inherently deceitful;
Harmony among the praiseworthy,
attachment to virtue among unguents of sandalwood etc.,
a daughter among causes of grief,
the dunce among those deserving pity;
Wealth among good destinies,
popularity among the roots of renown,
drink among zombies,
hunting among *yakshas* in the elephant wilderness;

Praśamaḥ svāsthya|karāṇām|
ātma|ratis tīrtha|sevānām
lubdhaḥ phala|rahitānām
ācāra|vivarjitaḥ śmaśānānām;

10.35 Nītiḥ strī|rakṣaṇānām
indriya|vijayaḥ prabhāvāṇām
īrṣyā yakṣma|śatānām|
ayaśaḥ kusthāna|maraṇānām;

Mātā maṅgalyānāṃ
janakaḥ sukṛt'|ôtsav'|ôpadeśānām
ghātas tīkṣṇa|śarāṇāṃ
marma|cheda|sit'|âsi|śastrāṇām;

Praṇatir manyu|harāṇāṃ
sauhārdaṃ kṛcchra|yācñānām
prabhu|bhaktir nītānāṃ
yuddhi nidhanaṃ saukhya|vīthīnām;

Puṇyaṃ prāpyatamānāṃ
jñānaṃ parama|prakāśānām
kīrtiḥ saṃsāre 'smin
sāratarā sarva|lokānām.

Jñeyaḥ kalā|kalāpe|
kuśalaḥ sarv'|ârtha|tattva|vijñātā
pravarataro loke 'smin|
brāhmaṇa iva sarva|varṇānām.

10.40 Ity uktaṃ śatam etad
yo vetti śubh'|âśubh'|ôdaya|kalānām
tasy' âiva vyavahāre|
dṛṣṭā dṛṣṭa|prayojanā lakṣmīḥ.

Tranquility among health-tonics,
delight in the self among visits to sacred fords,
the hunter among those without merit,
the dissolute among burning grounds;
Prudence among ways to protect women, 10.35
conquest of the senses among mighty deeds,
jealousy among the hundred forms of consumption,
disrepute among inglorious deaths;
A mother among blessings,
a father among teachings for the festivity of good deeds,
murder among sharp arrows,
severing of the vital ligatures among bright razor weapons;
Deference among appeasers of anger,
friendship among things difficult to ask for,
devotion to God among guiding principles,
death in battle* among paths to happiness;
Merit among things one must attain,
knowledge among the brightest illuminations,
which is most precious to all people.

An adept at this whole collection of arts,
who discerns the truth of all things,
must be acknowledged as unsurpassed in this world,
just as a brahmin is among all the castes.

Fortune smiles, making her intention clear, 10.40
upon the endeavours of those alone who know
the one hundred arts just revealed,
which lead to either fortune or misfortune.

Uktv" êti Mūladevo|
    visṛjya śiṣyān kṛt'|ôcit'|ācāraḥ
kiraṇa|kalikā|vikāsāṃ
    nināya nija|mandire rajanīm.

Kelī|mayaḥ smita|vikāsa|kal"|âbhirāmaḥ
    sarv'|āśray'|ântara|kalā|prakaṭa|pradīpaḥ
lok'|ôpadeśa|viṣayaḥ sukathā|vicitro
    bhūyāt satāṃ dayita eṣa Kalā|vilāsaḥ.

Kalā|vilāsaḥ Kṣemendra|
    pratibh"|âmbhodhi|nirgataḥ
śaś" îva mānas'|āhlādaṃ
    karotu satataṃ satām|

iti mahā|kavi|śrī|Kṣemendra|viracite
Kalā|vilāse
sakala|kalā|nirūpaṇaṃ nāma
daśamaḥ sargaḥ.

This said, Mula·deva
dismissed his pupils with the appropriate rite,
and spent the remainder of the night,
which blossomed with clusters of rays,
in his own palace.

May this "Grace of Guile" be dear to the good:
Made up of amusements,
merry with the art of wide smiles,
a bright lamp on the inner workings of all dispositions,
meant as instruction for the public
relieved by edifying tales.

May the "Grace of Guile,"
which has come forth
from the ocean of Ksheméndra's talent,
ever delight the minds of the good,
as does the moon.

The tenth canto,
named the description of all arts,
in the "Grace of Guile" composed by
the great poet Kshemméndra.

NILA·KANTHA: MOCKERY OF THE KALI ERA

PAṆḌITĀḤ

Na bhetavyaṃ na boddhavyaṃ
na śrāvyaṃ vādino vacaḥ
jhaṭiti prativaktavyaṃ sabhāsu vijigīṣubhiḥ!
Asaṃbhramo, vilajjatvam, avajñā prativādini,
hāso, rājñaḥ stavaś c' êti pañc' âite jaya|hetavaḥ.

Uccair udghoṣya jetavyaṃ madhya|sthaś ced apaṇḍitaḥ
paṇḍito yadi tatr' âiva pakṣa|pāto 'dhiropyatām.
Lobho hetur dhanaṃ sādhyaṃ dṛṣṭāntas tu purohitaḥ
ātm"|ôtkarṣo nigamanam anumāneṣv ayaṃ vidhiḥ.

5 Abhyāsyaṃ lajjamānena tattvaṃ jijñāsunā ciram
jigīṣuṇā hriyaṃ tyaktvā kāryaḥ kolāhalo mahān.
Pāṭhanair grantha|nirmāṇaiḥ pratiṣṭhā tāvad āpyate
evam ca tathya|vyutpattir āyuṣo 'nte bhaven na vā?

Stotāraḥ ke bhaviṣyanti mūrkhasya jagatī|tale?
na stauti cet svayaṃ ca svaṃ kadā tasy' âstu nirvṛtiḥ?
«Vācyatāṃ! samayo 'tītaḥ. spaṣṭam agre bhaviṣyati.»
iti pāṭhayatāṃ granthe kāṭhinyaṃ kutra vartate?
Agatitvam atiśraddhā jñān'|ābhāsena tṛptatā
trayaḥ śiṣya|guṇā hy ete mūrkh'|ācāryasya bhāgya|jāḥ.

MĀNTRIKĀḤ

10 Yadi na kv' âpi vidyāyāṃ sarvathā kramate matiḥ
māntrikās tu bhaviṣyāmo yogino yatayo 'pi vā.
Avilambena saṃsiddhau māntrikair āpyate yaśaḥ
vilambe karma|bāhulyaṃ vikhyāpy' âvāpyate dhanam.

ACADEMICS

If you want to triumph in a meeting, do not be afraid, do not pay attention, do not listen to the opponent's arguments,—just immediately contradict them! Unflappability, shamelessness, contempt for the adversary, derision, and praise of the king: these five are the grounds of victory.

If the arbitrator is not learned, one wins by shouting. If he is learned one has only to insinuate bias: "Greed" is the premise, "money" is the probandum, "the priest" is the example, "personal advance" is the result: such is the correct syllogistic procedure.*

The humble seeker after wisdom must ponder the truth 5
for a long time; the careerist has to set aside modesty and cause a great commotion. A reputation is above all won by composing works and by teaching; and might perhaps even true erudition be achieved in this manner before the end of life, or not?

Who, on this earth, will praise a fool? Were he not to praise his own work, could he ever be happy? "Read on! We are behind time. It will become clear further on,"—with such a method of teaching, what could prove difficult in a text? Resourcelessness, excessive faith, satisfaction with the appearance of knowledge—these three qualities in a student are a blessing for a dimwitted teacher.

SORCERERS*

Should our intellect absolutely fail to penetrate any sci- 10
ence at all, then we can always become mantra-sorcerers, yogins, or ascetics. When success is immediate, mantra-

Sukhaṃ sukhiṣu duḥkhaṃ ca jīvanaṃ duḥkha|śāliṣu
anugrahāyate yeṣāṃ te dhanyāḥ khalu māntrikāḥ.
Yāvad ajñānato maunam ācāro vā vilakṣaṇaḥ
tāvan māhātmya|rūpeṇa paryavasyati māntrike.

JYAUTIṢIKĀḤ

Cārān vicārya daiva|jñair vaktavyaṃ bhūbhujāṃ phalam
graha|cāra|parijñānaṃ teṣām āvaśyakaṃ yataḥ.
15 «Putra ity» eva pitari «kanyak" êty» eva mātari
garbha|praśneṣu kathayan daiva|jño vijayī bhavet.
Āyuḥ|praśne dīrgham āyur vācyaṃ mauhūrtikair janaiḥ
jīvanto bahu|manyante mṛtāḥ prakṣyanti kaṃ punaḥ?
Sarvaṃ koṭi|dvay'|ôpetaṃ sarvaṃ kāla|dvay'|âvadhi
sarvaṃ vyāmiśram iva ca vaktavyaṃ daiva|cintakaiḥ.
Nirdhanānāṃ dhan'|âvāptiṃ dhaninām adhikaṃ dhanam
bruvāṇāḥ sarvathā grāhyā lokair jyautiṣikā janāḥ.
Śatasya lābhe tāmbūlaṃ sahasrasya tu bhojanam
daiva|jñānām upālambho nityaḥ kārya|viparyaye.
20 Api sāgara|paryantā vicetavyā vasun|dharā
deśo hy aratni|mātre 'pi n' âsti daiva|jña|varjitaḥ.
Vārān ke cid grahān ke cit ke cid ṛkṣāṇi jānante
tritayaṃ ye vijānanti te vācas|patayaḥ svayam.

sorcerers become celebrities; when there is a delay, exorbitant rituals are prognosticated and they make money.

Blessed indeed are mantra-sorcerers, whose livelihood benefits from both the happiness of the well-off and the misery of the wretched. Provided the sorcerer keeps quiet in his ignorance or adopts bizarre behavior, his greatness is ensured.

ASTROLOGERS

Because insight gained from the movements *(cāra)* of the planets is indispensable for them, astrologers announce a prediction to the king after consulting spies *(cāra)*.

When asked about a pregnancy, the astrologer wins if he tells the father: "A son!" and the mother: "A daughter!" When asked about the length of life, the astrologer predicts a long life. Those who survive will be in awe of him. Who will the dead call to account?

Astrologers should say that everything has two sides, everything happens within two time-limits, and everything appears to be in flux. The people will always welcome astrologers who predict a gain of wealth to the impoverished, and even more wealth to the wealthy. For a predicted gain of a hundred, an astrologer earns some betelnut, for a predicted gain of a thousand a meal, and for a predicted fiasco eternal censure.

One may scour the earth up to the edge of the sea, but nowhere is there even a single ell of land free from astrologers. Some know the days, some the planets, some the constellations,—those who know all three are veritable Vachas·patis.* Fortune-tellers, interpreters of dreams, and

Naimittikāḥ svapna|dṛśo devat"|ôpāsakā iti
nisarga|śatravaḥ sṛṣṭā daiva|jñānām amī trayaḥ.

BHIṢAJAḤ

Svasthair asādhya|rogaiś ca jantubhir n' âsti kiṃ cana
kātarā dīrgha|rogāś ca bhiṣajāṃ bhāgya|hetavaḥ.
N' âtidhairyaṃ pradātavyaṃ n' âtibhītiś ca rogiṇi
naiścintyān n' ādime dānaṃ nairāśyād eva n' ântime.

25 Bhaiṣajyaṃ tu yathā|kāmaṃ pathyaṃ tu kaṭhinaṃ vadet
ārogyaṃ vaidya|māhātmyād anyathātvam apathyataḥ.

Nidānaṃ roga|nāmāni sātmy'|âsātmye cikitsitam
sarvam apy upadekṣyanti rogiṇaḥ sadane striyaḥ.
Jṛmbhamāṇeṣu rogeṣu mriyamāṇeṣu jantuṣu
roga|tattveṣu śanakair vyutpadyante cikitsakāḥ.

Pravartan'|ârtham ārambhe madhye tv auṣadha|hetave
bahu|mān'|ârtham ante ca jihīrṣanti cikitsakāḥ.
Lipsamāneṣu vaidyeṣu cirād āsādya rogiṇam
dāyādāḥ saṃprarohanti daiva|jñā māntrikā api.

30 Rogasy' ôpakrame sāntvaṃ
madhye kiṃ|cid|dhana|vyayaḥ
śanair anādaraḥ śāntau
snāto vaidyaṃ na paśyati.

priests;* these three natural enemies have been created for astrologers.

PHYSICIANS

The healthy and the terminally ill are of no interest, doctors thrive on hypochondriacs and those suffering from chronic diseases. The patient must neither be given too much hope nor too much fear. In the first case he will not pay up because he has no worry, in the second because he has no hope. .

A doctor prescribes medicine ad libitum, but insists on 25
a difficult, meager diet. If health is restored it is by the greatness of the physician, if not, the dietary regimen was not followed.

Pathology, diagnostic, what is agreeable and disagreeable, treatment,—the women in the patient's house will instruct him in all.* As epidemics spread, as people succumb, doctors learn, eventually, about the nature of diseases.*

Initially to make a housecall, in the interim for medicine, at the end out of gratitude,—physicians demand payment. When doctors, greedy for money, have at last secured a patient, two co-inheritors pop up: the astrologer and the mantra-sorcerer.*

At the onset of the disease the patient shows him kind- 30
ness, in the middle stage he parts with some money, as health returns he looses interest in him, after the bath of convalescense the physician has become a *persona non grata*.

KAVAYAḤ

Daiva|jñatvaṃ māntrikatā bhaiṣajyaṃ cāṭu|kauśalam
ek'|âikam artha|lābhāya dvi|tri|yogas tu durlabhaḥ.
Anṛtaṃ cāṭu|vādaś ca dhana|yogo mahān ayam
satyaṃ vaiduṣyam ity eṣa yogo dāridrya|kārakaḥ.
Kātaryaṃ durvinītatvaṃ kārpaṇyam avivekatām
sarvaṃ mārjanti kavayaḥ śālīnāṃ muṣṭi|kiṃkarāḥ.
Na kāraṇam apekṣante kavayaḥ stotum udyatāḥ
kiṃ cid astuvatām teṣāṃ jihvā phuraphurāyate.
Stutaṃ stuvanti kavayo na svato guṇa|darśinaḥ
kītaḥ kaś cid «aliḥ» nāma—kiyatī tatra varṇanā?
Ek" âiva kavitā puṃsāṃ grāmāy' âśvāya hastine
antato 'nnāya vastrāya tāmbūlāya ca kalpate.
Śabd'|ākhyam aparaṃ Brahma saṃdarbheṇa pariṣkṛtam
vikrīyate katipayair vṛth" ânyair viniyujyate.
Varṇayanti nar'|ābhāsān Vāṇīṃ labdhv" âpi ye janāḥ
labdhv" âpi kāma|dhenuṃ te lāṅgale viniyuñjate.
Praśaṃsanto nar'|ābhāsān pralapanto 'nyath" ânyathā
kathaṃ tarantu kavayaḥ kāma|pāramya|vādinaḥ?.
Yat sandarbhe yad ullekhe yad vyaṅgye nibhṛtaṃ manaḥ
samādher api taj jyāyāḥ Śaṅkaro yadi varṇyate.

POETS

Astrology, sorcery, medicine, skill in flattery: each on its own is profitable, but it is rare to find two or three together. Dishonesty and flattery are a great conjunction auguring wealth; the conjunction of honesty and erudition leads to poverty. Cowardice, barbarity, avarice, and lack of judgment, poets can expunge it all, hirelings for a handful of rice. Poets, poised to praise, require no reason: when they are not praising something their tongues vibrate. Poets praise what is already praised, they are not in fact appreciative of virtues: there is a gnat called "bee," —and what poetic labor is wasted in its portrayal?

"Unique" is the poetry which men compose in return for a village, for a horse, an elephant, when it comes to it for a meal, for clothing, for some betel. The second Brahman called "Speech," arranged beautifully in poetic composition, is peddled by some, is squandered in vain by others. These wretches who, attaining the Goddess "Speech," abuse her to eulogise would-be heroes, they might even yoke a wish-granting cow to the plow!

Praising reprobates, twisting everything with their prattle, how can poets find salvation, professing that desire is supreme?* Captive attention on whatever composition, on whatever description, on whatever suggestion, is superior to meditative trance, if Shiva is the topic.

BANDHAVAḤ

Gṛhiṇī bhaginī tasyāḥ śvaśurau śyāla ity api
prāṇinām kalinā sṛṣṭāḥ pañca prāṇā ime 'pare.
Jāmātaro bhāgineyā mātulā dāra|bāndhavāḥ
ajñātā eva gṛhiṇāṃ bhakṣayanty ākhu|vad gṛhe.
Mātulasya balaṃ mātā jāmātur duhitā balam
śvaśurasya balaṃ bhāryā svayam ev' âtither balam.
Jāmātur vakratā tāvad yāvac chyālasya bālatā
prabudhyamāne sāralyaṃ prabuddhe 'smin palāyanam.
Bhāryā jyeṣṭhā śiśuḥ śyālaḥ śvaśrūḥ svātantrya|vartinī
śvaśuras tu pravās" îti jāmātur bhāgya|dhoraṇī.*.
Bhūṣaṇair vāsanaiḥ pātraiḥ putrāṇām upalālanaiḥ
sakṛd āgatya gacchantī kanyā nirmārṣṭi mandiram.
Gṛhiṇī sva|janaṃ vakti śuṣk'|āhāraṃ mit'|āśanam
pati|pakṣyān tu bahv|āśān kṣīra|pāṃs taskarān api.
Bhārye dve putra|śālinyau bhaginī pati|varjitā
aśrānta|kalaho nāma yogo 'yaṃ gṛha|medhinām.
Bhārye dve bahavaḥ putrā dāridryaṃ roga|saṃbhavaḥ
jīrṇau ca mātā|pitarav ek'|âikaṃ narak'|âdhikam.

UTTAMA'|RṆĀḤ

Smṛte sīdanti gātrāṇi, dṛṣṭe prajñā vinaśyati
aho! mahad idaṃ bhūtam uttama|rṇ'|âbhiśābditam.
Antako 'pi hi jantūnām anta|kālam apekṣate
na kāla|niyamaḥ kaś cid uttama|rṇasya vidyate.

RELATIVES

A wife, her sister, her parents, and the brother-in-law: these five additional vital breaths Kali has created for men. Sons-in-law, nephews, maternal uncles, the in-laws, feed in the house-holder's home like rats without his knowledge. The mother is the power behind the maternal uncle, the daughter is the power behind the sons-in-law, the wife is the power behind the father-in-law, the guest is his own power. While the son-in-law is young—the brother-in-law is deceitful; when he begins to understand—he is forthright; when he has grown to understand—he takes flight.

A wife who is the eldest daughter, a brother-in-law who is a child, a wilful mother-in-law, a father-in-law abroad, this is an easy ride for the son-in-law. In just one visit, a daughter departs with jewellery, garments, vessels, and children's toys,—pillaging the home.

A wife claims that her parents eat dry scraps, sparingly, but that her husband's parents are gluttons, drink milk, or may even be thieves. Two wives blessed with many children, and a sister without husband: this is a conjunction called "incessant quarrel" for the house-holder. Two wives, many children, poverty, disease, an aged father and mother, each one is worse than hell.

MONEY-LENDERS

When he is remembered, the limbs hang loose, when he is seen, the spirit perishes. Lo! Mighty is the wraith called "money-lender." Even Death awaits the last days of creatures, but a money-lender is not bound by time. We cannot detect a fang in his mouth, nor a noose in his fist, never-

Na paśyāmo mukhe daṃṣṭrāṃ na pāśaṃ vā kar'|âñjale
uttama|rṇam avekṣy' âiva tath" âpy udvejite manaḥ.

DĀRIDRYAM

Śatrau sāntvaṃ pratīkāraḥ sarva|rogeṣu bheṣajam
mṛtyau Mṛtyuñ|jaya|dhyānaṃ dāridrye tu na kiṃ cana.
Śaktiṃ karoti saṃcāre śīt'|ôṣṇe marṣayaty api
dīpayaty udare vahniṃ dāridryaṃ param'|âuṣadham.
Giraṃ skhalantīṃ mīlantīṃ dṛṣṭiṃ pādau visaṃsthulau
protsāhayati yācñāyāṃ rāj'|ājñ" êva daridratā.
Jīryanti rāja|vidveṣā jīryanty avihitāny api
ākiṃcanya|bal'|āḍhyānām antato 'śm" âpi jīryati.
N' âsya corā na piśunā na dāyādā na pārthivāḥ
dainyaṃ rājyād api jyāyo yadi tattvaṃ prabudhyate.

DHANINAḤ

Prakāśayaty ahaṃkāraṃ pravartayati taskarān
protsāhayati dāyādāl̄ lakṣmīḥ kiṃ|cid|upasthitā.
Viḍambayanti ye nityaṃ vidagdhān dhanino janāḥ
ta eva tu viḍambyante śriyā kiṃ|cid|upekṣitāḥ.
Prāmāṇya|buddhiḥ stotreṣu devatā|buddhir ātmani
kīṭa|buddhir manuṣyeṣu nūtanāyāḥ śriyaḥ phalam.
Śṛṇvanta eva pṛcchanti paśyanto 'pi na jānate
viḍambanāni dhanikāḥ stotrāṇ' îty eva manvate.
Āvṛtya śrī|maden' ândhān anyo'|nya|kṛta|saṃvidaḥ
svairaṃ hasanti pārśva|sthā bāl'|ônmatta|piśāca|vat.

theless, as soon as the money-lender is spotted the heart convulses.

POVERTY

Against an enemy peace-negotiations are the remedy, there is a medicine for every disease, to ward off death there is the Mrityuñ·jaya mantra, but against poverty there is nothing. It gives one the strength to make one's rounds, even makes heat and cold bearable, kindles the digestive fire,—poverty is the ultimate medicament.

Stammering words, lowered eyes, tottering feet—poverty spurs one on to beg as does a royal condemnation. Those abounding in utter destitution can digest the contempt of the king, they can digest what is beyond the pale, and in the end they can even digest stones. For him there are no thieves, no denouncers, no inheritors, no kings,—poverty is superior to kingship if seen for what it is.

THE RICH

A slight increase in prosperity heightens egoism, encourages thieves, and emboldens inheritors. But the rich who always belittle the learned, are themselves derided when fortune no longer smiles upon them. Believing flattery to be fact, considering oneself divine, thinking common people to be worms,—such is the result of new money.

Though they can hear they moot the question, though they see they do not understand, the rich take even mockery to be praise. Hangers-on, colluding with each other in secret, laugh freely at those blind with the intoxication of wealth, as if they were children, deranged or demonically possessed.*

Stotavyaiḥ stūyate nityaṃ sevanīyaiś ca sevyate
na bibheti na jihreti tath" âpi dhaniko janaḥ.
Kṣaṇa|mātraṃ grah'|āveśo yāma|mātraṃ surā|madaḥ
lakṣmī|madas tu mūrkhāṇām ā|deham anuvartate.
65 Śrīr māsam ardha|māsaṃ vā ceṣṭitvā vinivartate
vikāras tu tad|ārabdho nityo laśuna|gandha|vat.

Kaṇṭhe madaḥ kodrava|jo hṛdi tāmbūla|jo madaḥ
lakṣmī|madas tu sarv'|âṅge putra|dāra|mukheṣv api.
Yatr' āsīd asti vā lakṣmīs tatr' ônmadaḥ pravartatām
kule 'py avataraty eṣa kuṣṭh'|âpasmāra|vat katham?
Adhyāpayanti śāstrāṇi tṛṇī|kurvanti paṇḍitān
vismārayanti jātiṃ svāṃ varāṭāḥ pañcaṣā kare

Bibhartu bhṛtyān dhaniko dattāṃ vā deyam arthiṣu
yāvad yācaka|sādharmyaṃ tāval loko na mṛṣyati.

PIŚUNĀḤ

70 Dhana|bhāro hi lokasya piśunair eva dhāryate
kathaṃ te taṃ laghū|kartuṃ yatante 'parathā svataḥ?
Śram'|ânurūpaṃ piśune kim upakriyate nṛpaiḥ?
dvi|guṇaṃ tri|guṇaṃ v" âpi Kṛt'|ânto lālayiṣyati.

He is ever lauded by those he ought to praise, he is served by those deserving his service, despite this the wealthy man knows no fear and no shame. Possession by an astrological demon lasts but a moment, drunkenness lasts for a watch, but the foolish are intoxicated with wealth for as long as
the body endures. The goddess of wealth lends a helping 65
hand for a month or perhaps for half a month and then withdraws, but the change she brings to pass lasts for ever, like the stench of garlic.

The inflammation wrought by ditch millet* numbs the throat, betel-nut stuns the heart, but the stupor caused by wealth affects the whole body, even the faces of wives and children. It makes sense that delirium afflicts someone who once was or still is wealthy, but how can it spread in a family, like leprosy or epilepsy? Five or six small coins in the hand give licence to lecture on science, consider the learned as chaff, let one forget one's caste.

The wealthy man may support his dependents, may give charity to beggars, but as soon as he looks like he might ask for a favor, nobody will suffer his presence.

INFORMERS

Surely, the world's burden of wealth is borne by informers 70
alone; otherwise why are they striving all by themselves to lighten it? Does the king compensate the informer with a reward appropriate to his effort? Twice, and even three times more, Death will care for him.

Go|karṇe Bhadra|karṇe ca japo duṣkarma|nāśanaḥ
rāja|karṇe japaḥ sadyaḥ sarva|karma|vināśanaḥ.
Na sv'|ârthaṃ kiṃ cid icchanti na preryante ca kena cit
par'|ârtheṣu pravartante śaṭhāḥ santaś ca tulya|vat.
Kāl'|ântare hy anarthāya gṛdhro geh'|ôpari sthitaḥ
khalo gṛha|samīpa|sthaḥ sadyo 'narthāya dehinām.

LOBHINAḤ

75 Śuṣk'|ôpavāso dharmeṣu bhaiṣajyeṣu ca laṅghanam
japa|yajñaś ca yajñeṣu rocate lobha|śālinām.
«Kiṃ vakṣyat' îti?» dhanikād yāvad udvijate 'dhanaḥ
«kiṃ prakṣyat' îti?» lubdho 'pi tāvad udvijate tataḥ.
Sarvam ātithya|śāstr'|ârthaṃ sākṣāt kurvanti lobhinaḥ
bhikṣā|kavalam ek'|âikaṃ ye hi paśyanti Meru|vat.
Dhana|pālaḥ piśāco hi datte svāminy upasthite
dhana|lubdhaḥ piśācas tu na kasmai cana ditsate.
Dātāro 'rthibhir arthyante dātṛbhiḥ punar arthinaḥ
kartṛ|karma|vyatīhārād aho nimn'|ônnataṃ kiyat!
80 «Svasminn asati n' ârthasya rakṣakaḥ saṃbhaved iti»
niścity' âivaṃ svayam api bhuṅkte lubdhaḥ kathaṃ cana.
Prasthāsyamānaḥ praviśet pratiṣṭheta dine dine
vicitrān ullikhed vighnāṃs tiṣṭhāsur atithiś ciram.

Murmuring mantras at the sacred fords called "Cow-ear" and "Lucky-ear" annihilates past misdeeds. Murmuring into the king's ear at once annihilates all deeds. *They have no interest in their own affairs, they cannot be guided by anyone, they meddle in other people's business*, the wicked as well as the good, *who for themselves want nothing, are not goaded by anyone else, and act from the highest motives.* It seems a vulture perched on the house is an omen for some future disaster, but a villain loitering near the house heralds immediate doom.

THE AVARICIOUS

The avaricious favor the meager fast among religious ob- 75
servances, starving the system among medical cures, murmured prayers among sacrifices. Just as the pauper dreads the rich: "What will he say?" so the avaricious dreads the pauper: "What will he ask for?" The avaricious directly perceive the scriptural teaching* concerning hospitality, for they perceive each mouthful of almsfood to be like Mt. Meru.

The demon "treasurer" gives when his lord arrives, the demon "miser" wants to give to nobody whomsoever. The charitable are implored by the needy, then the needy by the charitable. Lo! in this reversal of subject and object,—what ups and downs!

Reasoning in this way: "If I were no longer alive, there 80
would be no guardian for my wealth," the miser somehow forces himself to eat. Day by day, on the verge of departing,* he comes back in and stays put, pointing out all manner of impediments,—he is a guest eager to draw out his visit.

DHĀRMIKĀḤ

Pradīyate viduṣy ekaṃ, kavau daśa, naṭe śatam
sahasraṃ dāmbhike loke śrotriye tu na kiṃ cana.
Ghaṭakaṃ samyag ārādhya vairāgyaṃ paramaṃ vahet
tāvad arthāḥ prasiddhyanti yāvac cāpalam āvṛtam.

«Ekataḥ sarva|śāstrāṇi tulasī|kāṣṭham ekataḥ»
vaktavyaṃ kiṃ cid ity uktaṃ vastutas tulasī parā.
Vismṛtaṃ Vāhaṭen' êdaṃ tulasyāḥ paṭhatā guṇān
viśva|saṃmohinī vitta|dāyin" îti guṇa|dvayam.
Kaupīnaṃ bhasit'|ālepo darbhā rudr'|âkṣa|mālikā
maunam ek'|āsikā c' êti mūrkha|saṃjīvanāni ṣaṭ.

Vāsaḥ puṇyeṣu tīrtheṣu prasiddhaś ca mṛto guruḥ
adhyāpan'|āvṛttayaś ca kīrtanīyā dhan'|ârthibhiḥ.
Mantra|bhraṃśe saṃpradāyaḥ prayogaś cyuta|saṃskṛtau
deśa|dharmas tv anācāre pṛcchatāṃ siddham uttaram.
Yathā jānanti bahavo yathā vakṣyanti dātari
tathā dharmaṃ caret sarvaṃ na vṛthā kiṃ cid ācaret.
Sadā japa|paṭo haste madhye madhye 'kṣi|mīlanam
«sarvaṃ Brahm' êti» vādaś ca sadyaḥ|pratyaya|hetavaḥ.
Ā|madhy'|âhnaṃ nadī|vāsaḥ samāje devat"|ârcanam
santataṃ śuci|veṣaś c' êty etad dambhasya jīvitam.
Tāvad dīrghaṃ nitya|karma yāvat syād draṣṭṛ|melanam
tāvat saṃkṣipyate sarvaṃ yāvad draṣṭā na vidyate.

THE PIOUS

One gives one to the learned, ten to the poet, a hundred to the actor, a thousand to the horde of sanctimonious hypocrites, but nothing to the orthodox brahmin.* After petitioning the pimp,* one should show off extreme austerity. Fortunes are gained, as long as the duplicity remains concealed.

"On the one hand there are all the scriptures, on the other there is the wood of the holy basil. "* This is just a
figure of speech: in reality holy basil is supreme. Váhata,* 85
enumerating the properties of the holy basil, had forgotten this pair of properties: the power of universal delusion and the ability to provide wealth. A loin-cloth, a dusting of ash, sacred *darbha*-grass, a rosary of *rudráksha* beads, a vow of silence, and sitting in solitude,*—six are the livelihoods of the fool.

Lodging at sacred fords, a famous but dead guru, repeated cycles of teaching, these are valued among people on the make. When the mantra is wrong, it is "a tradition," when there are lapses in the rites, it is "an applied procedure," when the comportment is improper, it is "a local custom"—this is the effective answer to those who protest. All religion should be practised so that many know of it, so that they report it to a donor; do nothing pointlessly.
The rosary-veil ever in hand, closing the eyes from time to 90
time, prattling that "everything is Brahman," these are the causes for instant confidence.* Loitering by the river until midday, worshipping the gods in public gatherings, always wearing a religious costume, this is the life of hypocrisy.

Ānanda|bāṣpa|romāñcau yasya svecchā|vaśaṃ|vadau
kiṃ tasya sādhanair anyaiḥ—kiṃkarāḥ sarva|pārthivāḥ.

DURJANĀḤ

Daṇḍyamānā vikurvanti lālyamānās tatas tarām.
durjanānām ato nyāyyaṃ dūrād eva visarjanam.

Adānam īṣad|dānaṃ ca kiṃ|cit|kopāya durdhiyām
saṃpūrṇa|dānaṃ prakṛtir virāmo vaira|kāraṇam.

Jyāyān asaṃstavo duṣṭair īrṣyāyai saṃstavaḥ punaḥ
apatya|saṃbandha|vidhiḥ sv'|ânarthāy' âiva kevalam.

Jñāteyaṃ jñāna|hīnatvaṃ piśunatvaṃ daridratā
milanti yadi catvāri tad diśe 'pi namo namaḥ.

Para|chidreṣu hṛdayaṃ para|vārtāsu ca śravaḥ
para|*marmāsu* vācaṃ ca khalānām asṛjad vidhiḥ.

Viṣeṇa puccha|lagnena vṛścikaḥ prāṇinām iva
Kalinā daśam'|âṃśena sarvaḥ Kālo 'pi dāruṇaḥ.

Yatra bhāryā|giro Vedā yatra dharmo 'rtha|sādhanam
yatra sva|pratibhā mānaṃ tasmai śrī|Kalaye namaḥ!

Kāmam astu jagat sarvaṃ Kālasy' âsya Vaśaṃ|vadam
Kāla|kālaṃ prapannānāṃ Kālaḥ kiṃ naḥ kariṣyati?
Kavinā Nīlakaṇṭhena Kaler etad viḍambanam
racitaṃ viduṣāṃ prītyai rājāsthān'|ânumodanam.

Long-winded daily ritual while there is a crowd of onlookers—when nobody is watching all is abbreviated.

For one who can shed tears of bliss and whose hair stands on end at will, what need is there for other practices,—all kings are his lackeys.

THE WICKED

Punishment makes them worse, kindness even more so.
Therefore, for the wicked the rule is distant exile. Giving 95
nothing and giving little provokes the anger of the evil-minded just somewhat. They take giving to satiety for granted, a cessation of gifts turns them rabid. Better no dealings with the wicked, familiarity engenders their jealousy. A marital alliance with their offspring leads only to ruin.

Family, ignorance, slander, poverty, if these four meet in the same person, then "Hail to the horizon."*

The creator fashioned the heart of the wicked for the *bodily openings : failings* of others, their ear for the rumors of others, and their voice for the vulnerable points* of others.

Just as the whole scorpion terrifies living beings with the poison lodged in its tail, so the whole of Time terrifies
living beings with its tenth part, the Kali era. Hail to the 100
glorious Kali era, where the words of the wife are the Veda, where religion is a means to making money, where one's own fantasy is the law!

Granted, the world may be under the sway of this era, but what can Time do to us who are sheltered by the Slayer of Time, Shiva? The poet Nila·kantha composed this Mockery of Kali for the delight of the learned and the pleasure of royal court.

NOTES

Bold *references are to the English text;* ***bold italic*** *references are to the Sanskrit text. An asterisk (*) in the body of the text marks the word or passage being annotated. Bh= "The Hundred Allegories of Bhállata"; G= "The Grace of Guile"; M= "Mockery of the Kali Era"*

Bh 1 **Shárada** is the patron Goddess of Kashmir, often identified with Sarásvati, the Goddess of eloquence.

Bh 2 The commentary of Maheśvara [Mah] notes that such face-reddening was customary at the celebrations for the birth of sons.

Bh 4 Mah: *te 'nye dehino (hastacara)ṇādyavayavasya śarīrabhārasya voḍhāra eva,* "They are mere bearers of the burden of the body with its limbs such as hands and feet etc."

Bh 5 Mah: "If a wicked person attains a minor position he strives to rise higher and higher."

Bh 6c ***abhyupakāra°*** can mean both "embellishment" and "assistance, usefulness."

Bh 9 Maheśvara comments: *dinānte svatejo ravir nikṣipatīti lokavādah,* "It is popularly believed that the sun deposits its brilliance into fire at the end of the day."

Bh 9 The alleged misdemeanours of the sun punningingly describe the antics of a drunkard. It may be possible to read *loka* as having a second sense of "light" too but that struck me as weak.

Bh 16 **Faint of light**: the unexpressed second subject is the ignoramus scholar and his "trifling knowledge."

Bh 17 Mah: *dhīraṃ dhīra eva vetti na mūrkhaḥ,* "Only the brave have profound experiences, not fools."

Bh 18 The commentator Mahéshvara explains the intended sense as follows: *etad uktaṃ bhavati: manasvī mānaṃ vihāyāvanatiṃ karoti cet sarvatra loke sulabham eva jīvanaṃ, tathāpi manasvī na karoty avanatiṃ maraṇam eva kartum adhyavasyatīti,* "This is what is meant: If a learned man were to give up his pride and humble himself, he could easily get a living anywhere. If a learned man, despite this does not humble himself, then he is determined to die." A.A. RAMANATHAN translates as follows in the MaSuSaṃ: "Let the young cātaka bird cultivate friendship with one who holds his head high like himself, for, if he is so inclined, where will water pure, cool and sweet, not be available in the broad expanse of the sky." This implies that he had read *svasyeva* but did not correct the text.

Bh 21 **One-eyed** crows are believed to roll their single eye from one side of their head to the other.

Bh 23 **Lotus-stalk:** Secondarily, *kamala / nālasya* shifts its sense to something like "scion of the Kamala dynasty."

Bh 25 *Subhāṣitāvalī* 922. This verse is not commented on by Maheśvara. Lakṣmī, the Goddess of fortune, is in this verse portrayed as a fickle woman fearing her beauty would be outshone by the lotus.

Bh 31 *Intertwining venomous serpents* through secondary indication *(lakṣaṇā)* needs to shift its sense to something like: "is beholden to evil men who have made pacts with each other." I could not produce this required sense by punning alone *(śleṣa)*.

Bh 32 **Khádira:** =*Acacia Catechu,* an ugly, thorny hardwood tree.

Bh 45 The sage Agastya who drank the whole ocean.

Bh 48 My translation avoids the technical terminology of Sanskrit philosophy used here. An *upādhi* is a "limiting adjunct," a mark which lies somewhere between a "property" *(dharma)* or "characteristic" *(lakṣaṇa)*, and an "adventitious mark" *(upalakṣaṇa)*. It serves to distinguish objects it qualifies but need not perdure until the action it is involved in is completed. The commonly given example is that of a row of crystals *(sphaṭika)* placed before a row of china-rose blossoms *(japākusuma)*. The colour transmitted to the crystal by the blossom serves to distinguish the crystals, but once a crystal is selected and removed the colour vanishes.

Bh 51 **Electric tourmaline:** Sometimes known as the "electric stone," tourmaline becomes statically charged when heated or rubbed, attracting dust, bits of straw etc. The word tourmaline itself is derived from *tṛṇa/maṇi*.

Bh 65 Mahéshvara explains this apparent paradox by the fact that the eyes do not function at night and are thus debased to the state of all the other organs, yet they are not the same because the other organs still function in the dark.

Bh 66 **Tourmaline:** See note to 51.

Bh 88 The sage Agástya.

Bh 88 *Ghasmara:* Mahéshvara takes this either as the submarine fire or as Samhára·rudra. I follow GAI in taking it as an adjective describing Agástya.

Bh 89 Read *jala* for *jaḍa* in this pun.

Bh 98 The verse alludes to the tales of "Víkrama and the vampire."

Káustubha: Vishnu bears on his chest the fabulous Kaustubha jewel, churned from ocean of milk, *cf.* *Rāmāyaṇa* 1.44.24.

G 1.2 **Śeṣa:** The world-serpent Śeṣa or Ananta bears the earth at the behest of Brahmā, *cf.* *Mahābhārata* 1.32.18–24. *Vibhajya*: This is appropriate, for Shesha is said to have one thousand heads.

G 1.3 **Gleam:** *virājati*. This *Parasmaipada* form of the root *rāj* with the prefix *vi-* is not a grammatical lapse on Kshemēndra's part. The form is attested in the *Chāndogyopaniṣad*, the *Mahābhārata* and the *Rāmāyaṇa*.

G 1.4 **God of love:** Kshemēndra is alluding to Śiva's destruction of the God of love with the fire shooting from his third eye (*Brahmapurāṇa* 36.1–135 etc.). See *Kumārasambhava* 1–8 for the most attractive retelling of this episode.

G 1.7 *Dhārāgṛha:* sometimes also described as "shower-rooms," *cf.* Mallinātha to *Meghadūta* 1.64.

G 1.8 *Apsarases* are celestial nymphs of surpassing beauty born from the churning of the ocean by the Gods and Asuras, *cf. Rāmāyaṇa* 1.44.18ef; *Agnipurāṇa* 3; *Nāṭyaśāstra* 1.45ff.

G 1.9 **Mula·deva:** A legendary rogue, see BLOOMFIELD (1917:619ff.).

G 1.10 **Remote lands:** This is reminiscent of the opening of the Prakrit Dhuttakhāṇa of Haribhadra (*fl.* late eighth to early ninth cent.) where hundreds of rogues headed by Mūlasirī (Mūlaśrī= Mūladeva), Kaṇḍarīa, Elāsāḍha, Sasa, Khaṇḍavaṇā, gather in a garden pavilion outside Ujjainī. For the very similar virtues of the ideal emperor who receives tribute from distant feudatories, see *Arthaśāstra* 6.1.6.

G 1.11 *Sahṛdaya*: a sensitive reader of poetry, or person of refined taste. Such connoisseurship is defined as 'the ability of attaining identity with the heart of the poet' (*Abhinavabhāratī* vol. 2 p. 339: *kavihṛdayatādātmyāpattiyogyatā*).

G 1.13 **Bṛhaspati:** The preceptor of the Gods and also the name of the author of the root-text of the Cārvāka materialists, the *Bṛhaspatisūtra*.

G 1.16 The stages of life parody verses such as *Vairāgyaśataka* 50, where it is life itself that is uncertain, even in the midst of wealth. The simile of water on lotus-leaves/petals is a distortion of *Bhagavadgītā* 5.10. See also *Deśopadeśa* 3.28.

G 1.18 **Dhūrtakarakandukānām:** A gambling game? LAPANICH believes this to be *kandukakrīḍā* a "game famous among boys and girls." Sanskrit poets often describe the graceful ball-play of young ladies (see LIENHARD (1999:403–418)) but this seems rather inappropriate here and I thus consider emending to *dhūrtakarakaṇṭakānāṃ*, e.g. the "fingernails of villains" with a transferred sense of: "there is no release from the clutches of villains."

G 1.25 Ked glosses: *timirasamūha eva hastī*, e.g. a metaphor *(rūpaka)*: "the elephant who was a mass of darkness." *Cf.* also *Śiśupālavadha* 4.20. The mountain-elephant simile is appropriate because the eight points of the compass are believed to be supported by elephants. The name of the western elephant is Añjana. This in itself alludes to the famous Añjanādri, Mountain of Antimony, *cf. Kathāsaritsāgara* VIII,108. *Mātaṅga:* from *Dvirada* by *lakṣaṇā*. Punningly we may read the verse as: "When the man who occupied her days had gone to sleep, lady Sandhyā's chest shone, as if with the pale red lustre of a vermillion body-paste because she was embracing an extremely dark-skinned outcaste."

G 1.26 The tragic love of the sun and twilight is a popular topos among Sanskrit poets, *cf. Dhvanyāloka* 1.13e, 3.34.

G 1.30 **Night-maker:** The moon.

G 1.30 **chakravaki:** The shelldrake, or brahmany duck. It is a Kāvya convention that monogamous shelldrake *(cakravāka)* couples are doomed to spend each night in separation, calling out to each other with plaintive cries.

G 1.31 **Ladies of the compass points:** *digvanitā*. The eight points of the compass *(āśā, diś)* are in Sanskrit poetry often personified as beautiful ladies who are amorously involved with various celestial bodies.

G 1.32 **Celestial river:** The river Ganges has three currents *(trisrotā)*: the earthly Gaṅgā, the celestial Mandákini and the subterranean Bhagírathi. *Cf. Rāmāyaṇa* 1.43.6: *gaṅgā tripathagā nāma divyā bhāgīrathīti ca/ tripatho bhāvayantīti tatas tripathagā smṛtā*. To complete the simile in the formal manner of the rhetoricians: the subject of comparison *(upameya)* is that the moon must be shining at the border of the Milky Way, the object of comparison *(upamāna)* is a flamingo on the banks of a river, the common property *(sādhāraṇadharma)* is "being encircled with rays," and the word triggering the simile *(upamādyotaka)* is "like" *(iva)*. Since all of these four elements are explicitly mentioned, the simile is what later rhetoricians term "complete" *(pūrṇopamā).*

G 1.33 The poetic ornament Kshemендra employs here is called a "garland-metaphor" *(mālādīpakālaṅkāra), cf. Kāvyaprakāśa* 10.18ab.

G 1.35 **Female skull-bearing ascetic**: Kāpālika ascetics take on the vow of wearing the "six accoutrements" *(ṣaṇmudrā)* made of human bone. Kshemendra here repeats a common simile, *cf.* e.g. *Kāvyaprakāśa* 10.7cd: *a*. It is remarkable that literary references to female skull-bearing ascetics tend to focus not on the sinister but on their beauty. Kshemendra, of course, also condemns the fierce Kāpālika ascetic, wearing a bone necklace, as someone to be shunned (*Darpadalana* 7.14, 7.63). At *Nītikalpataru* 84.19 he describes the Kāpālika as follows: ***pitṛvanavāso mālā narāsthibhiḥ pāraṇā surāmāṃsaiḥ / pātraṃ kapālam arghyo narabalinā bhairavo devaḥ /***, "He lives in the forest dedicated to the manes, wears a necklace of human bones, he nourishes himself with liquor and meat, his begging-bowl is a skull, his respectful offering is made with human phlegm, his God is Bhairava."

G 1.41 *Nidhānakumbho*: The urn in which the ashes of the deceased are deposited after cremation until they are dispersed in the Ganges or some other sacred ford, *cf. Viṣṇudharma* 19.11. **Dambha** conveys the senses of "religious hypocrisy," "priggishness" and "smugness." The arrogance of religious hypocrites is also the topic of the final chapter of Kṣemendra's *Darpadalana*.

G 1.45 *Dambhodaya*= Dambhódbhava, the invincible but arrogant and quarrelsome emperor, *cf. Mahābhārata* 5.94.5–35. He was finally tamed by the two Ṛṣis Nara and Nārāyaṇa. Note the six *-ambha* alliterations *(anuprāsa).* Kshemendra himself has retold Dambhódbhava's tale at *Darpadalana* 5.29–45.

G 1.46 **Circular reasoning:** as a technical term in Nyāya-logic denotes the fallacy of circular argument. The verse further parodies logical treatises such as the *Hetucakra*, an investigation of admissible syllogistic reasons used by logicians to ascertain the validity of propositions.

G 1.47 I suspect an emendation is here required. Something like *udbāhu*? *Tree:* With the simile of the flourishing tree Ksheméndra may be alluding to a well-known verse in the *Manusmṛti* 9.255: *nirbhayaṃ tu bhaved yasya rāṣṭraṃ bāhubalāśritam/ tasya tad vardhate nityaṃ sicyamāna iva drumaḥ*, "A kingdom which is secure, protected by the might of its ruler's arm, will ever flourish, like a well-watered tree." Kshemendra is fond of the tree simile, in *Darpadalana* 1.37 he describes a similar tree sprouted from arrogance.

G 1.48 To adjust the sense for the heron we must read *vrata* with secondary sense of "always eating the same food," attested only in lexicons. **Smugness of the heron:** *Cf.* *Rājataraṅgiṇī* 5.305. Kṣemendra also uses the same metaphor for an aging courtesan who pretends to be a widow, dresses in white and who then performs religious ceremonies for her supposedly departed husband at a sacred ford. In this way she ensares a wealthy man who believes her to be pious (see *Samayamātṛkā* 2.28–30). **Smugness peculiar to cats:** A parody of the modest practise of keeping the gaze fixed on the ground when moving in public. *Cf.* the puns on cats and herons in the description on the Vātsyāyana sages, *Harṣacarita* 1, p. 18^{9-24}.

G 1.50 Here, Kshemendra does not intend to ridicule false ascetics, but merely hypocritical ascetics. Literary works attest to the proliferation of spies and criminals disguised as false ascetics (already mentioned in the *Arthaśāstra*). On hypocritical ascetics see also *Kathāsaritsāgara* II,2-5.

G 1.51 **Hemavallī:** *Hoya Viridiflora*. The practice of affixing apotropaic herbs on to auspicious knots *(maṅgalagranthi)* is described in the *Kṛtyacintāmaṇi* cited in the *Nirṇayasindhu*. It is possible that this is the same string referred to in the second chapter of the *Samayamātṛkā*. The prostitute, assuming the false name Ardhakṣīrā, becomes the nurse to the son of the minister Mitrasena. The boy wastes away with fever because of her neglect, and as he lies dying she does the most vile thing possible: she steals his protective *hemasūtrikā* (condemning him to certain death) and runs away at night: *dṛṣṭvā tatrāturaṃ bālaṃ tṛṇavat sutarāgiṇī / sā yayau nirdayā rātrau gṛhītvā hemasūtrikām* (*Samayamātṛkā* 2.73). *Cf.* also *Kuṭṭanīmata* 63. **Armpit:** Kṣemendra is here refining a motif he had already used at *Narmamālā* 1.73ab.

G 1.51 **Robe:** *Cf. Vasiṣṭhadharma*10.20b: *na śabdaśāstrābhiratasya mokṣo na cāpi lokagrahaṇe ratasya / na bhojanācchādanatatparasya na cāpi ramyāvasathapriyasya*, "There is no liberation for a man obsessed with grammar [and science], nor for a man fond of seeing people, nor for a man interested in food and clothing, nor for a man fond of beautiful dwellings."

G 1.52 **Squabbles:** *Cf. Manusmṛti* 6.50: "[The ascetic] must not seek to win almsfood by reading omens and portents, by astrology or physiognomy, by instruction or by debates."

G 1.55 **Crow's eye:** Crows are believed to have but one eye which they move from socket to socket. The emendation *kākaviṣṭām iva* may also be considered: "like crow's dropping fallen upon him." Meyer (1903:xlii) takes this to mean that he casts crow-glances around.

G 1.56 **Craves fame:** *cf.* Yama *cit. Yatidharmasamuccaya* 7.45ab: *lābhapūjānimittaṃ hi vyākhyānaṃ śiṣyasaṃgrahaḥ* "For the sake of profit and adulation, [false ascetics] discourse on scriptures and collect disciples."

G 1.58 **Jambha** was the leader of the Daityas who stole the nectar of immortality from Dhanvantari, *cf. Agnipurāṇa* 3.

G 1.59 **Snátaka:** A *brāhmaṇa* who has taken the ritual bath which marks the end of his studentship. The *Manusmṛti* 11.1–2 enumerates nine types, others give three. All support themselves by begging, Manu ordains that they must be given food and money in proportion to their learning.

G 1.60 **Cleansing clay:** Ksheméndra is here probably insinuating that the purity-manic appears to be continually smeared in clay which makes him look filthy.

G 1.60 **An enemy to all:** E.g. *viśva+amitra*. See *Mahābhārata* 13.95.35 for Viśvāmitra's own explanation of his name to the hag Yātudhānī: *viśvedevāś ca me mitraṃ mitram asmi gavāṃ tathā viśvāmitram iti khyātaṃ*, "I am called Viśvāmitra because the Viśvedevas are my friends, because I am a friend to cattle *(viś)*."

G 1.60 **The pure and the impure:** *Cf.* Viśvāmitra's justifications of his theft of dog-flesh from the Caṇḍāla in *Mahābhārata* 12.139.

G 1.60 **Different from his own kin:** Viśvāmitra was born as a Kṣatriya but later on became a Brahmin by his penance, *cf. Mahābhārata* 9.38.22cd.

G 1.63 The ornament is a *samāsoktyalaṅkāra*, or "compounded expression," in which the subject (serpent) has only one sense but all of the attributes are equally applicable to something not explicitly mentioned, namely, an "ascetic."

G 1.64 I am not sure which epic source Ksheméndra is following here. The *Bhāgavatapurāṇa* 4.8.2 *mṛṣā dharmasya bhāryāsīd dambhaṃ māyāṃ ca śatruhan/ asūta mithunaṃ tat tu*, makes Dambha the twin of Māyā and son of Adharma (son of Brahmā) and Mṛṣā. The sound Huṃ is also a commonly used destructive seed-mantra.

G 1.68 **Bundle:** *pūlī* f. "a bundle," not in MW. For the ascetic's paraphernalia *cf. Vaikhānasadharmasūtra* 2.6. In the *Darpadalana* 7.12–13 Kshemendra describes such vows and paraphernalia as a form of bondage if the ascetic should be devoid of holiness. **Burden of scriptures:** Vasiṣṭha, *cit.* in *Yatidharmasamuccaya* 7.47: *atrātmavyatirekeṇa dvitīyaṃ yadi paśyati/ tataḥ śāstrāṇy adhīyante śrūyate granthavistaraḥ*, "A person would undertake the recitation of texts and the study of a lot of books only if he regards something in this world as a second reality besides himself." **A horn:** This presumably refers to the prohibition on using the hands to scratch oneself during the *Jyotiṣṭoma* rite. Instead, the horn of a black antelope is to be used (*Taittirīya-saṃhitā* 6.1.3).

G 1.69 **Bunches of sacred grass:** *pavitraka*, two blades of kusha grass used at sacrifices in purifying and sprinkling ghee. What might be intended, is that these ear-ornaments reveal his status as one who has officiated at prestigious sacrifices. **Ritual-ring:** A *pavitra* is a ring worn on the ring-finger, made of twisted blades of Kuśa- or Darbha-grass, the tips of which project outwards into a sort of brush, which is used to wipe away or sprinkle *(prokṣaṇa)* water etc. in rituals. *Cf.* *Yājñavalkyasmṛti* 1.226. For a similar description of the ascetic's paraphernalia see *Darpadalana* 7.68.

G 1.70 **Neck stiff like a plank:** compare *Darpadalana* 1.24 (also 1.57: *akharvagalaḥ*), where Ksheméndra describes a stiff neck as a sign of arrogance. Similar is also *Narmamālā* 1.62: *kāṣṭhastabdhonnatagrīvaḥ*.

G 1.75 Ksheméndra is here using assonances *(anuprāsa-)* to provide fanciful new *nirvacana*-style etymologies for the sage's names: **graste** *'gastye*. **Devoured:** A further allusion to the myth of Agastya devouring the Asura Vātāpi, *cf.* *Mahābhārata* Araṇyakaparvan 3.94.97. For Vasiṣṭha Ksheméndra provides the following analysis: *alpa/tapo/vrata/lajjā/kuñcita/pṛṣ*the. **Hunched his back:** An allusion to Vasiṣṭha's birth from a pot.

G 1.76 Note the alliteration . . . *kutse*. . . *Kautse*. **Simple vow of silence:** An allusion to Kautsa's unwillingness to ask for money from Raghu. Note the alliteration *nirādare*. . . *Nārade.*

G 1.77 **Knee-caps:** Another alliterative play on the etymology of his name which Jamadagni gives to the hag Yātudhānī, *cf.* *Mahābhārata* 13.95.37: *jājamadyajajā nāma mṛjā māha jijāyiṣe jamadagnir iti khyātam ato māṃ viddhi śobhane*. **Trembled in**

fear: That the fearless Viśvāmitra should tremble in fear is a hyperbole *(atiśayokti)* demonstrating Dambha's ridiculous ascetic pomp. **Neck rolled about:** Gālava, son of Viśvāmitra, received his strange name because his mother, trying to raise money to feed her other children during a famine, tied a rope around his throat *(gala)* and in this manner led him to be sold. **Crushed:** Perhaps an allusion to the myth of Nandī breaking open the termite-hill which had risen up over the meditating Bhṛgu, *cf. Padmapurāṇa* 20.

G 1.82 Dambha is here outdoing even the law-books. Manu states that particles of water in the breath are not contaminating. This is the reason why Brahma suddenly recognises who Dambha is.

G 1.89 **Isolated:** Deriving *-bhajya* from the root *bhaj* cl. 1, "to share." **Devastated:** Deriving *-bhajya* from √*bhañj* cl. 7, "to break."

G 1.90 **Religious teachers:** At *Darpadalana* 2.50 Kshemendra makes Mati censure the sycophantic teacher who lives off his students. *pālaka = paripālaka, cf. Narmamālā* 1.62–70. *Niyogin*, "commissioner," a supervisor of villages who also settles civil and criminal cases. *Cf. Narmamālā* 1.97–127. **Initiates** into esoteric cults consider their religions superior to mundane religion.

The unexpressed second sense: "[Just as a serpent], after creeping into the cavities of all of the Jantu-trees, by squeezing itself in many ways, bit by bit, finally enters the hollows in trees full of nesting birds."

G 1.93 *Matsyārthī*: Hungering for fish or: "Someone observing the fish-vow *(matsyavrata)*." Or: "Supplicating with the Matsyasūkta."

G 1.94 **Clad in bark:** For garments of bark *(valkala)* see Emeneau 1962. The verse echoes Kṣemendra's own *Muktāvalī* as cited at *Aucityavicāracarcā* 29 (84).

The unexpressed second subject are penitent ascetics burdened with chunky matted locks, who wear bark garments, are continuously exposed to cold, heat and rain, and are eager for rewards in heaven.

G 1.95 Can also be read as **sadā+adambhaḥ**: Adambha is a name of Shiva. A parody of descriptions of Sadāśiva as *sarvajña, sarvaga* and *sarvakṛt*, *cf.* *Rauravatantra* Upodghāta 8.

G 1.96 **Wish-granting tree:** Five wish-granting trees are supposed to have been produced by the churning of the milk-ocean, these exist in the world of the Gods *(devaloka)*. **Dwarf:** Viṣṇu's incarnation as Vāmana, an ascetic dwarf, cheated Bali out of the possession of the three worlds by asking for only three steps of land. Bali readily acceeded to such a paltry demand but Viṣṇu then in three steps covered the entire triple universe.

G 2.2 *Cf.* *Arthaśāstra* 2.5.2–4 for details about the construction of a treasure vault. Kshemèndra is not exaggerating, Kauṭilya even recommends the construction of secret treasuries by condemned men who are then immediately put to death. Kshemèndra associates treasuries with death also in his *Darpadalana* 2.70–71, where the miser Nanda finally dies in his treasury, with his back resting against his pots of money, suffering because he was too stingy to pay for medicine.

G 2.4 Kshemèndra is here elaborating on Manu's twofold classification of thieves, those who steal openly *(prakāśavañcaka)* and those who do so in concealment, such as burglars, robbers, and thieves, *cf.* *Manusmṛti* 9.257.

G 2.5 For Kshemèndra the stinginess of merchants is proverbial. See especially *Darpadalana* 2.11–113. Kshemèndra there recounts the tale of the mean merchant Nanda, a miserable miser, who is reborn as a pitifully deformed and diseased Cāṇḍāla and is then raised with dog's milk. When he one day happens to beg for alms from his own former son Candana, he is brutally beaten. Just then the Buddha happens to be passing by. With a compassionate glance he cures the Cāṇḍāla's leprosy and reveals his former identity to his son. **Three cowries:** In Kshemèndra's

day, the cowrie was still in use as the lowest monetary unit
cf. STEIN (1961:308–328), *The Term Dīnnāra and the Monetary
System of Kaśmīr*. Ksheméndra describes a similarly tight-fisted
merchant in *Samayamātṛkā* 8.80.

G 2.6 **Fond of tales:** Kalhaṇa alleges that merchants like to listen
to the recitation of sacred texts because they are embezzlers
and hope for purification *Rājataraṅgiṇī* 8.708cd. **Black cobra:**
In the *Darpadalana* Ksheméndra again associates misers with
black cobras, but there it is the miser himself who appears to
others like the ominous serpent.

G 2.7 **Donate:** See KANE, *History of Dharmaśāstra* V. pp. 212, 243–5.
In his *Darpadalana* 6.8 Ksheméndra criticises those who think
that giving alms during a solar eclipse constitutes liberality.
Rather, giving alms on such occasions was considered to profit
the donor. The merchant in the present verse is too greedy
to realise this. That it was common to consider all kinds of
contributing factors (such as the position of the sun) before
giving alms is evident also from *Darpadalana* 6.11. Ksheméndra himself recounts his father Prakāśendra's liberality during
a solar eclipse in the *Bhāratamañjarī* Kavipraśasti 4: *sūryagrahe
tribhir lakṣair dattvā kṛṣṇājinatrayam / alpaprado 'smīty abhavat
kṣaṇaṃ lajjānatānanaḥ,* "On the occasion of the solar eclipse
after he gave away three hundred thousand black antelope[-
skins], he stood with his head bowed in shame, thinking: 'I
have given but little.'"

G 2.9 **Deposit:** Laws regarding the guarding and return of sealed
deposits were stringent and detailed, *Cf. Manusmṛti* 8.179–
196.

G 2.11 A tale similar to the following is recounted by Kalhaṇa at
Rājataraṅgiṇī 8.123–158. **Viṣṭikaraṇa:** Viṣṭi is the seventh of
the immovable *karaṇas*. Each lunar day *(tithi)* is made up
of two *karaṇas*. Since Viṣṭikaraṇa is presided over by Yama,
the God of death, it is considered an extremely inauspicious
period for any new undertaking. *Bṛhatsaṃhitā* 99.4c: *na hi*

viṣṭikṛtaṃ vidadhāti śubhaṃ, "For something undertaken during *viṣṭi* does not produce an auspicious [result]."

G 2.14 *Bhadrā*: The merchant is deliberately using this alternate name for Viṣṭi because it also means "auspicious."

G 2.19 **Rats:** A rat infesting decrepit houses is occasionally encountered as a motif used to warn of the future suffering of a fallen ascetic. He is first reborn for sixty thousand years as a worm in excrement. "Then," says Śātātapa (*cit. Yatidharmasamuccaya* 7.54ab: *śūnyāgāreṣu ghoreṣu bhavaty ākhuḥ sudāruṇaḥ*), "he will become a horrible rat infesting dreadful abandoned houses." **Samsára:** The world of rebirth.

G 2.23 A *muhūrta* is more precisely a time-period of about forty-eight minutes.

G 2.31 **Haragupta:** The merchant of course intends *Haraguptakula* to mean "family protected by Śiva," but it can also mean a "secret gang of thieves," e.g. *haraṇaśīlānāṃ guptakulaṃ*.

G 2.35 **The gate of the royal court:** In the final instance, litigation can be taken to the king himself. The legal formula for this is a representation at the Royal Gate *(rājādvāra)*. Already in the third-cent. CE Kroraina Prakrit documents we repeatedly encounter the formula: *ko pacima kalaṃmi icheyati eta aṃñatha karaṃnae rayadvaraṃmi muhucotaṃ apramāna siyati taṃḍa prapta*, "Whoever, at a later time, wishes to make this [agreement] otherwise, his representations at the royal gate shall be without authority and he will be punished" (see BOYER, RAPSON SENART 1920). *Solemn fast to starvation (prāyopaveśa)*: for this emendation *cf. Rājataraṅgiṇī* 6.25–27 etc.

2.37–86 A retelling of a tale found in the *Mahābhārata*.

G 2.38 **Śukra:** The son of Bhṛgu and the teacher of the Daityas. *Vaiśravaṇa* or Kubera is the God of wealth.

G 2.44 I take the Bahuvrīhi cpd. *atyantasaṃbhṛtasneham* adverbially rather than adjectivally to *tvām*. **Essence of life:** That misers consider money to be the essence of life is another popular image in Ksheméndra's work, see for instance the words of the mean merchant Nanda in *Darpadalana* 2.25–26, who concludes that "poverty is death."

G 2.48 **Possessed:** The art of entering another's body (whether alive or dead) is described in Tantric texts such as *Mālinīvijayottara* 21.9–19 *(saṃkrāntividhi)*. See also *Kathāsaritsāgara* IV,46; VII,114–5.

G 2.51 Śaṅkha, Mukunda, Kunda, and Padma are the names of some of Kubera's fabulous treasures. Here, the beings presiding over them, who are part of Kubera's retinue, are intended.

G 2.68 To complete the metaphor *(sāṅgarūpaka)*, *yaśas*, "good reputation," must punningly also be taken as "water," and "good fortune" must be taken as the Goddess of fortune, Lakṣmī, who faints from noxious fumes.

G 2.79 Shukra here twists Shiva's words to mean the opposite. He can do this because the word *vitta* has the double sense of "wealth" and "fame."

G 2.83 *Dhāraṇā*: Shiva is evidently practising the "fire fixation" *(āgneyīdhāraṇā)* which raises up the abdominal fire. In Shaiva Ṣaḍaṅgayoga this is one of usually four or five "fixations which are counted as one of the six ancillaries *(aṅga)* of yoga." *Cf. Mātaṅgapārameśvara* YP 2.35c–65.

Nikāmaṃ: Hapax?

G 3.2 **By their hind-legs:** reading *abalābhiḥ* as *avarābhiḥ*. This is permissible since *va/ba* and *ra/la* may be interchanged under certain circumstances. A dual is not required as the elephants are plural. For such puns *(śleṣa)* see *Kāvyādarśa* 2.185 *(jaḍa/jala)* etc. It is possible that **men** (*kariṇo*, "handed creature") is not intended and that the ornament is thus a *samāsokti* (only the epithets have double meanings, not the subject "elephants") rather than a fully worked out simile. **Suitably lavish gifts:**

Su+ucita+dāna. There may be a further set of puns with sexual innuendos: °*huṃkāraiḥ* is a particular humming sound used in lovemaking, *cf.* *Kāmasūtra* 2.7 for the classification such sounds. The members of the compound *parimalalīnāli*° all are also technical terms of erotic science but I am not able to construe a convincing second meaning here.

G 3.3 **Sensual pleasures:** *viṣaya*. **Kicks:** Kicking forms part of ancient Indian love play. Less convincingly: "fall at her feet." **Bites and scratches with the nails:** *aṅkuśaghaṭana*, *cf.* *Kāmasūtra* 2.4 on the various techniques of amorous scratching *(nakhakarma)* and biting *(daśanacchedya)*. In the present case the more intense variety, which breaks the skin *(chedya)* and leaves painful marks *(kṣata, cihna)* is intended. **Entwining in erotic gymnastics:** e.g. an *arthaśleṣa*: *nigaḍa= bandha*.

G 3.5 The image occurs already in *Kuṭṭanīmata* 316cd. Ksheméndra uses similar imagery also at *Darpadalana* 4.5, courtesans, he says, devour the flesh and blood of men just as old age does.

G 3.11 **Dustbin:** *Dhūlipaṭala* may also mean "cloud of dust."

G 3.14 Ksheméndra has here reworked *Nītiśataka* 47. See STERNBACH 1953:

G 3.16 This indeed was the commonly understood duty of courtesans. A procuress advises the young courtesan Dohanī: *putri! kim etad yad ekam evāliṅgya yauvanaṃ viphalīkaroṣi ? veśyānām anekaiḥ saha ramaṇakrīḍocitā*, "Daughter! What is this, that you waste your youth embracing only one man? For courtesans, love-sport with many [men] is proper."

G 3.18 LAPANICH seems to read a double accusative construction with *kurute*: "compells *(sic)* her relative to perform the functions of a man in the house."

G 3.20 **Commissioner:** *niyogin* see note to 1.90. **Lecher:** *Lubdha* might equally be a "hunter" or a "greedy man."

G 3.25 Sāvitrī, the wife of Satyavān, by her virtue reprieved her husband from death, *cf.* *Mahābhārata* 3.281.

G 3.31 **Boasts of gifts:** not only are the gifts made to unworthy people, but *Manusmṛti* 4.236d (*na dattvā parikīrtayet*) strictly forbids publicizing charitable gifts. **Captivate:** *vaśīkaraṇa*: "magical subjugation."

G 3.37 **Amusement-terraces:** E.g. *vilāsamahī = vilāsavātāyanam.*

G 3.42 Note the skilful alliterations *(anuprāsa).*

G 3.46 *Ked* reads inappropriately *madhumada*: e.g. «eye-lotuses unsteady with sweet wine.»

3.48–52 Kalhaṇa describes in very similar terms the symptoms of the princess Anaṅgalekhā's secret affair with the minister Khaṅkha (*Rājataraṅgiṇī* 3.501–5).

G 3.49 For feigned anger *cf.* Dhanika to *Daśarūpaka* 4.58cd: *premapūrvako vaśīkāraḥ praṇayaḥ, tadbhaṅge mānaḥ praṇayamānaḥ*: "*Praṇaya* is the subjugation preceded by love, the disdain shown when it is interrupted is 'coquettish anger.'"

G 3.51 The poetic ornament is an "apparent paradox" *(guṇasya guṇena virodhābhāsālaṅkāraḥ).* The paradox is resolved by a slight shift in the meaning of *svatantra* to "unrestrained." *Cf.* *Kāvyaprakāśa* 10.24–25b.

G 3.55 **Flickered with a flash:** E.g. *cakita* < $\sqrt{}$*kan*, *cf.* *Dhātupāṭha* 1.488: *kanī dīptikantigatiṣu.* There is an indirect *(saṃlakṣyakrama)*, sense-based *(arthaśaktimūla)* suggestion based on subordinated denotation *(vivakṣitānyaparavācyadhvani)* of the theme *(vastu)* "stealthy love is thrilling" *(cauraratasya ramyataratvam).*

G 3.58 *Kara:* "ray," punningly also: "hand."

G 3.59 *Tamas* can mean both "darkness" and "ignorance."

G 3.60 **Wishing to die:** *vivaśā.*

G 3.69 The following story is also given in *Vetālapañcaviṃśatikā* (of Śivadāsa) pp. 15ff. and in *Kathāsaritsāgara* 77.48ff. etc. **Vetálas** are demons which animate dead corpses. The lady's hot, fragrant kisses are compared to the rites of the terrifying Vetāla-invocation, in which the adept makes offerings into a sacrificial fire lit in the mouth of a hanged criminal. The corpse then becomes animated by a Vetála, and its tongue begins to rise up. If the adept fails to cut it off, the Vetāla will eat him. If he succeeds, the tongue transforms into a magical sword which gives him supernatural powers. *Cf. Picumata* 15 (Mahāyāga-vetālasādhana), *Harṣacarita* 3. **Nose bitten off:** For this motif compare *Kathāsaritsāgara* 6.188; 9.76.

G 3.70 **Severed nose:** This is intended as a form of divine vengeance, for faithless wives were often punished by cutting off their noses, see *Kathāsaritsāgara* V,123. Also *Manusmṛti* 8.125.

G 3.72 **Sold in a foreign land:** Ksheméndra uses the same image of someone being sold in a foreign land in *Darpadalana* 3.15 to ridicule the beauty of an inarticulate fool.

G 3.76 A paraphrase of *Manusmṛti* 9.15–17.

G 4.1 **Courtesans:** The reader may wish to consult *Kāmasūtra* 4. Ksheméndra discusses courtesans also in the third chapter of the *Deśopadeśa* and he has even devoted an entire work to this subject, the *Samayamātṛkā*. **Vaiśravaṇa**, or Kubera, the God of wealth, is as notoriously stingy as prostitutes are said to be greedy for money (*cf. Mṛcchakaṭikā* 5.35–7, *Kuṭṭanīmata* 227–8, *Samayamātṛkā* 4.18–25, 4.80–93). *Ked* reads *śramaṇatām eti*, e.g. even "the God of wealth is reduced to a beggar-monk by their machinations." The morality Kshemendra puts forward here is more commonly found in prescriptions specific to ascetics, *cf.* Gālava, *cit. Yatidharmasamuccaya* 10.105: *sakṛt sādhāraṇīṃ gatvā brahmahatyāprāyaścittaṃ caret*, "If someone has intercourse with a prostitute just once, he should perform the penance prescribed for killing a Brahmin" (transl. OLIVELLE 1995:171). Dāmodaragupta's *Kuṭṭanīmata* gives probably the more popular view in Ksheméndra's time (789ab: *dāraratiḥ saṃtataye kaṇḍūpraśamāya ceṭikāśleṣaḥ*), "Love of one's wife serves to continue the family-lineage, courtesans are embraced to satisfy the itch."

4.2 Here and in the following verses Ksheméndra compares courtesans to rivers or streams. All of the descriptive epithets he lists may have been intended to bear double meanings, but some remain obscure to me. He makes a very similar punning comparison between loose women and rivers in *Darpadalana* 1.65. **Sixty-four arts:** Compare the list in *Kāmasūtra* 1.3.15. The various lists of these arts found in Sanskrit literature are discussed by Venkatasubbiah & Müller (1914:355–367).

G 4.5 **Scratching and biting:** *Cf. Kāmasūtra* 2.4.

G 4.8 **Menstruation:** An important skill, see *Arthaśāstra* 2.27.14–15 for the punishment of courtesans who refused to entertain their paramour. *Cf. Manusmṛti* 4.40–42 for the prohibition on connubial intercourse during the woman's courses. Ksheméndra accuses prostitutes of using this ploy also at *Deśopadeśa* 3.30.

G 4.12 **Men whose name and caste is unkown:** Prostitutes were required to serve all customers e.g. *Kuṭṭanīmata* 314ab: *ujjhitavṛṣayogā api ratisamaye naraviśeṣanirapekṣāḥ*. See the verses collected in STERNBACH (1953:64ff).

G 4.14 Based on *Kāmasūtra* 2.9.39cd.

4.15–39 The same tale is also found in Soma·deva's *Kathāsaritsāgara* (book 10) 58.2–53. There the minister's name is however Anantaguṇa and the courtesan is called Kumudikā.

G 4.17 **Arms reaching down to his knees:** Long arms were considered an outward sign of greatness, *cf. Bṛhatsaṃhitā* 57.45a.

G 4.25 Compare this with the tests and temptations advocated by Kauṭilya to ascertain a minister's loyalty, *Arthaśāstra* 10.

G 4.26 That she wore ornaments indicates that she was prepared to cast herself into the flames.

G 4.27 Self-immolation: in the *Samayamātṛkā* 2.32–36, Kshemēndra makes the courtesan Arghagharghāṭikā pretend to follow her wealthy husband of one month into the fire also. The king intervenes to save the apparently pious woman and she ends up inheriting his fortune.

G 4.29 For the historical truth behind such stories see for instance the courtesan Sāmbavatī's influence over the Tantrin soldiers, *Rājataraṅgiṇī* 5.296.

G 4.31 The use of chowries is usually reserved for royalty.

G 4.39 A parody of Viṣṇu's manifestation as Viśvarūpa, *cf. Bhagavadgītā* 11.16.

G 5.1 *Cf. Arthaśāstra* 2.7–8. *Kāyastha*s are bureaucrats, scribes, accountants etc. See the *Narmamāla* for their many grades and duties (*cf.* Baldissera 2000). In Kshemēndra's satires the scribe's career usually ends with imprisonment or worse, see e.g. *Darpadalana* 2.54.

G 5.2 My emendation *aindavakaleva* attempts to account for P's variant *raudra* and also to ensure that the simile is not defective. Both LAPANICH and the KM edition read *°kalā iva* and thus make the object of the simile formally a plural, (*pace* the translations of SCHMIDT and LAPANICH) but the subject *-sampattiḥ* is singular. This is a poetical defect because the words expressing the common property cannot be construed in concord with both the subject and the object of the comparison. This problem is discussed in the prose to *Kāvyaprakāśa* 10.55–6. **Rahu:** The severed head of the dragon-like demon *Rāhu*, who causes eclipses by swallowing the sun or moon, is the ascending node–the point in the ascending half of the moon's orbit at which it intersects the earth's orbital plane from below. *Divira*: Kshemēndra uses the word *divira* firstly in its conventional sense of "scribe" (< Old Persian *dibīr*) and secondly in its etymological sense of "sky-going" *(< divi-ra)*. Thus the metaphor *(rūpaka) divira-rāhu-kalā* must be interpreted in two ways: "the power of the sky-going Rāhu," and "the scribe's ingenuity at making things vanish."

G 5.5 **Black men:** *Kāla* denotes both the color "black" and the "God of death" (derived from *kal* meaning 'movement of time'). The scribes are evidently black because they are smeared with ink. The attendants of Death bear wooden staffs with which they strike down those whose span of life has reached its end. **Birchbark:** The prepared, soft inner bark of the birch tree (Skt. *bhūrja*) has been popular as a material for writing on in Northwestern India from before the common era until quite recently.

G 5.7 **Raped:** *khanyamānā*, lit. "being dug into." **The tears of Añjanā:** *Sāñjanāśru* Añjana was the mother of the monkey-god Hánuman. When she was pregnant, Valin poured molten metal alloys *(pañcaloha)* into her womb trying to abort his future rival.

G 5.11 *Citragupta:* The recorder of souls' good and bad deeds who lives in the realm of Yama, lord of the dead. *cf. Muṇḍakopaniṣat* 1.20. **By deleting a mere line:** For a recorded perpetration of this trick, see *Rājataraṅgiṇī* 6.39.

G 5.18 As is evident from this verse the preceding list needs to be punningly construed with the 16 digits of the moon as well.

G 5.33 **Lump of iron:** Kṣemendra has taken over this image from Śivasvāmin's *Kāpphiṇābhyudaya* 4.28cd: *draḍhimam ayamayo hi prājyatejo 'bhiṣaṅgād vighaṭitakaṭhinatvaṃ yāṭi karmaṇyabhāvam.*

G 5.41 **Partaking of a share:** e.g. *bhāgin + rathyā.*

G 6.3 The attributes used to describe this intoxication punningly describe the diametrically opposed restraint of the ideal yogin.

G 6.4 A parody of the inverted cosmic tree. See *Bhagavadgītā* 15.1–2, and *Kaṭhopaniṣad* 6.1.

G 6.5 In light of 6.7 it might be more appropriate to translate not as "pompous man" but "pomposity" itself (so also at 6.6.). But the English reads better with this license. On *saṃnipāta* as a cause of fever see *Carakasaṃhitā* Nidānasthāna 1.29. The symptoms of this incurable fever are also Kṣemendra's metaphors of choice to describe the arrogant "Superintendent" *(paripālaka)* at *Narmamālā* 1.62–64 (BALDISSERA 2000 fails to connect verses 1.62–3 to the simile in 1.64 as they clearly should be). **Impaled on a stake:** Or: *suffering from a colic (śūla).*

G 6.7 A parody of *Bhagavadgītā* 5.24: "He who is inwardly blissful, who delights in the self, who has an inward illumination, that Yogin, having become Brahma, goes to the Nirvāṇa of Brahman."

G 6.10 Again medical imagery: "[The patient's] eyes are reddened by the outbreak of a morbid disorder of the humors, he is unable to endure even the faintest sounds, and babbles." Compare Ksheméndra's description of the arrogant young Brahmin Tejonidhi at *Darpadalana* 1.46. A similar lampoon of a scholar is also given in the *Padmaprābhṛtaka* in the prose after 16 describing the grammarian Dattakalaśi who has just been defeated in a debate. *Ā+kopa*: "Outbreak of a disorder of the humors."

G 6.12 **An acute** *(mahā+ājñānaṃ yasya saḥ)* **vulture** *(dīrghadarśī).* This "delirium of noble lineage" is treated in greater detail in the *Darpadalana* 1.

G 6.14 A parody of Purāṇic cosmography. Just as the infinite world-serpent Ananta supports the earth, so "self-importance" is the base of the various trees of intoxication.

G 6.16 A parody of *Bhagavadgītā* 5.18: "The wise see as equal the learned and saintly brahmin, a cow, an elephant, a dog and a dog-cooker."

G 6.17 An allusion to the *Bhagavadgītā*'s description of the Yogin 6.8cd: . . . *yogī samaloṣṭāśmakāñcanaḥ*, ". . . the Yogi, considering as equal clods of earth, rocks and gold are the same."

Ksheméndra makes a similar allusion at *Darpadalana* 2.60 and at *Deśopadeśa* 1.6 he uses the image yet again to show that a rogue who cares not for friend or foe etc. is equivalent to an initiate who has received the highest liberating consecration (*nirvāṇadīkṣitaḥ*).

G 6.18 A parody of the symptoms of certain mystical states. See, for instance, *Kulasāra* fol. 25v: *udgiret kaulikīṃ bhāṣāṃ mudrābandhamanekadhā / hasate gāyate caiva nānāceṣṭāni kurvate*, "He speaks in mystical Kaulikī language, spontaneously manifests various yogic seals, laughs, sings and fidgets." Utpaladeva describes the Shaiva devotee very similarly at *Shivastotrāvalī* 15.3: *rudanto vā hasanto vā tvām uccaiḥ pralapanty amī / bhaktāḥ stutipadoccāropacārāḥ pṛthag eva te.* See also *Skandapurāṇa* 21.47ab, *Vādanyāya* 2.

G 6.21 A retelling of the story told in *Mahābhārata* 3.122ff., *Śatapathabrāhmaṇa* 4.1.5ff., *Jaiminīyabrāhmaṇa* 3.120ff.

G 6.25 Pralamba was a notorious demon slain by Balarāma.

G 6.28 Punningly: *appearing immobilised, bound by cords.*

G 7.2 **Riches:** *kamalā*. Third sense: *After completely mangling (jagdhvā) the collection of Kamaladhruvā songs, and then chewing up the Kumudadhruvā songs, the feeble (kṣīṇa) singer-drones now show an interest (praṇayitā) in the compositions of Mataṅga's Bṛhaddeśī.* Mataṅga is the author of an early musicological work: the *Bṛhaddeśī*. The impact of this verse occurs in two stages. 1. Initially the metaphor *gāyanabhṛṅga* "singer-bee," fuses two obvious parallel paranomastic interpretations of the epithets. [a] Thus we have *kamalākara* first as "a lotuspond," *koṣa* as "a bud," *kumuda* as "a waterlily" and *kṣīṇa* in the sense of "emaciated." The verbs *jhakṣ* and *ā+svād* retain theit literal meaning of "consuming." The subject *gāyanabhṛṅga* itself may be read as "humming bee." The bee's longing *(praṇayatā)* for the ichor of rutting elephants *(mātaṅga)* is a popular conceit in Sanskrit Kāvya. [b] Secondly *kamalākara* may be rendered as "a hoard of wealth," *koṣa* as a "treasury," *ku+mud* as "displeasure" and *kṣīṇa* as "impoverished." Due to an incompatibility of the primary sense *(abhidhā)* of the verbs *jhakṣ* and *ā+svād* with the contextual meaning of the verse *(anvaya)*—eg. wealth and displeasure are not edible—their literal sense is barred *(mukhyārthabāḍha)* and a secondary *(lākṣaṇika)* meaning is forced upon them: *jhakṣ* > "squander," much like the english devour can refer both to the act of consumption as also to destruction; *ā+svād* > "experience, suffer." The metaphor *gāyanabhṛṅga* becomes singer-rake (*bhṛṅga:* "a libertine") and *mātaṅga* denotes an outcaste of extremely low standing. The humor of the situation is that the licentious singers first ruin their patron, are driven out by him, and then, with no dignity or discernment, entreat even the lowliest outcastes.

G 7.3 **Troops:** *skandha*. **Wedge-formation:** *śakaṭa*. ***Ghaṭapaṭa:*** Not attested as a synonym for *paṭaha* kettledrums. **Quivers:** *kalāpa*. **Powerful missiles:** *īśaka*. **Arrows:** *muktaka*. **Regicidal:** *bhūpabhuj*. **Warriors of the God of war:** *Gāyana cf. Mahābhārata* 9.44.62a.

G 7.5 *Padas:* "musical phrases," see *Nāṭyaśāstra* 28.11, 16–17; 32.28–29. For the names of the notes *(svara)* see *Nāṭyaśāstra* 28.21. The concealed pun eludes me.

G 7.6 **Faulty:** *bhrānta*. **Revolving ornamentations:** *āvartaka* is one of the 33 tonal ornaments defined by Bharata, Mataṅga etc. See *Bṛhaddeśī* Varṇālaṅkāraprakaraṇa 6, Alaṅkāralakṣaṇa 23: *ārohāvarohābhyām aṣṭau svarān uccārya prākṣvaroccāraṇānte kramaśo 'ṣṭakala āvartakaḥ*. **Flute ornamentations:** I am taking *vaṃśa* as a synonym for the "flute-ornament" *veṇvalaṅkāra*. See *Bṛhaddeśī* Varṇālaṅkāraprakaraṇa 6, Alaṅkāralakṣaṇa 8: *ākṛīḍitavadārohāvarohakrameṇa saptakalo veṇuḥ*. **Opening theme:** *mukha*. **Reeling:** *bhrānta*. **Gyrations:** *āvarta*. **Spines:** *vaṃśa*.

G 7.8 Both because of the resultant higher taxation and because the wrongdoing of the king is believed inevitably to result in some sort of calamitous epidemic or natural disaster.

G 7.11 **Thrilling:** *sahāra*. **Love-sport:** *-keyūrāḥ*. **Sapped of essence:** *nirādhārāḥ*.

G 7.19 A parody of the Śaivasiddhānta's account of creation by eight "sovereigns of mantra," *(vidyeśvara, mantramaheśvara).*

G 8.1 **Visionary imagination:** *pṛthudhyāna*. **Yogins with the ability** *(kalā)* **to endure** *(āharaṇa)* **the hardship** *(kārā)* **of snow** *(hema):* An instance of *śabdabhaṅgaśleṣa*, read compounded as: *hemakārāharaṇakalāyoginaḥ*. **State:** *dhāmni*. **Replete with beatitude:** *bahalalakṣmyāḥ*. Ksheméndra has based some of his verses on chapters 2.13–14 of Kauṭilya's *Arthaśāstra*.

G 8.4 A reversal of *Arthaśāstra* 2.13.23–24: a touchstone *(nikaṣa)* with the color of elephant-skin tinged with green, and reflective *(pratirāgī)*, is good for assaying at the time of selling. A durable, rough, uneven-colored, and non-reflecting stone is good for buying.

G 8.5 The goldsmith had to buy his counterweights from the superintendent of weights and measures, the Pautava *(cf. Arthaśāstra* 2.14.15–16). Furthermore, they needed to be stamped, for a small fee, on a daily basis. To prevent the fiddles described by Ksheméndra, *Arthaśāstra* 2.19.10 recommends that counterweights should be made of iron or of stones coming from Mágadha or Mékala which do not increase in weight when soaked in water or decrease when heated.

G 8.6 **Double bottom:** Ksheméndra here intends the *mūkamuṣā* contraption mentioned at *Arthaśāstra's* 2.14.23. **Bursting asunder:** This is the trick called "bleeding" *(visrāvaṇa)* described in *Arthaśāstra* 2.14.24–25. The crucible is deliberately caused to burst open and some grains of gold are then removed by sleight of hand when it is fastened again. **Copper inlay:** *Cf.* the practise of "adulteration" *apasārita* explained at *Arthaśāstra* 2.14.20–22. **Led and alkaline salt powder:** *Cf.* the practices known as "folding" *(peṭaka)* and "counterfeiting" *(piṅka)* in *Arthaśāstra* 2.14.26–33 and 2.14.34–42.

G 8.7 I count as follows: [1.] a bent indicator, [2.] unevenly matched bowls, [3.] a perforated layer, [4.] they are loaded with mercury, [5.] they are bendable, [6.] have an inert scale *(-kakṣyā)*, [7.] (their cords are:) knotty, [8.] badly strung, and [9.] many-stranded, [10.] they are out of balance before used, [11.] can be disturbed by the wind, [12.] are too light, or [13.] too heavy, [14.] they retain gold-dust in their coarse bowls, and [15.] are (magnetically controlled to be) static, or [16.] volatile. **Perforated layer:** E.g. to siphon off gold-dust. **Loaded with mercury:** This probably corresponds to the *Arthaśāstra*'s 2.14.19 "hollowed out" *(upakaṇṭhī)* defect. A quantity of heavy mercury travels along the hollow arms of the scales, altering the balance. **Static or volatile:** The last two defects probably allude to the *Arthaśāstra*'s final defect: that of being controlled magnetically *(ayaskāntā ca duṣṭatulāḥ)*; see *Kalāvilāsa* 8.14. **Quarters:** *mukha*. **Hostile:** *vakra*. **Hollows:** *puṭa*. **Impassable:** *viṣama*. **Ground** *tala*. **Cracked open:** *suṣira*. **Quicksilver:** Kshemendra must somehow have taken *pāradā* as a synonym (or by *lakṣaṇā*) for "snow." **Severe:** *kaṭu*. **Wraps:** *kakṣyā*. **Knotted together:** *granthimatī*. **Indecorously looped around:** *kuśikyitā*.

G 8.10 **Copper dust:** See the note on *visrāvaṇa* to 8.6.

8.11–12 The *Arthaśāstra* (2.14.53) gives a similar list of behavioral oddities as signs from which to infer a goldsmith has been misusing alkaline salts etc. I understand these as indications not just of shiftiness and guilt but as symptoms of self-poisoning. It is possible that this was an inevitable occupational hazard, since gold was often obtained amalgamated with mercury *(rasaviddha)*, *cf. Arthaśāstra* 2.13.3. Note, finally, that with a little ingenuity this passage might equally be read as describing a dog.

8.16–17 These two verses must be corrupt, I cannot produce a satisfactory text ot translation.

G 8.21 **Veins:** *saṃdhi*, lit. "joints."

G 8.25 **Gods**: *tridaśa-* Kṣīrasvāmin's commentary on the *Amarakoṣa* claims that this term refers to the number of the Vedic gods, "the thirty": *trir daśa parimāṇam eṣāṃ tridaśāḥ*, but, as the scriptural evidence he adduces shows, there are of course thirty-three Gods (*trayastriṃsad vai dehāḥ somapāḥ*). Much more plausible is the explanation offered by Jātarūpa ad *Amarakoṣa* 1.1.7: *bālyayauvanapraudhatvākhyās tisro daśā eṣām iti tridaśāḥ*, "*Tridaśa-*, are those who have [only] three stages of life, childhood, youth and maturity [but no old age]."

G 8.28 According to *Manusmṛti* 12.61 rebirth as a goldsmith is a punishment for the theft of gems, coral or pearls in a previous life.

G 8.29 A sentiment echoing *Manusmṛti* 9.292: *sarvakaṇṭakapāpiṣṭhaṃ hemakāraṃ tu pārthivaḥ/ pravartamānam anyāye chedayel lavaśaḥ kṣuraiḥ*, "The king shall have the dishonest goldsmith, the most evil thorn of all, cut into pieces with razors."

G 9.1 The con-men described in this section are what Manu calls "thorns" *(kaṇṭaka)*, *cf. Manusmṛti* 9.253–60. By removing these "thorns," and by protecting the subjects, kings reach heaven.

G 9.2 *Vaidya:* "physician" derived from *vidyā (vidyā asty asya aṇ)*; and "belonging to the Veda" *(veda+aṇ)*.

G 9.6 The sixteenth lunar asterism. The moon is here fancied as the lover of the lady Viśākhā, and the astrologer is a voyeur. Wife: The choice of the word *gṛhiṇī* for "wife," is appropriate *(padaucitya)* because Viśākhā is also a *gṛhiṇī*, e.g. a "lunar mansion," of the moon. In the *Darpadalana* too, Kshemendra portrays the astrologer as an idiot-savant, for despite his astral science he cannot even figure out who is continuously robbing him.

G 9.7 *Kanakārthin:* also "greedy for gold." The problem appears to be that transmutational experiments required some gold as a catalyst. See *Kathāsaritsāgara* III,161/2. Medhātithi on *Manusmṛti* 9.58b: "alchemists who pretend to change base metals into precious metals." Kalhaṇa recounts that the king Jalauka was believed to have an alchemical substance which could transmute base metals into gold (*Rājataraṅginī* 1.110, also another account at 4.246–7).

G 9.9 **Bald:** Compare the story of the bald man and the hair-restorer at *Kathāsaritsāgara* V,83-4.

G 9.10 I have preferred the reading of *Ked*L because the contrast between the bright eyes of the celestial damsels and the lecher's blindness appears to be original.

G 9.11 **Sky-flower:** In Sanskrit philosophical texts sky-flowers and rabbit's horns are usually given as standard examples of completely non-existent entities *(atyantābhāva)*; one cannot even imagine them *(vikalpakajñāna)*, that is, one can imagine cow's horns on a rabbit, or pond-lotuses in the sky, but not horn of a rabbit or a flower which grows in the sky.

9.11–12 Sorcery of this kind is taught already in the *Atharvaveda*. One of the earliest sources to give more detailed recipes of magical power-substances is the *Arthaśāstra* 14.1–4. The efficacy of the magic Ksheméndra is describing in these two verses depends entirely on the power-substances, mantras etc. are not required.

G 9.14 **Root:** *Cf. Manusmṛti* 9.290c. The rites involving the burying of magical roots are meant to subjugate a person. The lawbooks permit these rites if practised against a husband or relative. Kṣemendra also intends love-potions made with such roots, *cf. Samayamātṛkā* 2.25, and especially *Daśavatāracarita* 8.509–513 on the diseases wives caused their husbands with such homemade concoctions.

G 9.17 In the divinatory practice of *prasenā* or *prasannā* an oracular apparition manifests in water, in a sword-blade, in a mirror, in the eye of a virgin, or in the thumb-nail smeared with oil, in the sun or moon etc. and there reveals the future or past events. The vision appears either to a mantra-adept, or to a girl or boy who has become possessed for the occasion.

G 9.18 In a story in the *Kathāsaritasāgara* (70.56–62) it is a high-born Kṣatriya boy who serves as the medium. Ksheméndra is probably insinuating that only a lowly spirit would possess a Ceṭa medium. On *nīcagraha*, "lowly possessing spirits" such as goblins, *cf.* *Abhinavabhāratī* 17.37 (those so-possessed speak vulgar Prakrit languages). ***dhūpa:*** a ball of incense paste, for most rituals preferably made of *yakṣakardama*, burned on coals in a censer *(dhūpapātra)*.

G 9.19 The earliest reference to the famous "collyrium of Nagárjuna" *(nāgārjunavarti)* is provided by Vṛnda's *Siddhayoga* 61.148–152 (repeated verbatim by Cakrapāṇi). He gives a recipe with 14 ingredients, including the expensive killed copper and blue vitriol.

G 9.20 Kshemēndra is here ridiculing the use of occult fumigants made with all sorts of weird and wonderful ingredients. That they should be peddled by "sons of *yakṣīs*" may intend that they are successful practitioners of rites to summon a *yakṣī*. At the first meeting the *yakṣī* is supposed to address the successful acolyte as: "*putra!*", "my son!" Another vague connection I see is that the most popular fumigant is called *yakṣakardama*. Or, perhaps *cf.* *Arthaśāstra* 13–14 for spies masquerading as Nāgas, Rākṣasas, Varuṇa and various Gods.

G 9.21 A man without a son may "appoint" his daughter as a so-called *putrikā*. Her sons subsequently inherit all of her father's wealth. If she dies without a son, her husband inherits. *Cf.* *Manusmṛti* 9.127–139.

G 9.22 **Reader of body-language:** *iṅgitavādin*. *Cf.* Kullūka to *Manusmṛti* 9.258d: *īkṣaṇikā hastarekhādyavalokanena śubhāśubhaphalakathanajīvinaḥ*, "Physiognomists are people whose livelihood it is to descry auspicious and inauspicious fortunes by investigating the lines on the palms etc." This was not only done with human beings but also with animals, chapters 91–92 of the *Bṛhatsaṃhitā* are devoted to auspicious and inauspicious marks of bovines and horses.

G 9.26 *Cf. Manusmṛti* 9.258b.

G 9.30 *Cf. Arthaśāstra* 2.1.7.11 for the difficulties of colonising virgin lands. Immigration by force or inducement is advocated.

G 9.34 The expression *abhinava/sṛṣṭiṃ* echoes a famous benediction verse composed by Ábhinava·gupta, who taught Kseméndra literature. Could this be intended as censure of his teacher?

G 9.39 This corresponds more or less to the *Kāmasūtra* (1.4.32) definition of the pimp.

G 9.40 **Commissioner:** See 1.90.

G 9.44 **Dream:** Kṣemendra is here by no means ridiculing the idea that deities may appear in dreams itself, rather just the exploitation of the faithful. Somendra records that Kṣemendra was encouraged in a dream by the Buddha to complete the *Avadānakalpalatā*. *Śārada: Adj.* meaning "shy" is attested only in lexicons.

G 9.52 **Rat:** Ksheméndra likes to introduce the image of rats when he describes treasuries. In *Darpadalana* 2.36 the miser Nanda's wife Mati points out that he stupidly starves himself taking only rice-water while rats carry off the jewels stored up in his treasury. The descriptive epithets shift their sense slightly when construed with the rat: ". . . whose snout and eyes always face downwards in case there might be something extra, who has an unclean body and nest, who appears in the pantry."

G 9.58 In the *Dhuttakhāṇa* 5.79–110 the cheat Khaṇḍavaṇā uses just such a ploy to blackmail a rich banker to pay her off. With a recently deceased infant swaddled in layers of cloth she accosts her victim. When his servants throw her out she wails that they have murdered her baby. Alarmed that the uproar may reflect badly on him the banker gives her a gold earring to remove the dead child.

G 9.60 **Dressed in respectable finery:** Ksheméndra is perhaps referring to what Manu calls the Bhadrā swindlers. *Cf.* Kullūka to *Manusmṛti* 9.258d: *bhadrāḥ kalyāṇākārapracchannapāpā ye dhanagrāhiṇaḥ*, "Respectable [thieves] are those who steal wealth conceiling their evil and appearing respectable."

G 9.64 This verse probably refers to the "extortionists" *(aupadhika)* mentioned in *Manusmṛti* 9.258a. Kullūka glosses: *aupadhikā bhayadarśanād ye dhanam upajīvanti*, "'Extortionists' are people who extort money by threats."

G 9.69 **Cheat:** *vañcaka*. Medhātithi *ad Manusmṛti* 9.258b glosses: "Men who promise to transact business for others, and do not keep their word."

G 9.70 Ksheméndra is fond of describing the failings of arrogant scholars. In the third chapter of his *Darpadalana* Ksheméndra portrays the career of Yavakrīta, the idiot son of the sage Bharadvāja. He performs penance and is rewarded with learning but then becomes an egomaniac and quarrelsome nuisance who irritates his own father by continuously babbling in difficult Sanskrit metres. Since his learning lacks "peace of mind" *(cetaḥśānti)* a tragedy ensues. *Malapatraka*: LAPANICH takes this as a synonym for *malapṛṣṭha*, "dust-jacket of a book." We may add that this *malapatra* does seem to have been inscribed, perhaps with summaries of contents or the like. See, for instance *Narmamālā* 2.36a, where Kṣemendra is ridiculing the imbecile Maṭhadaiśika who walks about with his *malapatra* which is there probably a kind of notebook or diary.

G 9.71 **Piercing initiation-guru:** A "piercing initiation" *(vedhadīkṣā)* is in Shaiva Tantric literature presented as a high salvific act performed by a guru for a fortunate chosen few. The preceptor enters the initiate's body and pierces various centres along the central channel of his subtle body. As Ksheméndra indicates, the initiate perceives signs, such as trembling, while this is taking place (*cf.* *Tantrāloka* 29.236–82). The context Kshéméndra describes appears to be much more humble: a low-life officiant does the rounds like a door-to-door salesman, tricking his gullible clients into parting with their money by planting stooges to demonstrate the efficacity of his technique. Sanderson has pointed out to me that the purpose of the *vedha* Ksheméndra describes is uncertain. Perhaps the guru comes to a house and performs a *vedhadīkṣā* for the household, the stooge serving to show that it is the real thing and perhaps to set off a chain reaction in which the conned will believe that they too have been touched by the Goddess. Or perhaps he comes and offers to bless the household by performing a simple *pūjā* of the Goddess, the stooge's performance being the proof that he has succeeded in summoning her.

G 9.72 **Shakuni**: There are several mythical Śakunis who could be meant but I take this as a more concrete reference to that Śakuni who is known from the *Rājataraṅgiṇī* as the great-grandfather of the famous emperor Aśoka. Lapanich, reading: *kāle śakuniṃ smarāmi*, translates: "I can summon a bird at the right time." This remains obscure to me. Schmidt believes the fraud to be boasting: "I know how to fly like a bird."

10.2–6 The four aims of life *(puruṣārtha)*.

G 10.6 The thirty-two arts are thus presented as thirty-two *kalā*s of a long mantra with four *pāda*s which the *mantrin (<vidyāvat)* manipulates in various ways *(krama, samasta)* for specific rewards.

G 10.7 A parallel to magical powers such as leaving the earth *(bhūmi-tyāga)*, poetic power *(kavitva)* etc. promised as *siddhi*s for the perfection of various mantras.

G 10.14 Verses 14–38 make up a single sentence containing an elaborate "consequential metaphor" *(paramparitarūpaka)*, *cf. Kāvyaprakāśa* 10.9. The structure of the sentence is: "In this world, it is renown, which is the Guru's word among truths. . . knowledge among supreme illuminations, that is indispensable for all people."

G 10.15 **Snares and black cobras:** I am assuming that Ksheméndra is here using a common epic metaphor, which EMENEAU (1960: 291–300) has shown to be a *pl. dvandva* compound, e.g. "snakes and bonds."

G 10.21 **chandálas**: In Kāvya literature outcastes are portrayed as inherently cruel. Ksheméndra follows this convention unquestioningly. In a story in *Darpadalana* 1, Ksheméndra uses this prejudice to show that the arrogant and cruel Brahmin Tejonidhi was in fact the son of a Cāṇḍāla (see especially *Darpadalana* 1.54–55). **Necromancer:** *māyāvin*, *cf. Kathāsaritsāgara* VI,35.

G 10.22 *Visarpa*, Erysipelas.

G 10.23 The eldest son performs the funeral rites.

G 10.31 **Kútaja** *Wrightia antidysenterica*, also known as Indrayava, "Indra's grain," the seeds of which are used as a vermifuge.

G 10.37 **Death in battle**: As Kṣemendra explains in *Darpadalana* 4.31, the fallen hero could expect to be welcomed into heaven by beautiful Apsarases such as Urvaśī.

M 4 A parody of the standard example of a **syllogistic inference** taught in Nyāya logic: the premise is smoke, the probandum is fire, the example is the kitchen, the conclusion is the presence of fire.

M 10 A **mantra-sorcerer** *(māntrika)* is an initiate into the cult of a mantra-deity who has achieved supernatural power *(siddhi)*.

M 21b **Vachas·pati:** the teacher of the gods.

M 22b **Priests:** FILLIOZAT takes *devatopāsakāḥ* as "mediums." I have translated as "priests" for that is closer to the literal sense: "worshippers of gods."

M 26 **All:** These are the five departments of Āyurvedic medicine.

M 27 Cf. *Kalāvilāsa* 9.4.

M 29 FILLIOZAT translates differently: *"Quand le médecin soutire l'argent d'un malade qu'il visite depuis longtemps..."*.

M 39 This is probably not a general statement about poets glorifying love but rather a dig at the rhetoricians' theories which teach that the aesthetic sentiment of love is the most important in poetry (cf. *Dhvanyāloka* 2.7).

M 45 **Dhoraṇī:** sv. *Amarakośa* 2.7.1048 *dhoraṇā*.

M 62 **Children etc.:** Nīlakaṇṭha is here alluding to a Smṛti list which is a shorthand for all utterly unreliable persons.

M 77 An allusion to the scriptural teaching that any food one gives to a mendicant becomes in the next world a reward of food the size of Mt. Meru and any water one gives an ocean (See *Parāśarasmṛti* 1.53).

M 81 **Departing:** or, reading *prasthāpyamānaḥ*: "Sent away each day. . . ."

M 82 **Orthodox brahmin:** A *śrotriya* is a brahmin learned in the Veda.

M 83 **Ghaṭaka:** A *ghaṭaka* is an agent who predominantly arranges marriages, but Nīlakaṇṭha here seems to consider him a kind of pimp.

M 84 **Wood of the holy basil:** The Tulasī tree is sacred to Vaiṣṇavas who fashion rosaries from its wood.

M 85 **Vāhaṭa** or Vāgbhaṭa is the author of a compendium of Materia medica.

M 86 **Ekāsikā:** sitting alone or sitting in one place.

M 90 **Sadyaḥpratyaya:** "giving immediate proof of efficacy."

M 97 **Hail to the horizon:** I assume Nīlakaṇṭha intends no more than: "I will flee," but it may be a reference to the *mahāpathaprasthāna*, the rite in which the elderly brahmin leaves his home and walks towards the Himālayas until he dies. FILLIOZAT translates: *'Je salue la direction oú ces quatre sont réunis'*.

M 98 Chidra means both 'bodily opening' and 'fault'.

BIBLIOGRAPHY

Adbhutasāgara of Niḥśaṅkaśaṅkara Ballālasena, ed. MURALĪDHARA ŚARMA, Kāśī 1905.

Aucityavicāracarcā ed. Kāvyamālā Guccha 1, Nirṇaya Sāgara Press, Bombay 1886.

Kalāvilāsa of Kṣemendra ed. PAṆḌITA DURGĀPRASĀDA & KĀŚĪNĀTHA PĀṆḌURĀṄGA PARAB, Kāvyamālā Part 1, Bombay 1886.

— *Kṣemendra: His Kalāvilāsa*, PRANEE LAPANICH, Pennsylvania dissertation, 1973.

— E.V.V. RĀGHAVĀCĀRYA & D.G. PADHYE 1961.

Kāpphiṇābhyudaya. Śivasvāmin's Kāpphiṇābhyudaya or Exaltation of King Kapphiṇa, ed. Gauri SHANKAR, with an appendix and revised romanized version of cantos 1–8 and 19 by M. HAHN, Delhi 1989.

Dhūrtākhyāna Dhuttakhāṇa of Haribhadra, ed. A.N. UPĀDHYE, Singhi Jain Series 19, Bombay 1944.

Deśopadeśa of Kṣemendra, ed. MADHUSŪDANA KAULA ŚĀSTRĪ, KSTS 40, Śrīnagara & Poona 1923.

Narmamālā of Kṣemendra, ed. MADHUSŪDANA KAULA ŚĀSTRĪ, KSTS 40, Śrīnagara & Poona 1923.

Nirṇayasindhuḥ of Kamalākara Bhaṭṭa, ed. KṚṢṆAṂBHAṬṬA NENE, GOPĀLAŚĀSTRĪ, Caukhambā Saṃskṛta granthamālā 265, Banārasa, 1930.

Bhāratamañjarī ed. M.M. PAṆḌIT ŚIVADATTA & KĀŚĪNĀTH PĀṆḌURANG PARAB, Kāvyamālā no. 64, Reprint Delhi 1984.

Manusmṛti with the Manubhāṣya commentary of Medātithi, ed. GANGANĀTHA JHĀ, Bibliotheca Indica no. 256, 2 vols., RASB, Calcutta 1932 & 1939.

— *with the Manvarthamuktāvalī commentary of Kullūkabhaṭṭa*, ed. J.L. ŚĀSTRĪ, New Delhi reprinted 1990.

Mahābhārata ed. V. SUKTHANKAR wuth the cooperation of S.K. BELVALKAR, A.B. GAJENDRAGADKAR, V. KANE, R.D. KARMARKAR, P.L.

VAIDYA, S. WINTERNITZ, R. ZIMMERMAN ETC., 19 VOLS., BORI, POONA 1927–59.

Rājataraṅginī of Kalhaṇa, ed. VISHVA BANDHU in collaboration with BHĪMA DEV, K.S. RĀMASWĀMI SĀSTRĪ and S. BHĀSKARAN NAIR, part 1 (taraṅga-s 1–7), Woolner Indological Series No. 5, VVRI, Hoshiarpur 1963; part 2 (taraṅga 8), Woolner Indological Series No. 6, VVRI, Hoshiarpur 1965.

Samayamātṛkā ed. M.M. PAṆḌIT ŚIVADATTA & KĀŚĪNĀTH PĀṆḌURANG PARAB, Kāvyamālā no. 10, Bombay 1925.

Siddhayoga of Vṛnda, Vṛndamādhavāparanāmā Siddhayogaḥ, ed. HANUMANTA ŚĀSTRĪ, Ānandāśramasaṃskṛtagranthāvalī 27, Puṇyākhyapattane (Poona) 1894.

Subhāṣitahārāvalī of Harikavi (Bhānubhaṭṭa), ed. JAGANNĀTHA PĀṬHAKA, GaṅgānāthaJhāKendriyaSaṃskṛtavidyāpīṭham, Text Series No. 19, Allahabad 1984.

Sūktimuktāvalī of Bhagadatta Jalhaṇa, ed. E. KRISHNAMACHARYA, Gaekwad's Oriental Series 82, Baroda 1938.

Bāṇa's Harṣacarita ed. P.V. KANE, Bombay 1918.

SECONDARY LITERATURE

M.B. EMENEAU *Nāgapāśa, nāgabandha, sarpabandha and related words,* Bulletin of the Deccan College Research Institute 20.1–4, Poona 1960, pp. 291–300.

— *Barkcloth in India– Sanskrit Valkala,* JAOS 82.1, 1962, pp. 167–170.

M. HARA *Tapo-dhana*, Acta Asiatica 19, 1970, pp. 58–76.

S. LIENHARD *Kanyākandukakrīḍā– Ballspiel junger Damen, Zur Entwicklung eines Motivs der klassischen Sanskrit-Dichtung*, Nachrichten von der Akademie der Wissenschaften in Göttingen. Philologisch-Historische Klasse ; Jahrg. 1999, Nr. 8, Göttingen 1999.

VICTOR H. MAIR & TSU-LIN MEI Sanskrit and Recent Style Poetry, *Harvard Journal of Asiatic Studies,* Vol. 51, no. 2, 1991, pp. 382–3.

J.J. MEYER *Kṣemendra's Samayamātṛkā*, Altindische Schelmenbücher 1, Leipzig 1903.

B. Mookerji *Rasa-jala-nidhi*; or, Ocean of Indian Chemistry & Alchemy, Calcutta 1926.

Prafulla Chandra Ray *A history of Hindu Chemistry from the Earliest Times to the Middle of the 16th Century* A.D., 2 Vols., Calcutta 1904–9.

E.V.V. Rāghavācārya & D.G. Padhye *Minor Works of Kṣemendra*, Hyderabad 1961.

L. Sternbach *Unknown verses attributed to Kṣemendra,* Akhila Bharatiya Sanskrit Parishad, Lucknow 1979.

— *Gaṇikā-Vṛtta-Saṃgrahaḥ or Texts on Courtezans in Classical Sanskrit*, Vishveshwaranand Indological Series No. 4, Hoshiarpur 1953.

Sūryakānta *Kṣemendra Studies*, Poona 1954.

A. Venkatasubbiah & E. Müller *The Kalās*, JRAS 1914, pp. 355–367.

P.C. Dandiya & Y.M. Chopra *CNS-active drugs from plants indigenous to India*, Department of Pharmacology, S. M. S. Medical College, Jaipur, Ind. J. Pharmac. 1970, 2 (3), 67–90.

INDEX

INDEX

Sanskrit words are given according to the accented CSL pronuncuation aid in the English alphabetical order. They are followed by the conventional diacritics in brackets.

					ṃṣ	ṃ	ṣ	aṣ	aṣ	ṭ/ṭh
g	ḍ	ḍ	b	ṅ	ṇ	ṃ	r	ā	o	ḍ/ḍh
k	ṭ	t	p	ṅ	ṃs	ṃ	s	ās	as	t/th
g	ḍ	d	b	ṅ	n	ṃ	r	ā	o	d/dh
k	ṭ	t	p	ṅ	n	ṃ	ḥ	ā	aḥ	p/ph
g	ḍ	d	b	ṅ	n	ṃ	r	ā	o	b/bh
ṅ	ṇ	n	m	ṅ	n	ṃ	r	ā	o	*nasals* (n/m)
g	ḍ	d	b	ṅ	n	ṃ	r	ā	o	y/v
g	ḍ	d	b	ṅ	n	ṃ	*zero*[1]	ā	o	r
g	ḍ	l	b	ṅ	l̃[2]	ṃ	r	ā	o	l
k	ṭ	c ch	p	ṅ	ñ ś/ch	ṃ	ḥ	āḥ	aḥ	ś
k	ṭ	t	p	ṅ	n	ṃ	ḥ	āḥ	aḥ	ṣ/s
gg h	ḍḍ h	dd h	bb h	ṅ	n	ṃ	r	ā	o	h
g	ḍ	d	b	ṅ/ṅṅ[3]	n/nn[3]	m	r	ā	a[4]	*vowels*
k	ṭ	t	p	ṅ	n	m	ḥ	āḥ	āḥ	*zero*

[1] ḥ or r disappears, and if a/i/u precedes, this lengthens to ā/ī/ū. [2] e.g. tān+lokān=tāl̃ lokān.
[3] The doubling occurs if the preceding vowel is short. [4] Except: aḥ+a=o '.

Permitted finals: *(Except āḥ/aḥ)*

k	ṭ	t	p	ṅ	n	m	ḥ/r	āḥ	aḥ	*Initial letters:*
k	ṭ	t	p	ṅ	n	ṃ	ḥ	āḥ	aḥ	k/kh
g	ḍ	d	b	ṅ	n	ṃ	r	ā	o	g/gh
k	ṭ	c	p	ṅ	ṃś	ṃ	ś	āś	aś	c/ch
g	ḍ	j	b	ṅ	ñ	ṃ	r	ā	o	j/jh
k	ṭ	t	[illegible]	[illegible]	[illegible]	[illegible]	[illegible]	[illegible]	[illegible]	